WINTER RECREATION
IN
CALIFORNIA
AND WESTERN NEVADA

by   D.J. Dirksen & R.A. Reeves

Sail Sales Publishing
P.O. Box 1028
Aptos, California 95001
Phone: 408-662-2456

**First Edition
1986 - 1987**

ISBN 0-943798-09-4

CREDITS

MAPS by RENEE REEVES

CARTOONS by GREG DIRKSEN

PRINTING by DELTA LITHOGRAPH COMPANY

**ALL FEES AND INFORMATION
ARE SUBJECT TO CHANGE**

MAPS ARE NOT TO SCALE

ORDER FORM

"WINTER RECREATION IN CALIFORNIA"

FIRST EDITION

TO: SAIL SALES PUBLISHING
      P.O. Box 1028
      Aptos, CA 95001

$10.95	Book
.71	Tax
1.84	Postage & Handling
$13.50	CHECK ENCLOSED

NAME: _____

ADDRESS: _____

_____

ACKNOWLEDGEMENTS

We are grateful to the many people who have contributed to "Winter Recreation in California". Ed Corbett, an avid skier and outdoorsman, gave us the idea and inspiration. The United States Forest Service, the National Parks System, and the California Department of Parks and Recreation, provided a wealth of indispensable information. The various Chambers of Commerce and Visitors Bureaus were always available and supportive. A special thanks must go to the many resorts who filled out our questionnaires and patiently answered our numerous questions about their facilities. Kimberly Davis' and Matt Herbberd's long, and often trying, hours were an invaluable contribution. Again we must give our readers a special thanks; your continuing support of our other publications has made this book possible.

Especially helpful in the development of the latter sections of this book were the USDA – Forest Service publications "Winter Sport in the National Forests of California" and "Winter Recreation Safety Guide". For copies of these informative pamphlets contact:

Office of Information
Pacific Southwest Region
USDA – Forest Service
630 Sansome Street
San Francisco, CA 94111

INTRODUCTION

Can you imagine a major winter sports area in the mountains above Los Angeles, a serene tour amid the winter splendor of Yosemite, or an alpine ski resort just minutes away from the desert of Las Vegas! Yes, there is snow in California and Western Nevada, and a vast amount of developed facilities awaiting the many who enjoy them.

We are pleased to present these facilities in this first edition of "Winter Recreation in California". Using the same concise format as our other publications, "Recreation Lakes of California" and "Recreation on the Colorado River", this comprehensive guide describes the abundance and variety of winter activities. Alpine and nordic Resorts, cross-country and snowmobile wilderness trails, and other snow sports are featured on each page. Each resort and the surrounding area is described and mapped according to location, size, support facilities and services.

When you think of winter recreation, alpine or downhill ski resorts usually come to mind. Skiers will not be disappointed in California and Western Nevada, where these areas are in abundance. From the locally used basic facilities at Coppervale to the complete destination facilities at Kirkwood, there is a tremendous variety of choices. Mammoth Mountain, Heavenly Valley and Squaw Valley are all World Class Resorts. While some areas are separated, there is a great variety of Resorts at Tahoe and Big Bear areas. Needless to say, the choice is yours, but it is not easy, for there are so many from which to choose.

The cross-country enthusiast will find an even greater variety. Royal Gorge, the site of the Subaru/USSA Cross-Country Championships, is America's premier nordic resort, with excellent facilities and 255 kilometers of groomed trails. Castle Lake near Mount Shasta, Montecito/Sequoia in the Sequoia National Forest, and Granlibakken near Tahoe City, are representative of the many fine nordic resorts throughout the state. Our public lands offer hundreds of miles of marked wilderness trails for this fast growing winter sport.

While skiing is a prime winter sport, it has no monopoly on winter fun. There are miles of snowmobile and ATV runs leading into backcountry wilderness, and several centers offer professionally guided tours. The California Sno-Park program has opened acres of snow play areas where parking, once impossible, is now available for a small fee. There are privately operated snow play areas where you can sled or tube down a hill.

Be it a family day in the snow, Heli-Skiing at Mammoth, or nordic touring in Lassen Volcanic National Park, the opportunities are unlimited. So go out and enjoy the winter wonderlands of California and Western Nevada.

CALIFORNIA

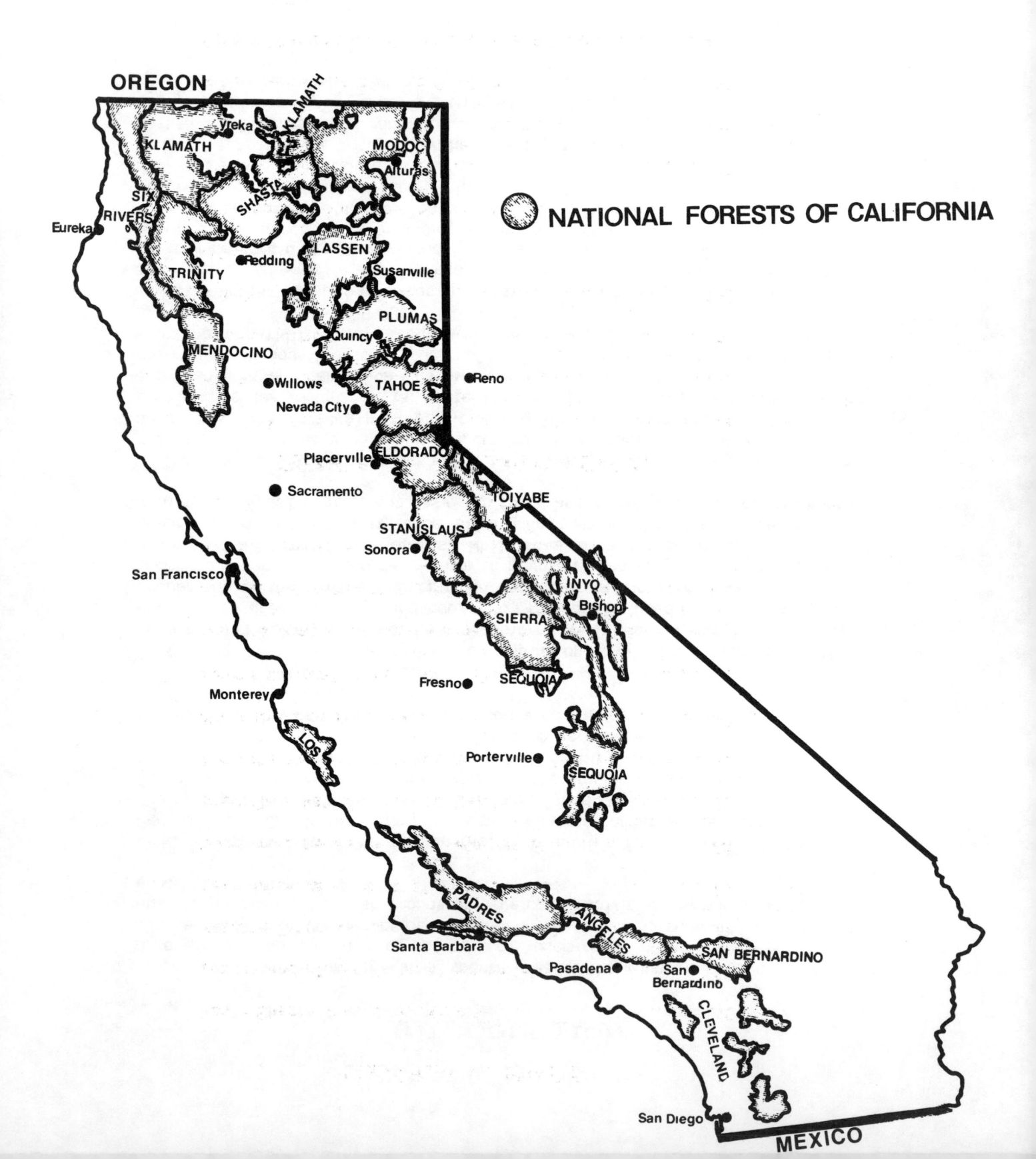

OREGON

KLAMATH
Yreka
MODOC
Alturas
SIX
RIVERS
Eureka
SHASTA
Redding
LASSEN
Susanville
TRINITY
PLUMAS
Quincy
MENDOCINO
Willows
TAHOE
Reno
Nevada City
Placerville
ELDORADO
Sacramento
TOIYABE
STANISLAUS
Sonora
San Francisco
INYO
Bishop
SIERRA
Monterey
Fresno
SEQUOIA
LOS
Porterville
SEQUOIA
PADRES
ANGELES
Santa Barbara
SAN BERNARDINO
Pasadena
San Bernardino
CLEVELAND
San Diego
MEXICO

◯ NATIONAL FORESTS OF CALIFORNIA

OVERALL MAPS

GENERAL INFORMATION

ALPINE RESORTS

Alpine Meadows	46	Mount Shasta Ski Area	11
Badger Pass	94	Mount Shasta Ski Park	14
Boreal Ski Area	32	Mount Waterman	125
Coppervale Ski Area	20	Mountain High-East & West	128
Cottage Springs	84	Northstar	39
Dodge Ridge	92	Plumas Eureka Ski Bowl	21
Donner Ski Ranch	35	Sierra Ski Ranch	67
Echo Summit	69	Sierra Summit	113
Goldmine Ski Area	135	Ski Green Valley	131
Granlibakken	48	Ski Incline	56
Heavenly Valley California	70	Ski Sunrise	129
Heavenly Valley Nevada	71	Slide Mountain	59
Homewood	50	Snow Forest	133
Iron Mountain	77	Snow Summit	134
June Mountain	106	Snow Valley	132
Kirkwood	75	Soda Springs	31
Kratka Ridge	126	Squaw Vallley	43
Lassen Park	16	Stover Mountain	19
Lee Canyon	138	Sugar Bowl	33
Mammoth Mountain	104	Tahoe Donner	40
Mount Baldy	127	Tahoe Ski Bowl	51
Mount Reba	88	Wolverton	119
Mount Rose	58		

NORDIC SKI AREAS

Arroyo Seco	124	Mount Shasta Cross-Country	12
Badger Pass Nordic	95	North Tahoe Regional Park	41
Bear River	80	Northstar at Tahoe Nordic	38

NORDIC SKI AREAS continued:

Bear Valley Nordic	87	Palm Springs Nordic	137
Big Chief Nordic	42	Quiet Mountain	23
Calaveras Big Trees	83	Royal Gorge	29
Castle Lake	13	Sequoia National Forest	117
Childs Meadows	18	Shady Rest Area-Inyo National Forest	101
Clair Tappaan Lodge	34	Sierra Meadows	102
Donner Memorial State Park	36	Sierra National Forest	114
Eagle Mountain	24	Spooner Lake	55
Echo Summit	68	Squaw Valley Nordic	44
Giant Forest	118	Stanislaus National Forest	85
Grant Grove	116	Stanislaus National Forest-Summit District	93
Greenhorn Mountain	121	Strawberry Canyon	66
June Lake	105	Sugar Pine Point State Park	52
Kirkwood Cross-Country	76	Tahoe Donner	37
Lassen Volcanic National Park	17	Tahoe Meadows	57
Leland Meadows	91	Tahoe Nordic	45
Loon Lake	65	Tamarack Lodge	103
Lumberyard & Peddler Hill Trails	79	Tamarack Pines Lodge	86
Mount Pinos	122	Telemark Country Sports	72

SNO-PARK SITES

Blackwood Canyon	49	Lake Alpine	89
Bishop Creek	99	Lake Tahoe	53
Carson Pass	74	Rancheria	112
Donner Summit	30	Rock Creek	100
Eagle Lake	25	Taylor Creek	54
Eastwood	111	Western Devide	120
Grass Lake	73	Yuba Pass	26
Iron Mountain	78		

MT. SHASTA AREA

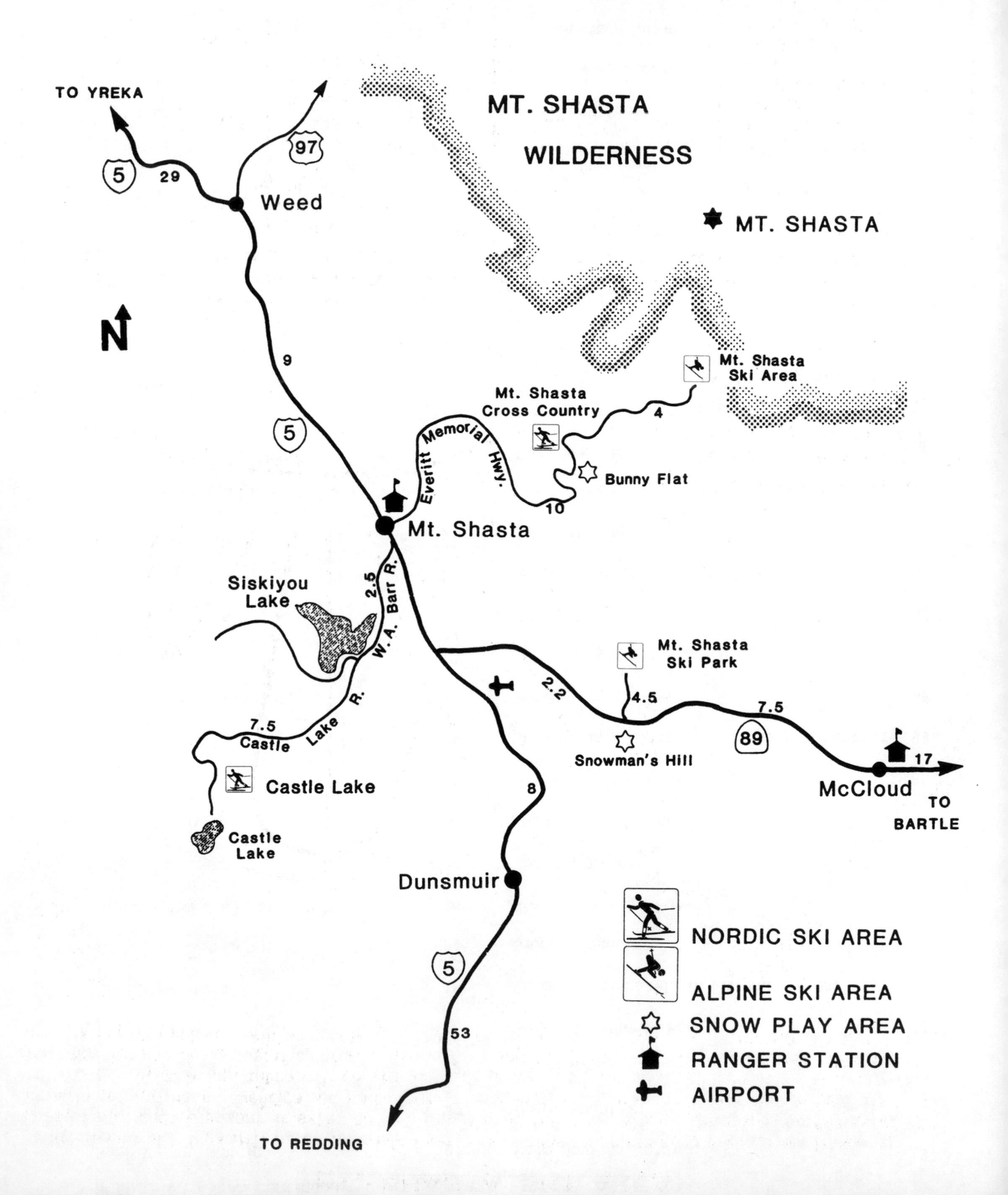

TO YREKA

5 29

97

Weed

MT. SHASTA

WILDERNESS

★ MT. SHASTA

N

9

5

Everitt Memorial Hwy.

Mt. Shasta
Cross Country

Mt. Shasta
Ski Area

4

☆ Bunny Flat

10

Mt. Shasta

2.5

W. A. Barr R.

Siskiyou
Lake

Lake R.

Castle

7.5

Castle
Lake

Castle
Lake

8

Dunsmuir

5

53

Mt. Shasta
Ski Park

4.5

2.2

☆
Snowman's Hill

7.5

89

17
McCloud

TO
BARTLE

NORDIC SKI AREA

ALPINE SKI AREA

☆ SNOW PLAY AREA

RANGER STATION

AIRPORT

TO REDDING

MT. SHASTA SKI AREA

Mt. Shasta Ski Area will be California's newest ski resort for both nordic and downhill skiers. Phase I of its development is expected to be completed for this season. There will be 565 acres of skiable terrain down a vertical of 1,400 feet. There will be 21 miles of trails challenging all levels of ability. In addition, there will be ten miles of groomed nordic track. There is a 15,000 square foot day lodge. While specific information on fees and facilities are to be determined, this new ski area is sure to enhance winter sports opportunities in one of California's most beautiful scenic areas.

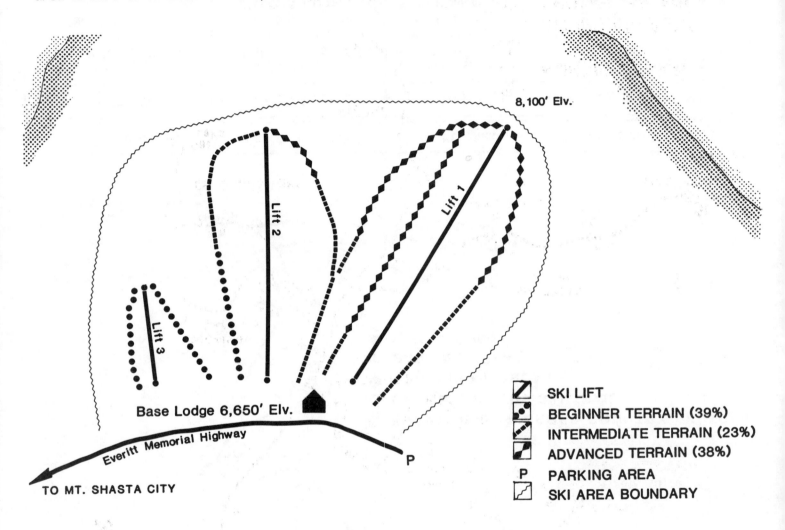

8,100' Elv.

Lift 2

Lift 1

Lift 3

Base Lodge 6,650' Elv.

Everitt Memorial Highway

TO MT. SHASTA CITY

P

	SKI LIFT
	BEGINNER TERRAIN (39%)
	INTERMEDIATE TERRAIN (23%)
	ADVANCED TERRAIN (38%)
P	PARKING AREA
	SKI AREA BOUNDARY

INFORMATION: Mt. Shasta Ski Area, P. O. Box 238, Mt. Shasta 96067, Ph: 916-926-4033

SKIING	RENTALS & LESSONS	RECREATION	ACCOMMODATIONS

Alpine:
  2 Chairlifts
  1 Rope Tow
Fees: Adults-$16-$18
Children-$8-$10
Seniors - Free
Nordic:
  10 Miles Groomed
  Trails
  Fee
Season: Mid-November
  to May
	Ski School:
	  Alpine –
	  Group & Private
	  Lessons
	Rentals:
	  Alpine & Nordic
	  Combinations
		Nearby:
		  Ski Touring
		  Mountaineering
		  Snow Play Areas
		  Snowmobiling
			Day Lodge
			
			Full Facilities in
			Mt. Shasta City
			Contact:
			Mt. Shasta Chamber of
			Commerce
			300 Pine St.
			Mt. Shasta 96067
			Ph: 916-926-4865

MT. SHASTA CROSS COUNTRY AREA

Mt. Shasta, at 14,162 feet, displays a majestic prominence over this beautiful area in the Shasta-Trinity National Forest. The varied terrain and predictable snowfall has long attracted nordic skiers. Beginner and intermediate cross country skiers will find the southwestern slopes of the mountain above Everett Memorial Highway a gentle challenge. The 2,000 acres offers 3 miles of marked trails. The unmarked areas north and east of Bunny Flat are for more experienced skiers. Ski mountaineers with expert skills will find the upper slopes of Mt. Shasta and the surrounding peaks and ridges demanding. There are snowplay areas at Bunny Flat, and snowmobilers can also enjoy this area.

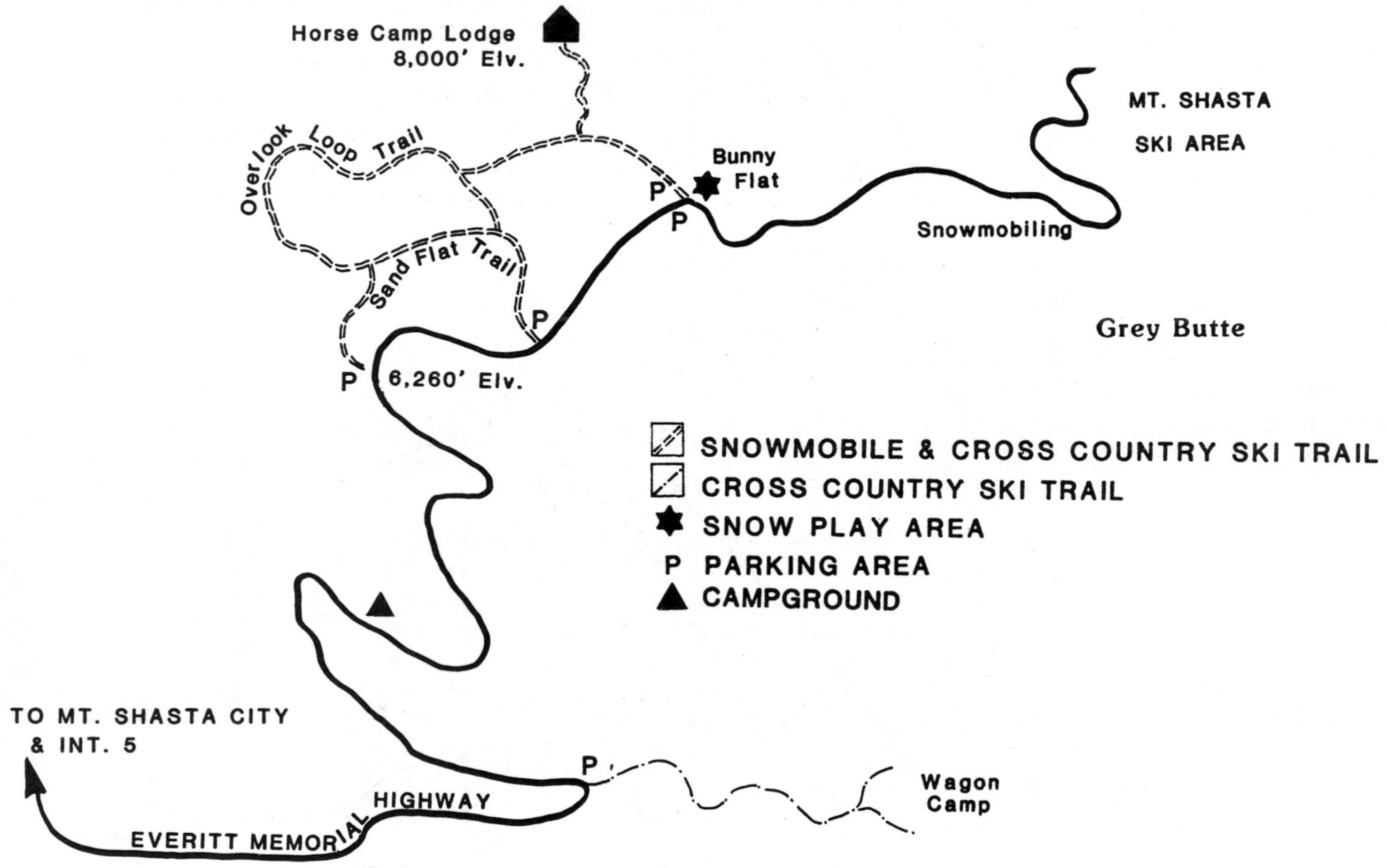

Horse Camp Lodge
8,000' Elv.

Overlook Loop Trail

Sand Flat Trail

Bunny Flat

P

P

P

P 6,260' Elv.

MT. SHASTA SKI AREA

Snowmobiling

Grey Butte

⊠ SNOWMOBILE & CROSS COUNTRY SKI TRAIL
☐ CROSS COUNTRY SKI TRAIL
✶ SNOW PLAY AREA
P PARKING AREA
▲ CAMPGROUND

TO MT. SHASTA CITY & INT. 5

P

Wagon Camp

HIGHWAY

EVERITT MEMORIAL

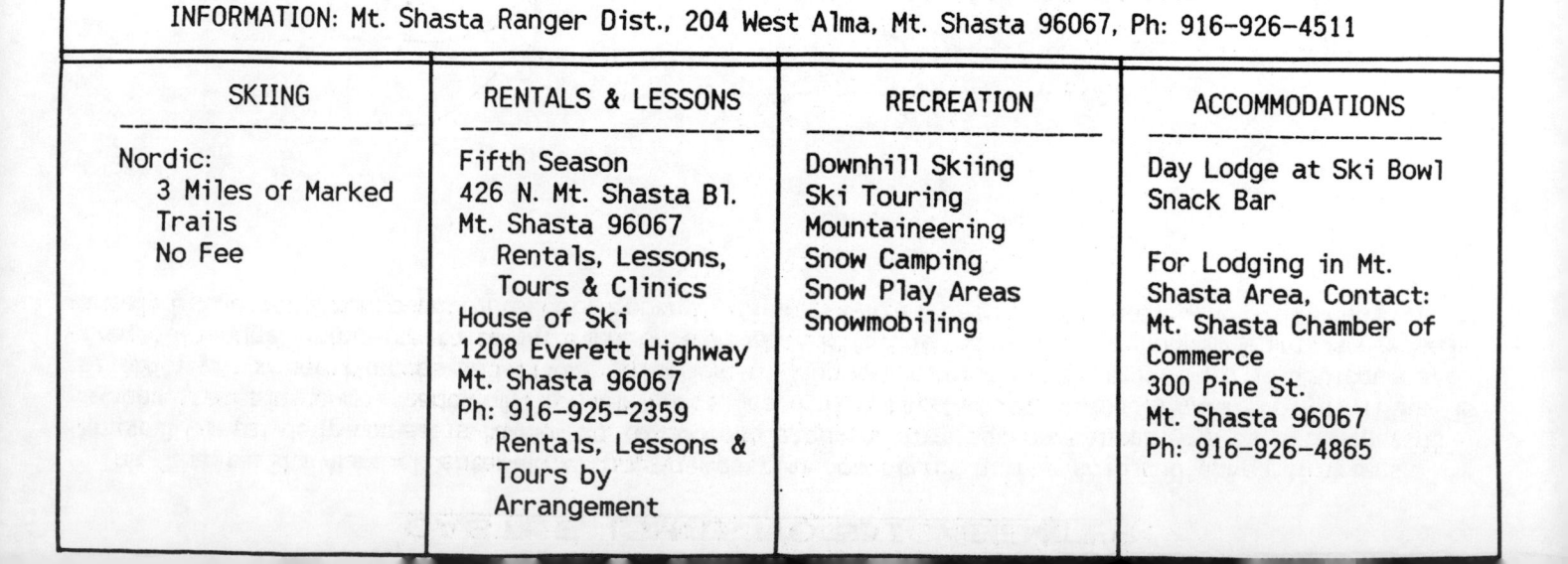

INFORMATION: Mt. Shasta Ranger Dist., 204 West Alma, Mt. Shasta 96067, Ph: 916-926-4511

SKIING	RENTALS & LESSONS	RECREATION	ACCOMMODATIONS
Nordic: 3 Miles of Marked Trails No Fee	Fifth Season 426 N. Mt. Shasta Bl. Mt. Shasta 96067 Rentals, Lessons, Tours & Clinics House of Ski 1208 Everett Highway Mt. Shasta 96067 Ph: 916-925-2359 Rentals, Lessons & Tours by Arrangement	Downhill Skiing Ski Touring Mountaineering Snow Camping Snow Play Areas Snowmobiling	Day Lodge at Ski Bowl Snack Bar For Lodging in Mt. Shasta Area, Contact: Mt. Shasta Chamber of Commerce 300 Pine St. Mt. Shasta 96067 Ph: 916-926-4865

CASTLE LAKE NORDIC CENTER

The Castle Lake Nordic Center is a complete destination resort in the scenic Shasta-Trinity National Forest. This area is famous for excellent snow and beautiful scenery. The 50 miles of well groomed trails through meadow, forest and ridge are well marked and patrolled. A variety of challenges from steep drops and climbs to gentle rolling slopes await skiers of all levels. There are several downhill areas for telemark enthusiasts. The ski school offers both group and private lessons as well as guided back country tours. There is also a special junior ski program.

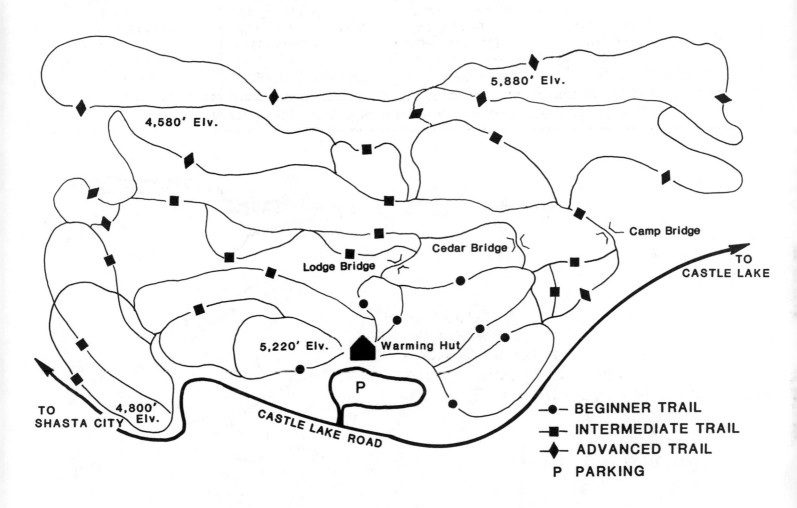

SKIING	RENTALS & LESSONS	RECREATION	ACCOMMODATIONS
Nordic: 　50 Kilometers of 　Double Track, 　Patrolled Trails Fees: Adult-$6.50 Jr.(8-12yrs)-$5 Children (7 & 　under)-free Season: Mid-Nov. to 　Mid-April Ph: 916-926-5555	Nordic Ski School Group Lessons: 　Level: 　A (1.5 hrs.)-$8 　B (3hrs.)-$12 Private Lessons: 　1 hour-$12 Rentals: 　Adults-$9 　Juniors-$6	Nearby: 　Alpine Skiing 　Ski Touring 　Ski Mountaineering 　Snow Camping 　Snow Play 　Snowmobiling 　Ice Skating 　Ice Fishing	Warming Hut 　Snack-bar, Hot 　Drinks

INFORMATION: Castle Lake Nordic Center, P.O. Box 600, Mt. Shasta, CA. 96067 Ph:916-926-3606

Mt. Shasta Ski Park is one of California's newest ski areas. Located beneath the majestic slopes of Mt. Shasta, the all new facility offers a full service day lodge with complete conveniences and a friendly atmosphere. There are 160 acres of varied terrain. From wide open gentle slopes, tree lined runs, and long open runs, there is ample challenge for all levels of ability. The vertical of Douglas Butte is 1,100 feet. While many of the more popular slopes are groomed on a daily basis, there are others which are left in their natural state for those who prefer such a challenge. The ski school offers a beginner's special plus a children's program and race clinics.

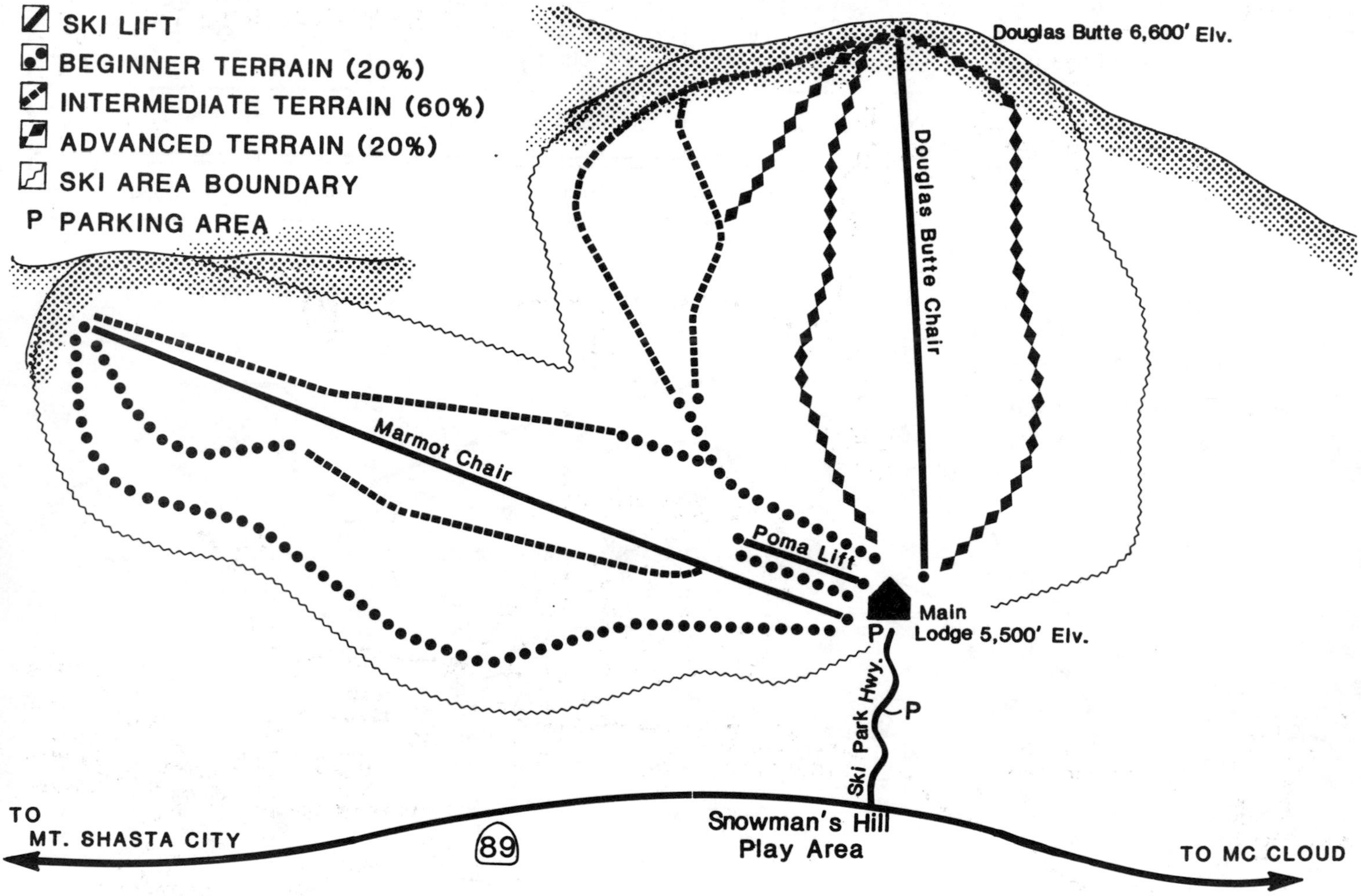

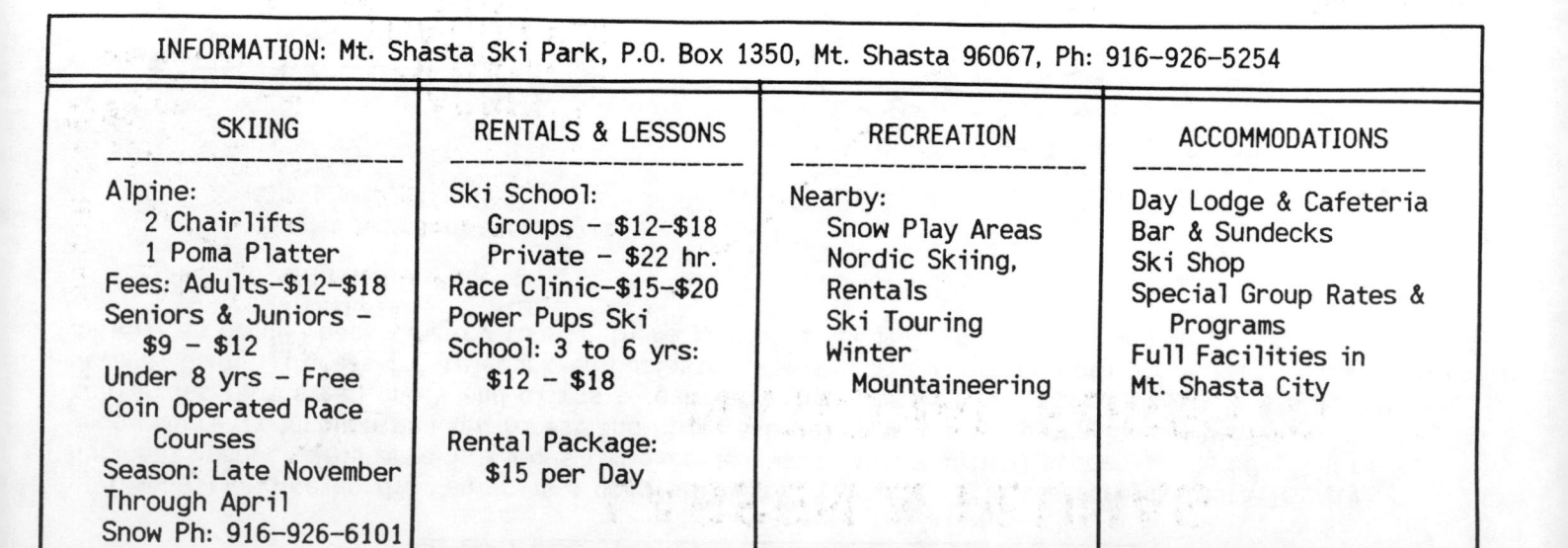

◩ SKI LIFT
⬚ BEGINNER TERRAIN (20%)
◪ INTERMEDIATE TERRAIN (60%)
◪ ADVANCED TERRAIN (20%)
◱ SKI AREA BOUNDARY
P PARKING AREA

Douglas Butte 6,600' Elv.

Douglas Butte Chair

Marmot Chair

Poma Lift

Main Lodge 5,500' Elv.

Ski Park Hwy.

TO MT. SHASTA CITY

(89)

Snowman's Hill Play Area

TO MC CLOUD

INFORMATION: Mt. Shasta Ski Park, P.O. Box 1350, Mt. Shasta 96067, Ph: 916-926-5254

SKIING	RENTALS & LESSONS	RECREATION	ACCOMMODATIONS

Alpine:
   2 Chairlifts
   1 Poma Platter
Fees: Adults-$12-$18
Seniors & Juniors -
   $9 - $12
Under 8 yrs - Free
Coin Operated Race
   Courses
Season: Late November
Through April
Snow Ph: 916-926-6101
	Ski School:
	   Groups - $12-$18
	   Private - $22 hr.
	Race Clinic-$15-$20
	Power Pups Ski
	School: 3 to 6 yrs:
	   $12 - $18
	
	Rental Package:
	   $15 per Day
		Nearby:
		   Snow Play Areas
		   Nordic Skiing,
		   Rentals
		   Ski Touring
		   Winter
		     Mountaineering
			Day Lodge & Cafeteria
			Bar & Sundecks
			Ski Shop
			Special Group Rates &
			   Programs
			Full Facilities in
			Mt. Shasta City

LASSEN & PLUMAS NATIONAL FORESTS

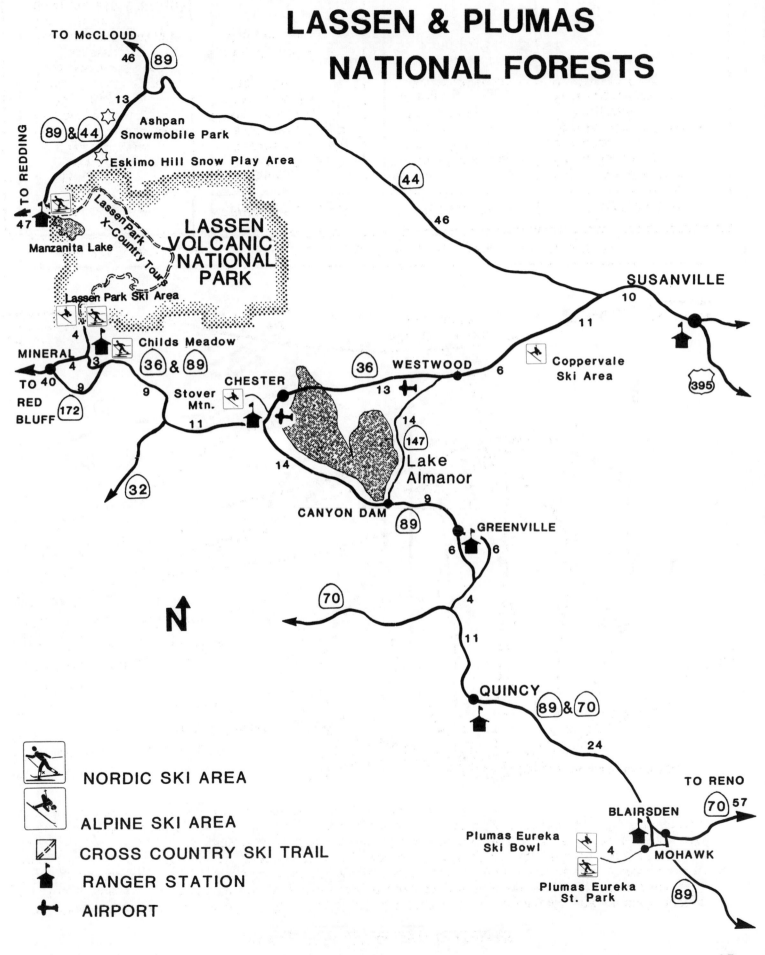

TO McCLOUD

46 (89)

13

(89)&(44)

Ashpan
Snowmobile Park

Eskimo Hill Snow Play Area

TO REDDING

47

Manzanita Lake

Lassen Park X-Country Tours

LASSEN VOLCANIC NATIONAL PARK

(44)

46

SUSANVILLE

10

11

Lassen Park Ski Area

4

4 3

9

MINERAL

TO 40

RED BLUFF

(172)

Childs Meadow

(36) & (89)

Stover Mtn.

9

11

(32)

14

CHESTER

Lake Almanor

(36) WESTWOOD

13

6

Coppervale Ski Area

395

14

(147)

CANYON DAM

9

(89)

6

GREENVILLE

6

(70)

4

11

QUINCY

(89)&(70)

24

TO RENO

(70) 57

BLAIRSDEN

Plumas Eureka Ski Bowl

4

MOHAWK

Plumas Eureka St. Park

(89)

NORDIC SKI AREA

ALPINE SKI AREA

CROSS COUNTRY SKI TRAIL

RANGER STATION

AIRPORT

N

15

Lassen Park Ski Area is a full service day use facility offering both alpine and nordic skiing. Located inside the southwest entrance of Lassen National Park, this family oriented facility offers a variety of downhill terrain suitable for all levels of ability. All seven runs are well groomed except when there is a good powder snowfall when a few are left untouched. The vertical is 600 feet. The Ski School offers group and private lessons for cross-country and alpine skiing. The "Kids are People, Too" Children's School is divided into two groups — beginner and more advanced. There is also a coin operated race course.

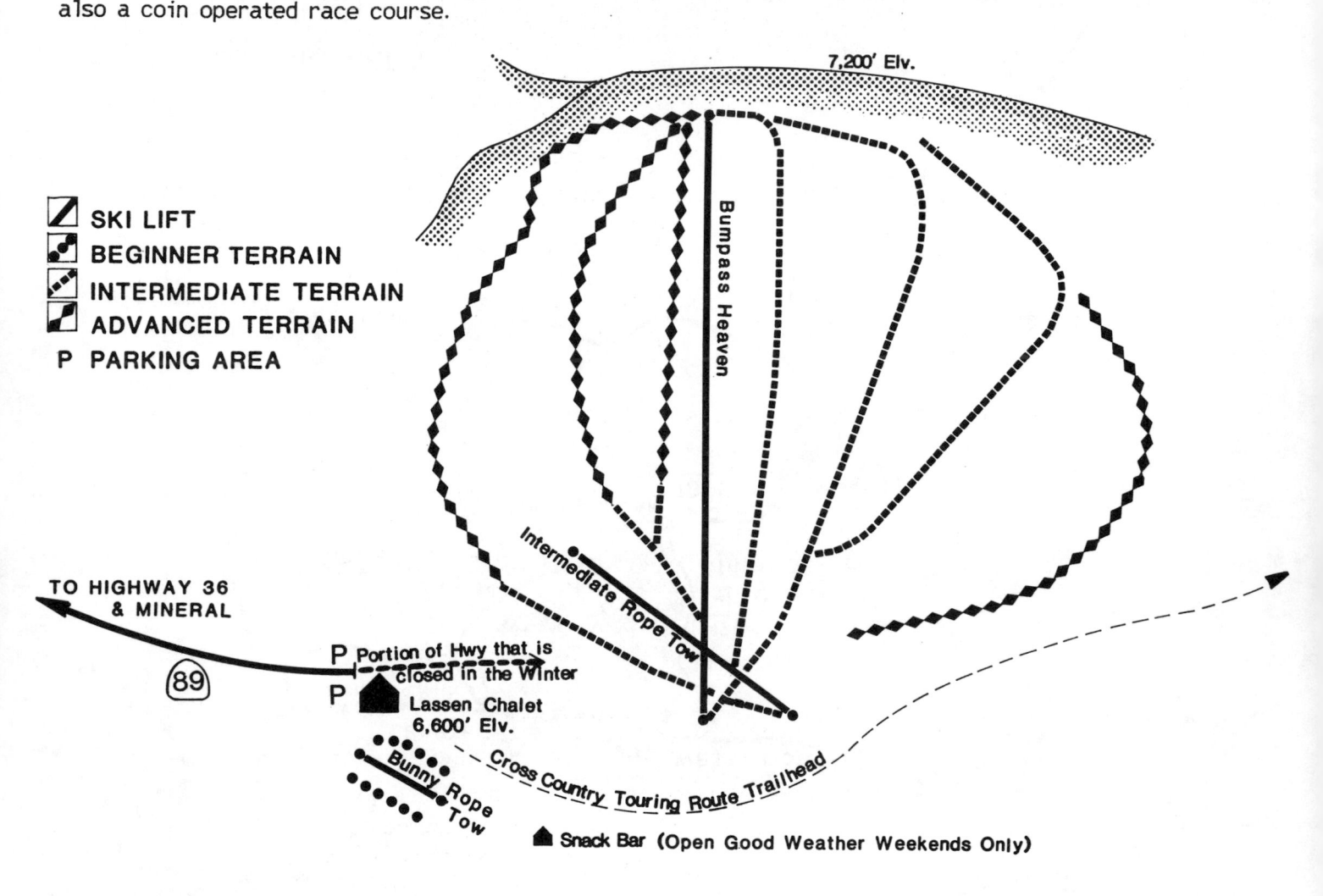

- ◢ SKI LIFT
- ◢ BEGINNER TERRAIN
- ◢ INTERMEDIATE TERRAIN
- ◢ ADVANCED TERRAIN
- P PARKING AREA

7,200' Elv.

Bumpass Heaven

TO HIGHWAY 36 & MINERAL

(89)

P Portion of Hwy that is closed in the Winter

P Lassen Chalet 6,600' Elv.

Intermediate Rope Tow

Bunny Rope Tow

Cross Country Touring Route Trailhead

🏠 Snack Bar (Open Good Weather Weekends Only)

INFORMATION: Lassen Park Ski Area, 2150 N. Main St.,#7, Red Bluff 96080, Ph: 916-595-3376

SKIING	RENTALS & LESSONS	RECREATION	ACCOMMODATIONS
Alpine: 　1 Triple Chairlift 　Adults –$15 　Child/Senior–$10 　2 Surface Tows: 　Adults – $8 　Child or Senior–$7 Nordic: Marked Trails Season : Mid. Nov.– 　　　Easter	Ski School: 　Alpine – Group: $11 　Private – $20 Hr. 　"Kids" 4 – 10yrs: 　Full Day Lesson, 　Lunch, Ticket, 　Rentals–$27 　Nordic–Group: $10 　Private – $15 Hr. Rentals: 　Alpine Comb:$14 　Nordic Comb:$10	N.P.S. Ranger Led: 　Snow Shoe Walks 　　(Snow Shoes 　　Furnished) 　Winter Survival & 　Snow Shelter 　Programs Snow Play & Camping Sledding (Outside Ski 　Area)	Day Lodge Cafeteria Ski Shop & Repairs Gift Shop Nordic Center Limited Camping & Overnight Parking in Designated Areas

LASSEN VOLCANIC NATIONAL PARK

Lassen Volcanic National Park is a prime winter sports area. In addition to downhill skiing there are two nordic areas separated by the winter closure of Highway 89 within the park. These designated touring routes are the South Area Winter Touring Trails which offer a nordic center and the Manzanita Lake Winter Trails. Virtually the entire park is open to touring, although caution is advised to the danger of inclement weather and avalanche. Always check weather and snow conditions in advance, before venturing into the backcountry. Permits are required for all overnight tours and day users are required to sign in. Park Rangers conduct several environmental programs including a snowshoe walk and group cross-country tours.

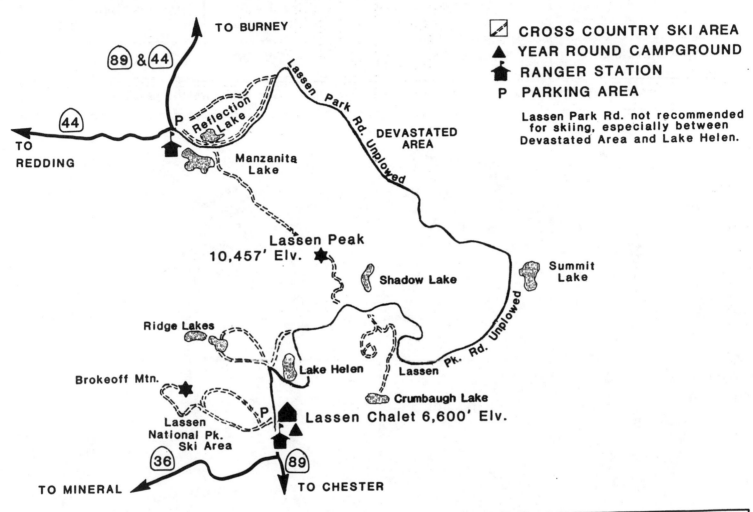

CROSS COUNTRY SKI AREA
▲ **YEAR ROUND CAMPGROUND**
RANGER STATION
P **PARKING AREA**

Lassen Park Rd. not recommended for skiing, especially between Devastated Area and Lake Helen.

INFORMATION: Lassen Volcanic Park, P.O. Box 100, Mineral, Ca. 96063 Ph:916-595-4444

SKIING	RENTALS & LESSONS	RECREATION	ACCOMMODATIONS
Nordic: 　50 Miles of 　Designated Trails Ski Touring Alpine:(see prev.pg.) Backcountry Weather and Avalanche Info: 　Ph: 916-595-4444 Ski Chalet: 　Ph: 916-595-3308 Manzanita R.S. 　Ph: 916-335-4266	Nordic Ski School: 　(At Ski Chalet 　Only) 　Group Lessons $10 　Private $15 　Tours with 　Equipment $20 Rentals: 　Adult: $9 　Senior/Child $5	Ranger Guided: 　Cross-Country Ski 　Tours (by Reserv.) 　Snowshoe Walking 　(Shoes Furnished) 　Winter Survival 　Program Other: 　Snow Play Nearby: 　Snowmobiling	At Southwest Area: 　Day Lodge/Cafeter. 　Ski Shop/ Repairs 　First Aid 　Gift Shop 　 Parking in 　Designated Areas 　For Lodging 　Outside Park See 　Following Pages.

Childs Meadows Cross Country Ski Area is in the Lassen National Forest off Highway 36–89 between Mineral and Chester. Located in a beautiful alpine setting at the base of Mt. Lassen, this popular nordic area offers a variety of cross-country skiing. There are 75 kilometers of marked trails, the majority of which are regularly groomed, but several are left in their natural state. From gentle groomed runs to ungroomed steeps, these trails offer a variety of terrain and challenges to all levels of skiing ability. There is a telemark practice hill and the Doe Mountain Downhill Run. Lessons are available for all levels of ability and guided snow camping and tours are offered.

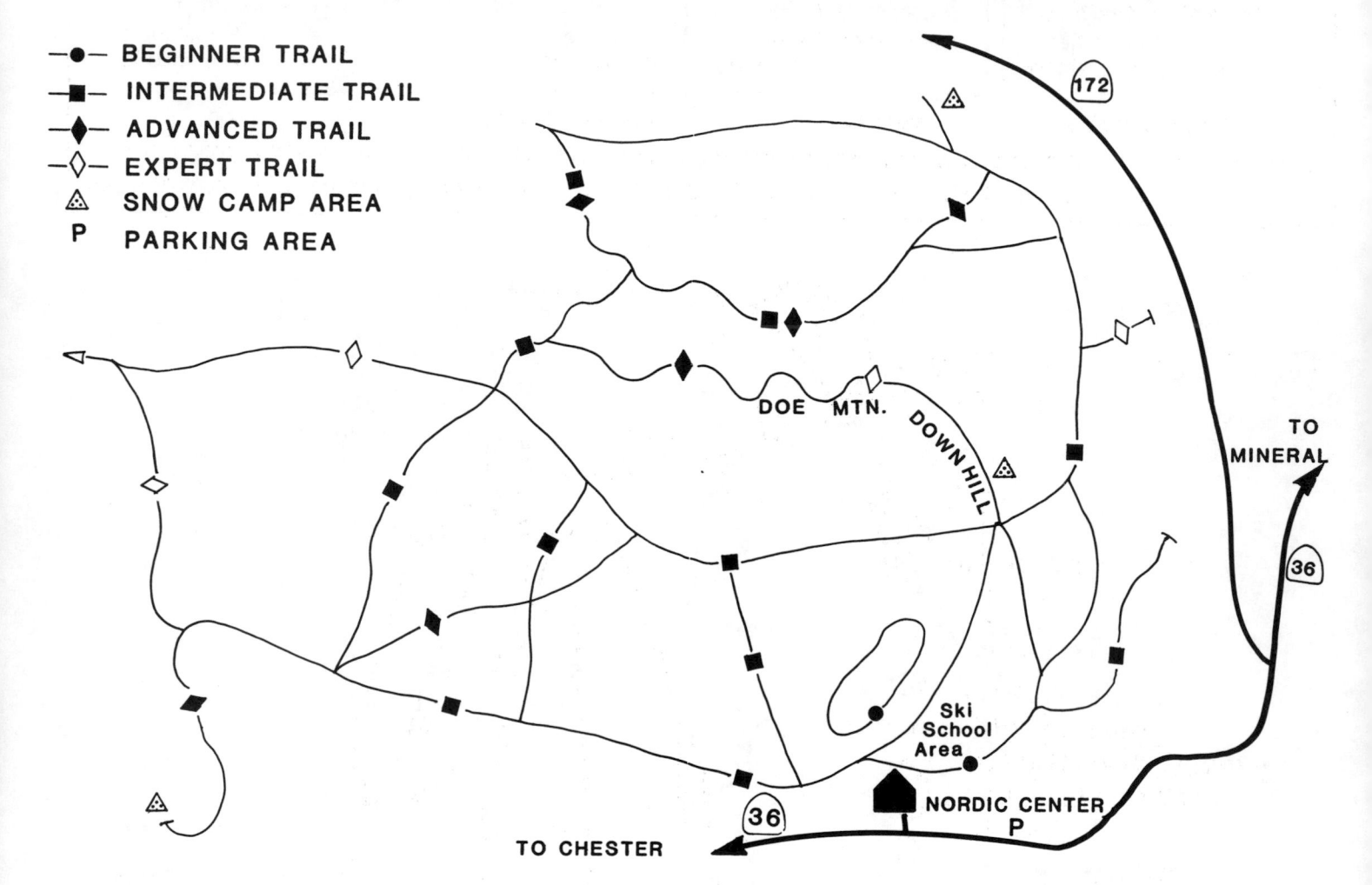

—●— BEGINNER TRAIL
—■— INTERMEDIATE TRAIL
—◆— ADVANCED TRAIL
—◇— EXPERT TRAIL
△ SNOW CAMP AREA
P PARKING AREA

DOE MTN. DOWNHILL

172

TO MINERAL

36

Ski School Area

NORDIC CENTER
P

36

TO CHESTER

INFORMATION: Childs Meadows Ski Area, P.O. Box 177, Mineral, Ca. 96063 Ph: 916-595-4411

SKIING	RENTALS & LESSONS	RECREATION	ACCOMMODATIONS

Nordic:
  75 Kilometers
  Groomed, Marked
  Trails
  Telemark Practice
  Area
Fee:All Day/Half Day
  Adult:$5/$3.50
  Child:$2.50/$2
Season–Mid-November
Through April
	Nordic Lessons:
	  Group $10
	  Private $18
	Tours:(1–10 People)
	  Half Day:$75
	  All Day:$125
	  Nordic, Alpine
	  Helicopter Tours
	Rentals Available
		Nearby:
		  Ski Touring
		  Downhill Skiing
		  Snow Play
		  Snowmobiling
			Day Lodge
			Snow Camping
			  (by 2 Week Advance
			  Reservation)

STOVER MOUNTAIN

Stover Mountain is a small privately operated ski facility in the Lassen National Forest. This area is three miles west of Chester on Chester Ski Road. This is a basic facility with a rope tow, poma lift, warming hut and sanitary facilities. Stover offers primarily beginner and intermediate runs for local skiers. It is only open on weekends and holidays. Cross country and ski touring on the back roads are popular especially off Butt Lake Road and the McGowan Lake Loop of Highway 89. Each year the Chester/Lake Almanor Chamber of Commerce sponsors the Winterfest, featuring dog-sled racing, snowmobile races and other festive events.

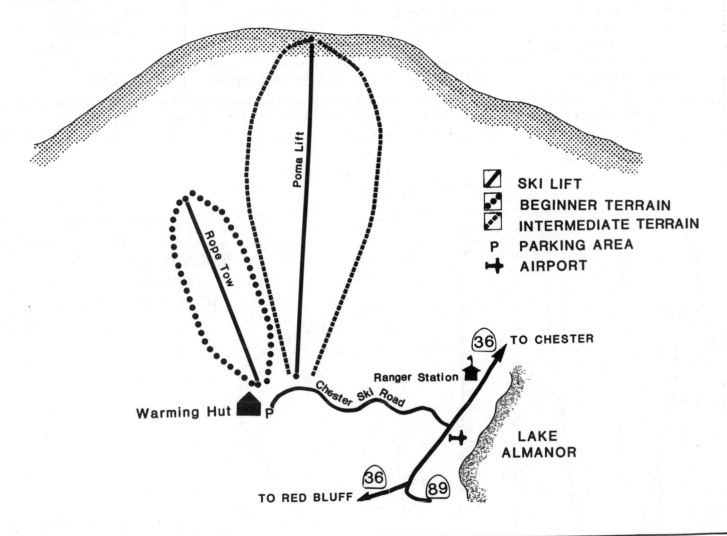

INFORMATION: Lake Almanor Chamber of Commerce, P.O. Box 1198, Chester 96020, Ph: 916-258-2426

SKIING	RENTALS & LESSONS	RECREATION	ACCOMMODATIONS
Stover Mountain: Alpine Skiing – 1 Poma Lift 1 Rope Tow	Not Available at Site	Nearby: Cross Country Skiing Ski Touring Snow Play Areas Snowmobiling	Small Warming Hut Lodging & Facilities in Chester

Coppervale is a small downhill ski area off Highway 36 between Westwood and Susanville. Just 5 miles east of Westwood in the Lassen National Forest, this local facility is operated by the Lassen Community College District. There is a rope tow and a poma lift. The vertical down the mountain is 600 feet offering varied runs for every level of ability. It is open on Tuesday and Thursday afternoons and all day during weekends and holidays. There are no accommodations so bring your own lunch and drinks. The Forest Service maintains a snow play area just up the road at Willards Hill.

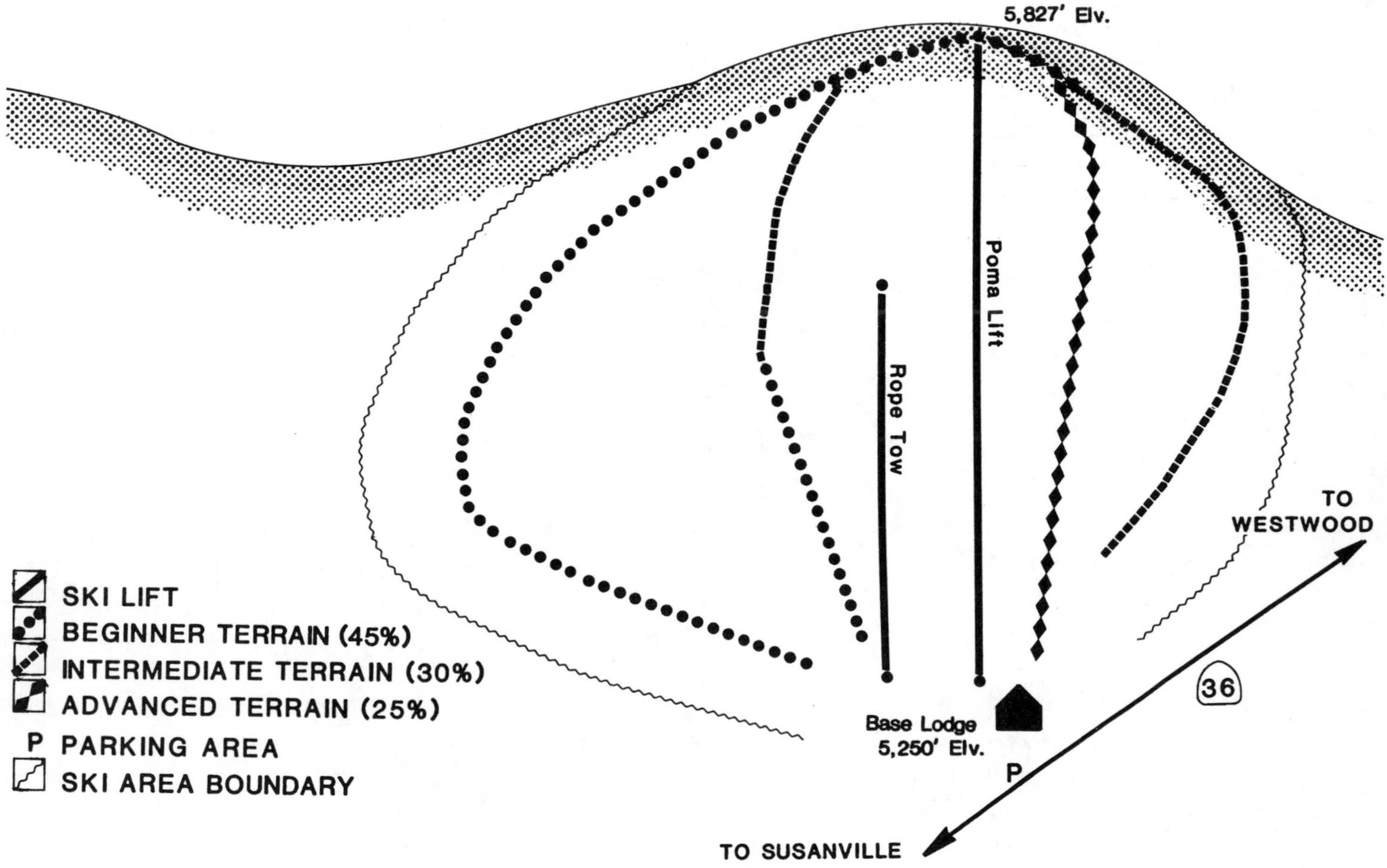

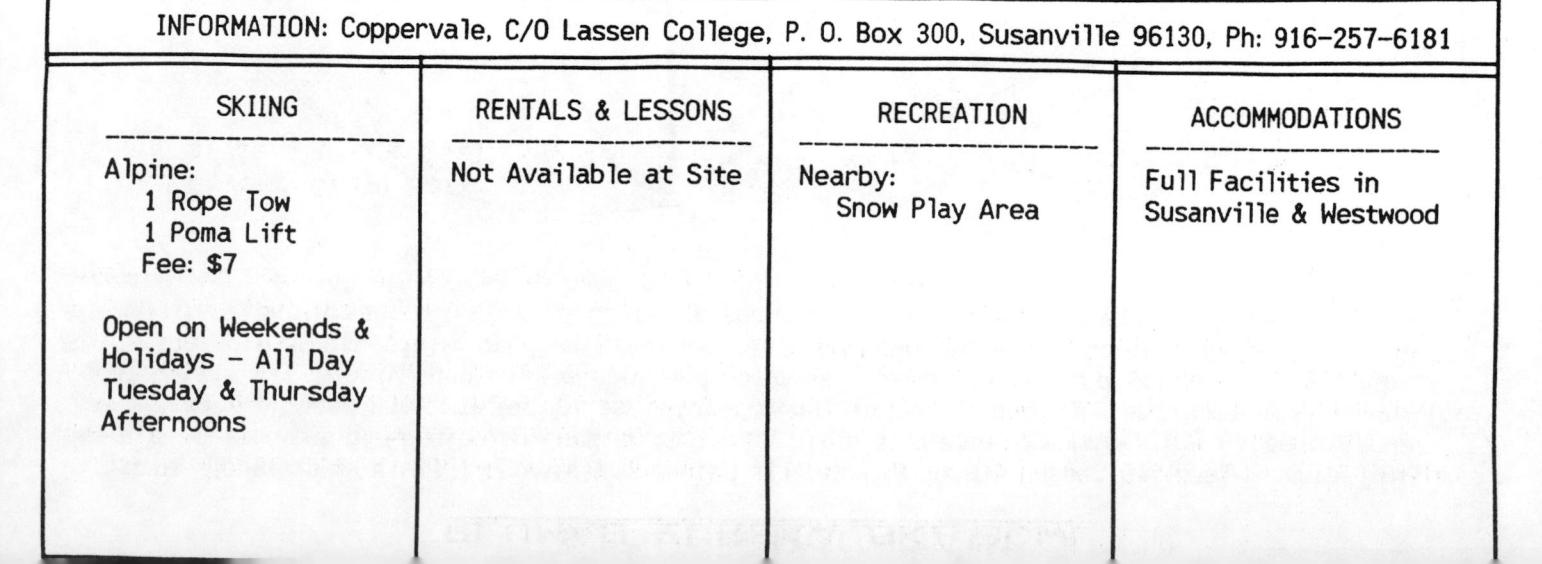

5,827' Elv.

Poma Lift

Rope Tow

TO WESTWOOD

36

Base Lodge
5,250' Elv.

P

TO SUSANVILLE

SKI LIFT
BEGINNER TERRAIN (45%)
INTERMEDIATE TERRAIN (30%)
ADVANCED TERRAIN (25%)
P PARKING AREA
SKI AREA BOUNDARY

INFORMATION: Coppervale, C/O Lassen College, P. O. Box 300, Susanville 96130, Ph: 916-257-6181			
SKIING	**RENTALS & LESSONS**	**RECREATION**	**ACCOMMODATIONS**
Alpine: 　1 Rope Tow 　1 Poma Lift 　Fee: $7 Open on Weekends & Holidays – All Day Tuesday & Thursday Afternoons	Not Available at Site	Nearby: 　Snow Play Area	Full Facilities in Susanville & Westwood

PLUMAS EUREKA SKI BOWL

The Plumas Eureka Ski Bowl is a small downhill area within Plumas Eureka State Park. This remote downhill facility is operated by the Plumas Ski Club primarily for local skiers and schools, but is open to the general public. There are six runs down a vertical of 600 feet, only half of these runs are groomed. Facilities are limited to a warming hut and snack bar. Snow play and cross-country skiing along the trails of the Park is popular. The Park is closed to camping in the winter. This area of the scenic Plumas National Forest offers limited winter recreation facilities, but those who enjoy a more basic nordic environment will find it a challenge.

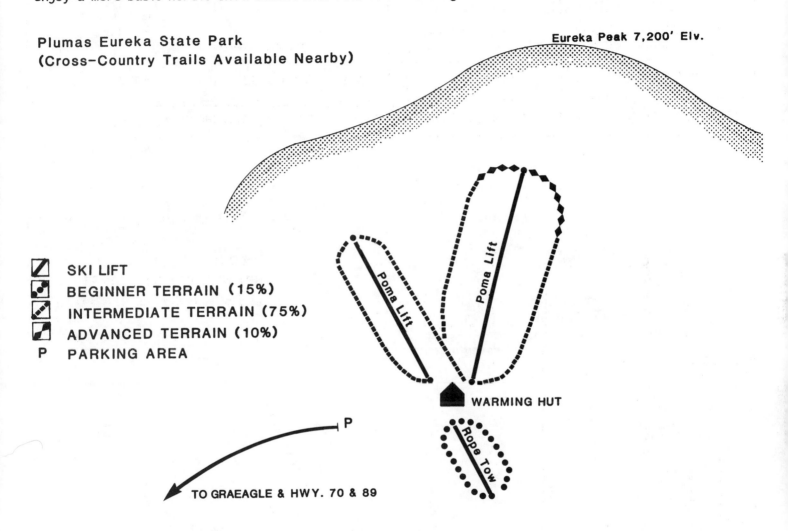

Plumas Eureka State Park
(Cross-Country Trails Available Nearby)

Eureka Peak 7,200' Elv.

SKI LIFT
BEGINNER TERRAIN (15%)
INTERMEDIATE TERRAIN (75%)
ADVANCED TERRAIN (10%)
P   PARKING AREA

Poma Lift

Poma Lift

WARMING HUT

P

Rope Tow

TO GRAEAGLE & HWY. 70 & 89

INFORMATION: Plumas-Eureka State Park, 310 Johnsville Rd., Blairsden 96103, Ph: 916-836-2380			
SKIING	RENTALS & LESSONS	RECREATION	ACCOMMODATIONS

Alpine:
  2 Poma Lifts
  1 Rope Tow
Fees: Adult – $10
Child Under 12 – $8
Rope Tow – $4
Open: Wednesdays,
Weekends & Holidays
Season:Mid-Nov.-Apr.
Snow Conditions are
Unpredictable
Snow Ph:916-283-1124
	None at this Site	Cross-Country Skiing
		Snow Play
		Nearby:
		  Ski Touring
		  Snow Camping
		  Snowmobiling
			Warming Hut
			Snack Bar
			National Ski Patrol
			
			Lodging & Facilities
			in Graeagle & Portola

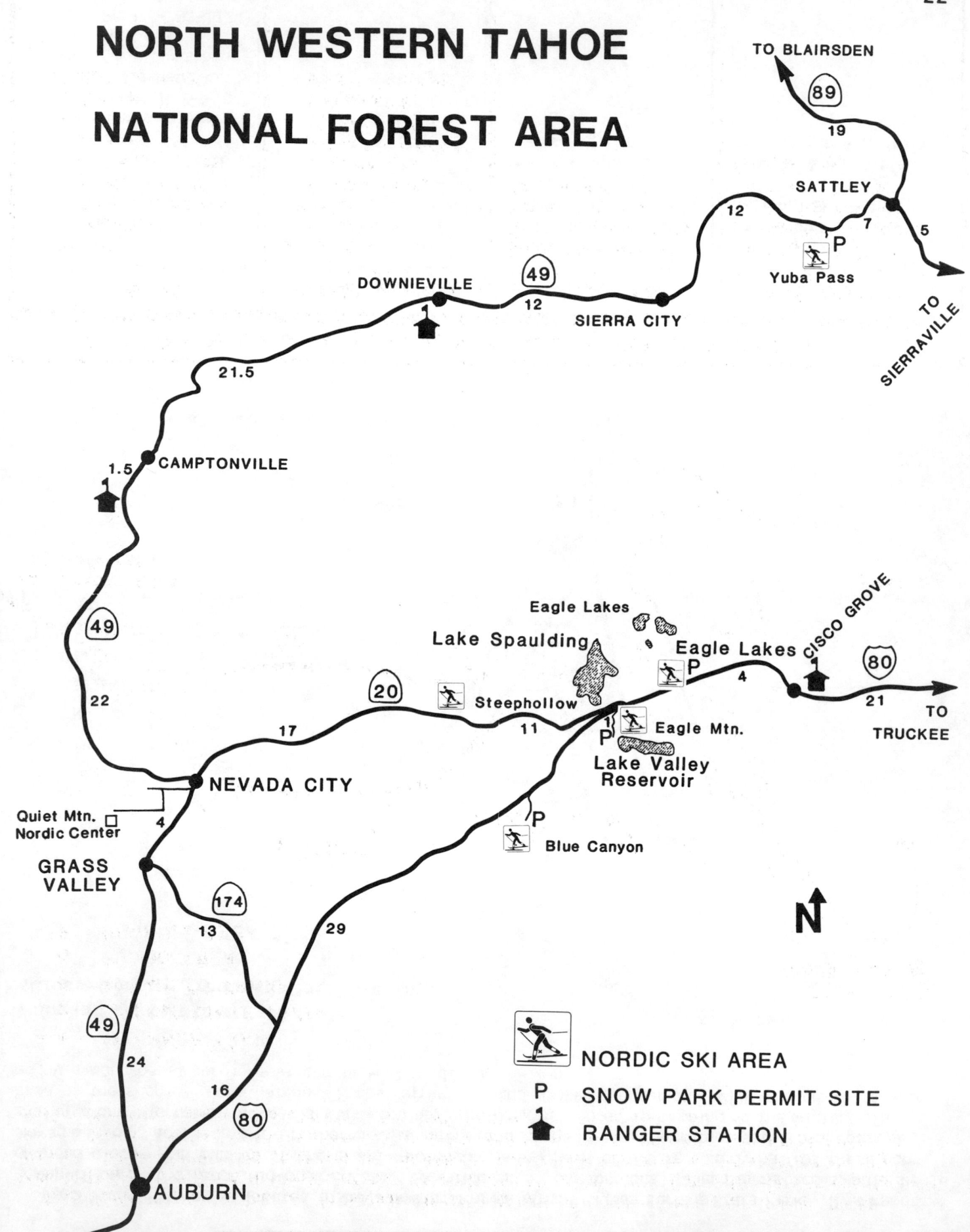

NORTH WESTERN TAHOE
NATIONAL FOREST AREA

TO BLAIRSDEN

89

19

SATTLEY

12

7

5

P

Yuba Pass

DOWNIEVILLE

49

12

SIERRA CITY

TO SIERRAVILLE

21.5

1.5 CAMPTONVILLE

49

22

Eagle Lakes

Lake Spaulding

CISCO GROVE

Eagle Lakes

80

20

P

4

21

Steephollow

11

TO TRUCKEE

Eagle Mtn.

P

Lake Valley
Reservoir

17

NEVADA CITY

Quiet Mtn.
Nordic Center

4

P

Blue Canyon

GRASS
VALLEY

174

13

29

N

49

24

16

80

NORDIC SKI AREA

P   SNOW PARK PERMIT SITE

RANGER STATION

AUBURN

TO ROSEVILLE

QUIET MOUNTAIN NORDIC CENTER

This Nordic Center is located in Nevada City and maintains trails 17 miles up Highway 20 at Steephollow in the Tahoe National Forest. Specializing in group tours, Quiet Mountain is popular with various clubs. The 9 miles of trails are marked for every level of cross-country skiing ability. Nevada City is located in the Mother Lode Country, and Quiet Mountain offers lodging packages in conjunction with some unique old Victorian style hotels.

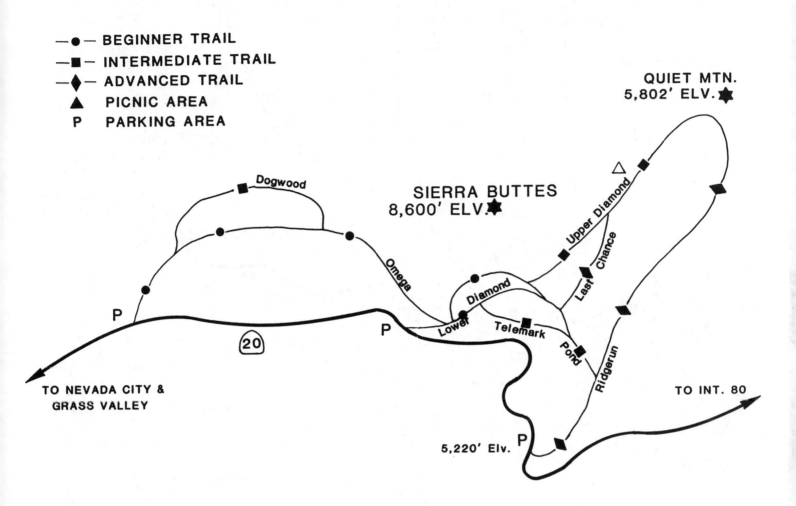

—●— BEGINNER TRAIL
—■— INTERMEDIATE TRAIL
—◆— ADVANCED TRAIL
▲ PICNIC AREA
P PARKING AREA

QUIET MTN.
5,802' ELV. ★

SIERRA BUTTES
8,600' ELV. ★

Dogwood
Omega
Upper Diamond
Last Chance
Diamond
Lower
Telemark
Pond
Ridgerun

P
P
P

20

TO NEVADA CITY &
GRASS VALLEY

TO INT. 80

5,220' Elv.

INFORMATION: Quiet Mountain, 419 Spring St. Nevada City 95959, Ph: 916-265-9186			
SKIING	**RENTALS & LESSONS**	**RECREATION**	**ACCOMMODATIONS**

Nordic:
  Beginner,
  Intermediate and
  Advanced–9 Miles
  of Marked Trails
  No Fee
Season: Mid–November
to Mid–April
Closed Tuesdays
	Ski School:
	  All Levels
	Rentals:
	  Cross-Country
	  Combinations
	  Adults: $7.50–$9.50
	  Children:$6.50
	  Groups of 12 or
	  more – Discounts
		Guide Service for
		Cross-Country Tours
		Mother Lode Country
		for Sight Seeing
			National Hotel
			  Historic Landmark
			  Ph: 916-265-4551
			Full Facilities in
			Nevada City

EAGLE MOUNTAIN NORDIC

Eagle Mountain Nordic is just 74 miles from Sacramento and is within a reasonable drive from the Bay Area. Located on a well-maintained road one mile off I 80 at the Yuba Gap Exit, this secluded forested area, surrounded by the Tahoe National Forest, provides some of the finest and most beautiful nordic trails in the Sierras. There are 20 groomed, marked trails meandering through snow-covered meadows, by frozen streams, climbing to spectacular vistas. There are 65 kilometers of set track varying in difficulty from novice to expert. This nice, friendly day use resort offers a variety of free programs and mid-week specials. There are two trailside warming huts with stoves and hot drinks and a cozy day lodge with cafe, ski rentals and accessories and a ski school.

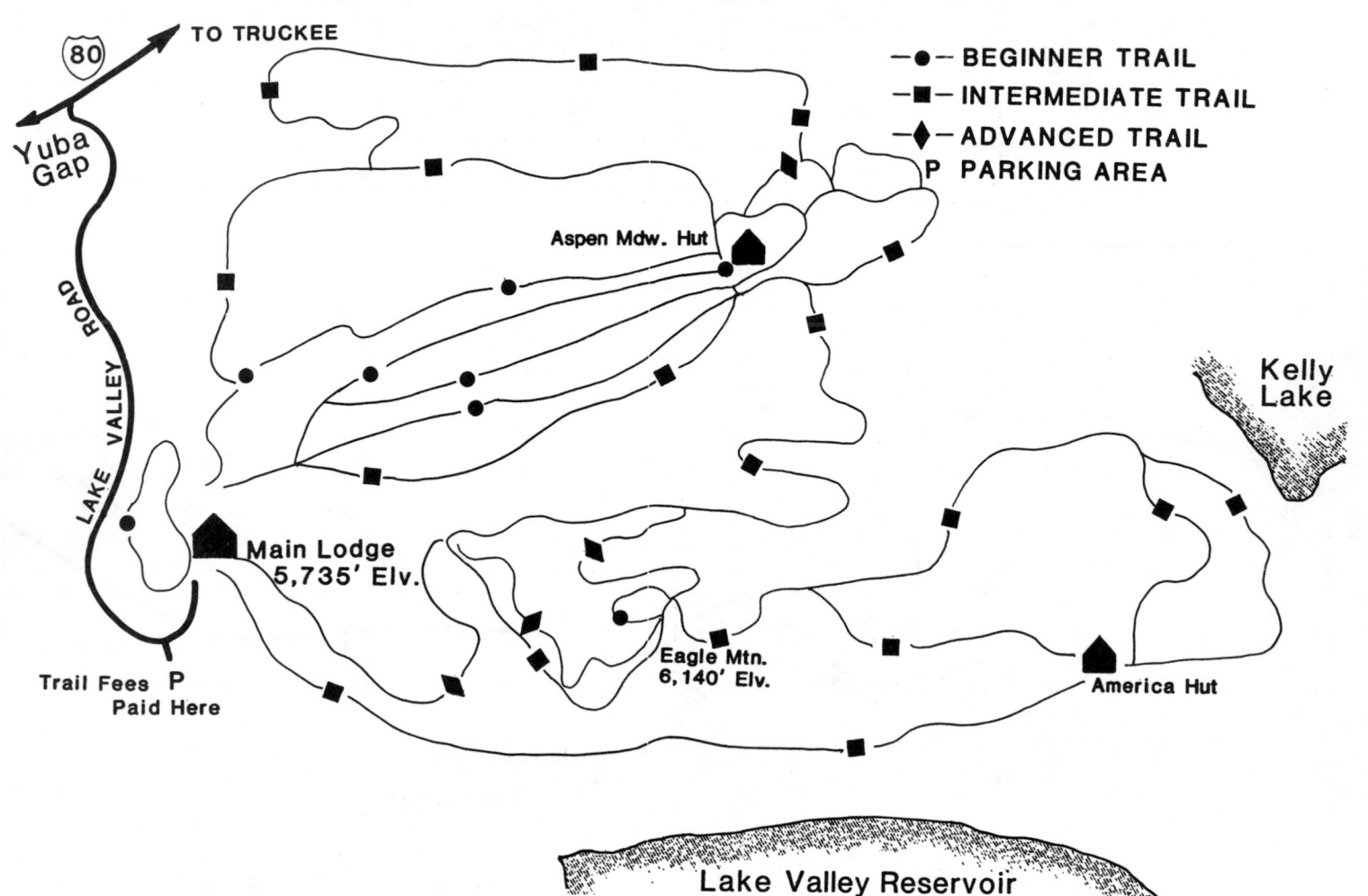

SKIING	RENTALS & LESSONS	RECREATION	ACCOMMODATIONS

Nordic:
  65 Kilometers of
  Groomed Set Track
Fees: Adults –
Full Day: $9.50
At 1 PM: $7.50
Juniors – 6–11 Yrs.:
Full Day: $5.50
At 1 PM: $3.50
5 & Under: Free
Season: Nov. to May
Snow Ph: 916–389–2255
	Ski School:
	  Basic Lesson – 2
	  Hrs. – $12
	  Skill Clinic – $9
	  Private – $18 Hr.
	  Children – $7
	Reservations Advised
	Rentals:
	  Adults: $7.50–$9.50
	  Junior: $5.50–$7.50
	  Demos: $15
	  Racing Skis: $10
		Free Programs:
		  Telemark Clinics –
		  Fri., Sat., Sun.
		  Ski–Skating Clinics
		  Daily
		  Mid Week Discounts
		  Guided Tours
		Nearby:
		  Snow Play
		  Ski Touring
		  Snow Camping
		  Snowmobiling
			Day Lodge & Cafe
			Warming Huts:
			Complimentary Hot
			Drinks
			Sun Deck
			Picnic Tables
			Group Discounts
			Nearest Facilities
			At Emigrant Gap and
			Cisco Grove. Also
			Along Hwy. 80 at Soda
			Springs & Norden

INFORMATION: Eagle Mountain Nordic, P.O. Box 89, Emigrant Gap 95715, Ph: 916–389–2254

EAGLE LAKES ROAD SNO-PARK SITE

A large plowed area at this Site is designated for 70 vehicles with Sno-Park Permits. Located just off Highway 80 on the Eagle Lakes Road at 5,600 feet elevation, this area offers excellent cross-country skiing to beautiful Eagle Lakes in the high Sierras. In addition, snowmobilers can follow a route along the South Yuba River. All around snow play is good after a heavy snowfall.

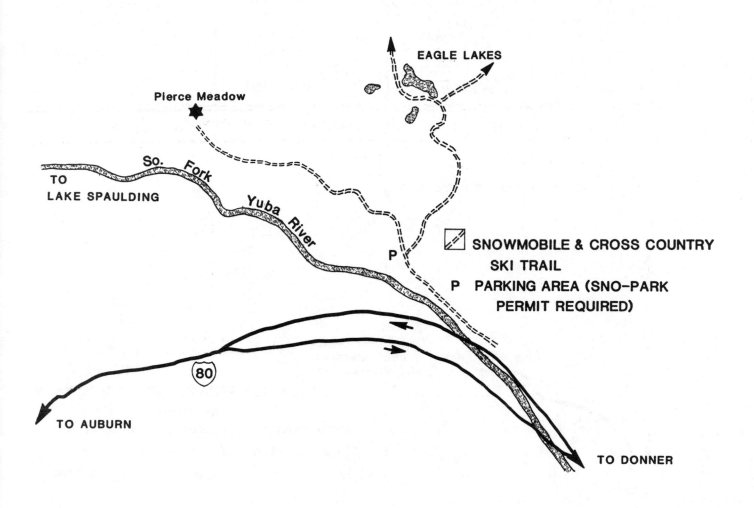

SNOWMOBILE & CROSS COUNTRY SKI TRAIL

P PARKING AREA (SNO-PARK PERMIT REQUIRED)

INFORMATION: Sno-Park Program, P. O. Box 2390, Sacramento 95811, Ph: 916-322-8993

SKIING	RENTALS & LESSONS	RECREATION	ACCOMMODATIONS
Nordic: Beginner, Intermediate & Advanced Trails 2-1/2 Miles to Eagle Lakes	Not Available at Site	Snow Play Area Snowmobiling	Parking: 70 Vehicles No Parking at End of Road Sno-Park Permit Fees: $2 - Day $10 - Annual Must Have Permit in Advance

Located about 10 miles west of Sierraville along Highway 49, the Yuba Pass Sno-Park Area normally has a heavy snowfall for a long season of snow play activities. Cross-country skiers will find terrain from unplowed roadways to the challenge of Mt. Haskell, a difficult 10 mile round trip. There is also a short loop which starts north and then cuts back along Lunch Creek. Skiers are asked to stay on the north side of Highway 49 while snowmobilers can follow routes on the south side into Lincoln Valley. A long tour via a marked trail passes through Jackson Meadow, by Webber Lake and back to Highway 49. This route is popular for snowmobiles. A Sno-Park Permit is required for use of this parking area so be sure to have one in your vehicle.

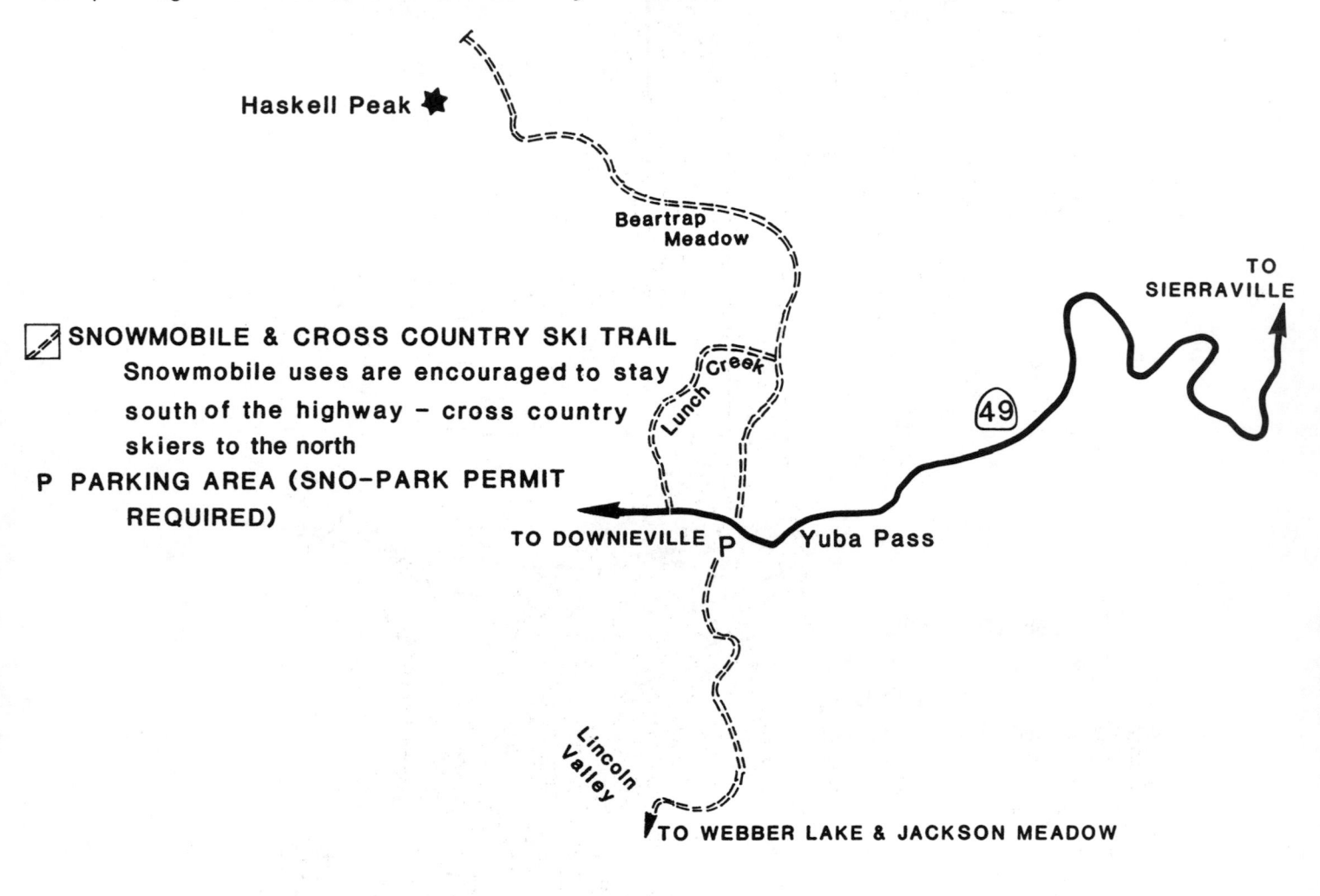

SNOWMOBILE & CROSS COUNTRY SKI TRAIL
Snowmobile uses are encouraged to stay south of the highway – cross country skiers to the north

P PARKING AREA (SNO-PARK PERMIT REQUIRED)

INFORMATION: USFS, P.O. Box 95, Sierraville 96126, Ph: 916-994-3401			
SKIING	**RENTALS & LESSONS**	**RECREATION**	**ACCOMMODATIONS**

Nordic:
  Beginner,
  Intermediate &
  Advanced Trails
	Not Available at Site	Snow Play Areas
		Snowmobiles:
		  Marked Trails
		
		SNO-PARK PERMITS
		ONLY:
		Contact –
		California Sno-Park
		Permit Program
		P. O. Box 2390
		Sacramento 95811
		Ph: 916-322-8993
			Parking: 30 Vehicles
			
			Sno-Park Permit Fees:
			  $2 – Day
			  $10 Annual
			Must Have Permit in
			  Advance

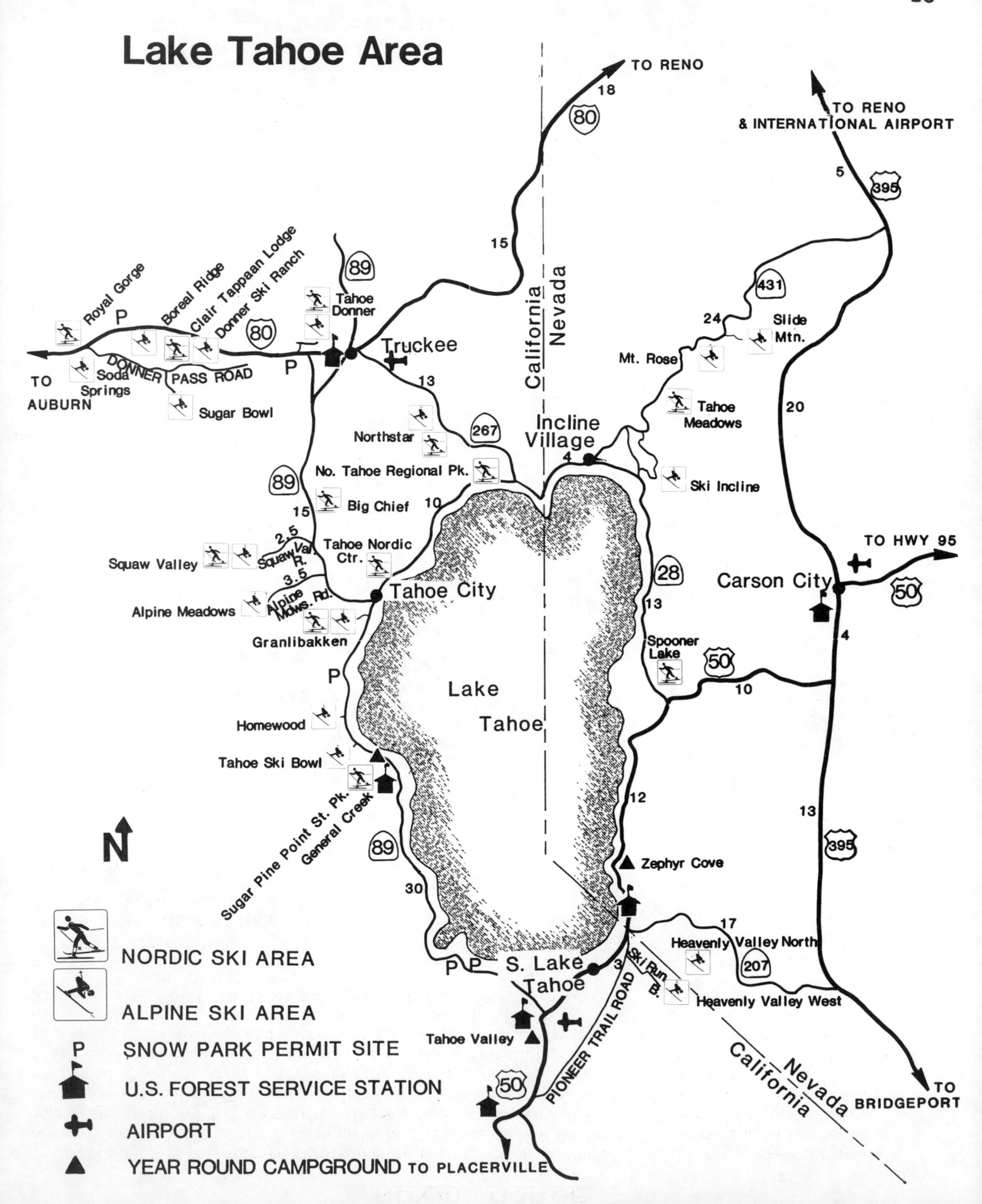

Lake Tahoe Area

TO RENO

18

80

TO RENO & INTERNATIONAL AIRPORT

5

395

15

89

431

24

Slide Mtn.

Royal Gorge

Boreal Ridge

Clair Tappaan Lodge

Donner Ski Ranch

P

Tahoe Donner

Mt. Rose

Tahoe Meadows

80

Truckee

California

Nevada

Incline Village

Soda Springs

DONNER PASS ROAD

P

TO AUBURN

Sugar Bowl

13

267

4

Ski Incline

20

Northstar

89

No. Tahoe Regional Pk.

10

15

Big Chief

Tahoe Nordic Ctr.

28

Carson City

TO HWY 95

50

2.5

Squaw Val. R.

Squaw Valley

13

3.5

Alpine Mdws. Rd.

Tahoe City

Spooner Lake

50

4

Alpine Meadows

Granlibakken

10

P

Lake Tahoe

Homewood

Tahoe Ski Bowl

General Creek

Sugar Pine Point St. Pk.

89

12

Zephyr Cove

13

395

N

30

17

Heavenly Valley North

207

NORDIC SKI AREA

ALPINE SKI AREA

P   SNOW PARK PERMIT SITE

U.S. FOREST SERVICE STATION

AIRPORT

YEAR ROUND CAMPGROUND

P P   S. Lake Tahoe

3

Ski Run B.

Heavenly Valley West

Tahoe Valley

California

Nevada

50

PIONEER TRAIL ROAD

TO BRIDGEPORT

TO PLACERVILLE

ROYAL GORGE

Royal Gorge is the premier cross-country ski resort in America. Located in the heavy snowfall area of Donner Summit, this huge nordic facility has modern grooming equipment and is continually improving on Mother Nature's gifts. There are 62 trails and 255 kilometers of double, triple or quadruple set and skating tracks. There are runs for all levels of ability. Six warming huts are scattered along the trails providing complimentary tea. In addition to the Summit Cafe at the trailhead, there is a wilderness lodge cafe in the heart of the trail system. The Ski School is geared to all levels of ability, and there is a special skating/telemark clinic. The European style wilderness lodge features French country cuisine, and visitors arrive by sleigh or snowcat. Royal Gorge is the site of the 1986, 1987 and 1988 Subaru/USSA Cross-Country Championships.

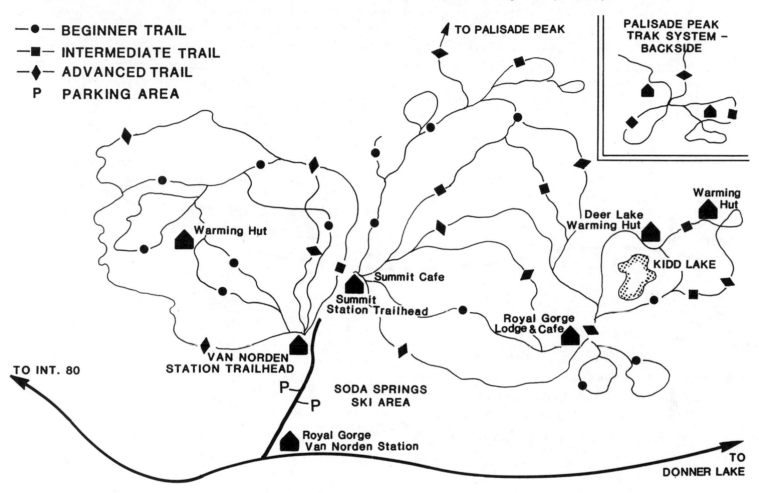

SKIING	RENTALS & LESSONS	RECREATION	ACCOMMODATIONS
Nordic:	Ski School:	Nearby;	6 Warming Huts
255 Kilometers of Groomed Track	Group – $12	Alpine Resorts,	Summit Cafe & Bar
62 Trails	Private – $20	Lessons & Rentals	Wilderness Cafe
Moonlight Tours	Children's Ski School/ Day Care – 5-9 Yrs.	Ski Touring	Retail Store
Fee: Adults –	Lesson, Lunch,	Snow Camping	Shuttle Bus
Full Day – $11.50	Rental – $24.50	Snowmobiling	Royal Gorge
Half Day – $8.50	Rentals:	Snow Play Areas	Wilderness Lodge:
Children – $6.50	Combinations –	Casinos	Dorms, Gourmet Meals,
Senior-$8.50 Midweek	$8.50 – $11	Dancing	Hot Tub & Sauna,
Season: November 15 to May 15	Special:Rental, Lesson & Trail Pass – $24.50	Live Entertainment	Sleigh & Snowcat Transportation

INFORMATION: Royal Gorge Resort, P. O. Box 178, Soda Springs 95728, Ph: 916-426-3871

DONNER SUMMIT SNO—PARK SITE

Castle Valley is a very popular cross-country area as the snow is usually excellent and the season is long. On the north side of Highway 80, a 3-mile trail begins for skiers up to the Peter Grubb Warming Hut and Castle Peak. On the west side of Castle Valley are open areas good for beginning cross-country skiers as well as snow campers. Snowmobiles are restricted to the west side of Andesite Peak along a designated route. Typical of the high Sierras, the scenery is spectacular. A Sno—Park Permit is required to use the Parking Area which has space for 50 vehicles.

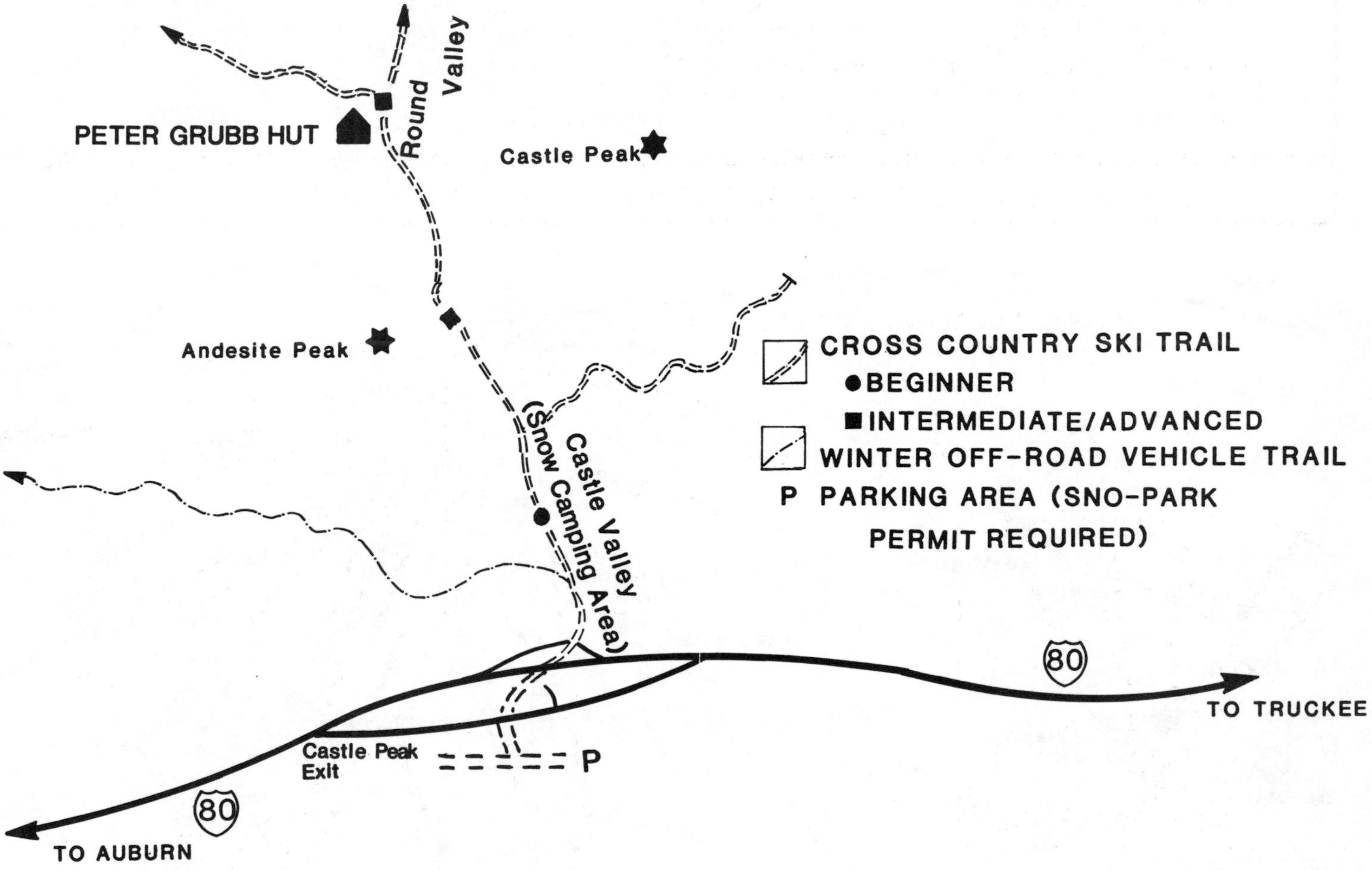

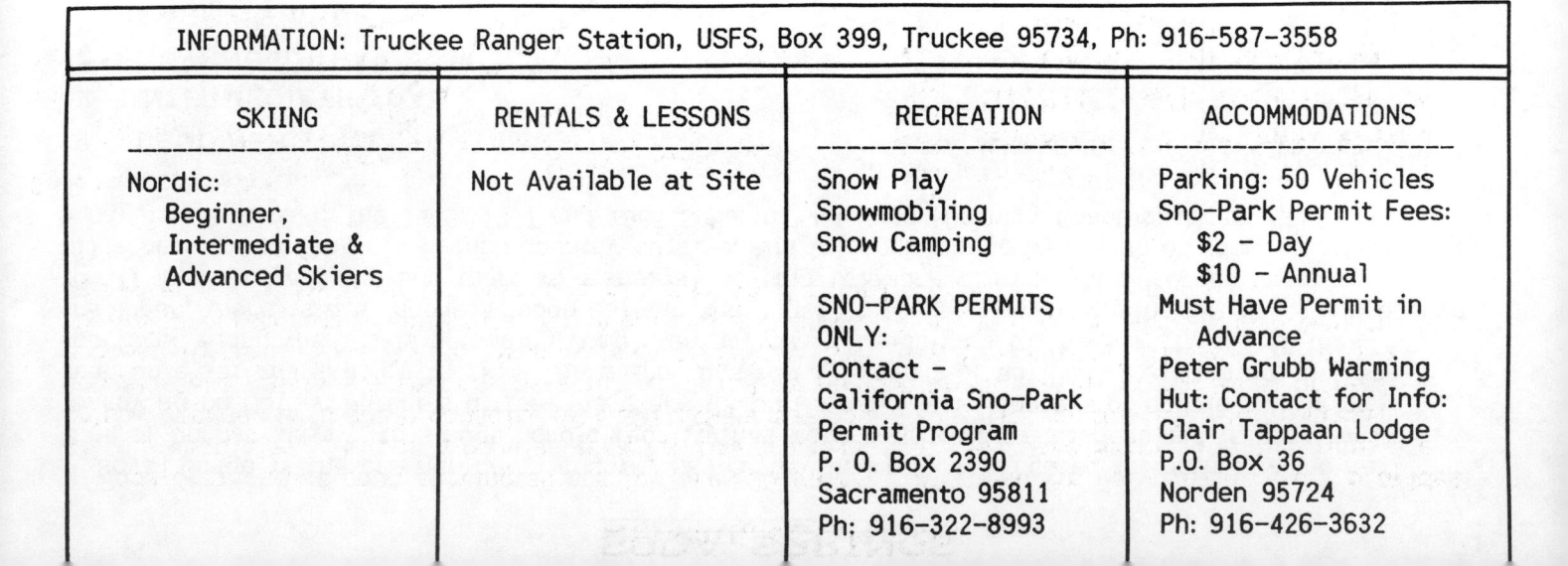

	SKIING	RENTALS & LESSONS	RECREATION	ACCOMMODATIONS
INFORMATION: Truckee Ranger Station, USFS, Box 399, Truckee 95734, Ph: 916-587-3558				

	Nordic:
	  Beginner,
	  Intermediate &
	  Advanced Skiers
		Not Available at Site	Snow Play
			Snowmobiling
			Snow Camping
			
			SNO—PARK PERMITS
			ONLY:
			Contact –
			California Sno—Park
			Permit Program
			P. O. Box 2390
			Sacramento 95811
			Ph: 916-322-8993
				Parking: 50 Vehicles
				Sno—Park Permit Fees:
				  $2 – Day
				  $10 – Annual
				Must Have Permit in
				  Advance
				Peter Grubb Warming
				Hut: Contact for Info:
				Clair Tappaan Lodge
				P.O. Box 36
				Norden 95724
				Ph: 916-426-3632

SODA SPRINGS

Soda Springs has been serving skiers for over 50 years. This pleasant, easy going resort provides all the amenities. This is a popular area for day trippers from the Tahoe Basin. The lift lines are seldom crowded with their capacity of 4,800 skiers per hour. The runs on this 652 foot vertical mountain are relatively short. The skier will find three open bowls within its 200 acres of well-groomed terrain. Soda Springs is only open on Friday, Saturday, Sunday and holidays. There is a special program for large groups, organizations and corporations that permits the entire facility to be rented for a day when the resort is not open to the public.

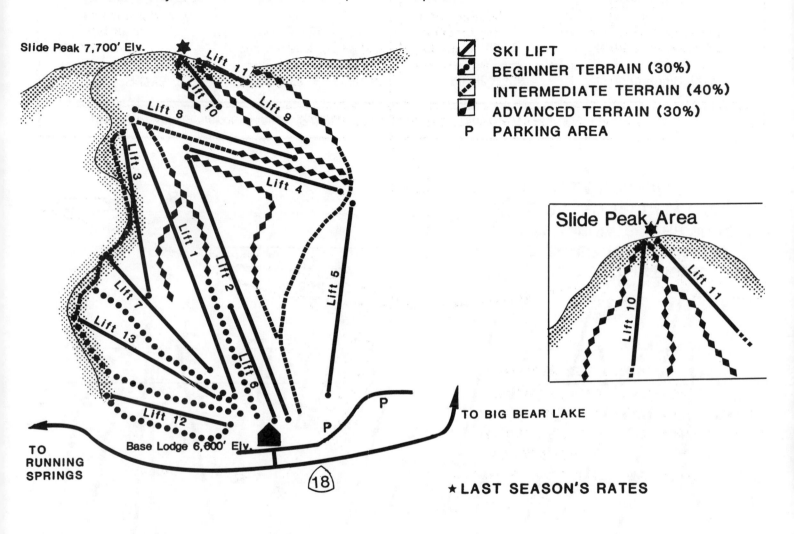

SKI LIFT
BEGINNER TERRAIN (30%)
INTERMEDIATE TERRAIN (40%)
ADVANCED TERRAIN (30%)
P PARKING AREA

Slide Peak 7,700' Elv.
Lift 11
Lift 10
Lift 8
Lift 9
Lift 3
Lift 4
Lift 1
Lift 2
Lift 5
Lift 7
Lift 13
Lift 6
Lift 12
Base Lodge 6,600' Elv.

Slide Peak Area
Lift 10
Lift 11

P
P
TO BIG BEAR LAKE

TO RUNNING SPRINGS
(18)

★ LAST SEASON'S RATES

INFORMATION: Soda Springs Ski Area, P.O. Box 67, Soda Springs 95728, Ph: 916-426-3666

SKIING	RENTALS & LESSONS	RECREATION	ACCOMMODATIONS

Alpine:
  3 Chairlifts
  Fees:* Adults –
    $10 – $14
    Children –
    $8 – $9
    Seniors – $9
Season: Thanksgiving
through Easter
Friday, Saturday,
Sunday & Holidays
Snow Ph: 916-426-3663
	Ski School:*
	  Group Lessons:
	  $14 – $21
	  Private Lessons:
	  $27 per hour
	  Learn to Ski
	  Package: $27
	  (All Day Lesson,
	  Lifts & Rentals)
	  Skiwee-4-12 yrs.
	Ski Equipment* – $14
	Snowboard Rentals
		Snowboarding: Rentals
		& Lessons
		Nearby:
		  Cross Country
		  Snow Play Areas
		  Snowmobile Rentals
		  ORV Trails
		  Casinos
			Cafeteria, Bar, Sun
			Deck, Sundries
			Repair Shop, First Aid
			Rent-a-Ski Area Day
			Boreal Motel –
			  Ski/Lodge Packages
			P.O. Box 39
			Truckee 95734
			Ph: 916-426-3211
			Other Lodging at
			Boreal, Truckee & N.
			Lake Tahoe

BOREAL SKI AREA

Boreal is the largest night skiing area in the Sierras. The lighted area covers acres of beginning, intermediate and advanced runs. Those skiers who have a late start may ski 'til ten at night. This full service facility provides over 300 acres of varied terrain. Located on the top of a long ridge on the Donner Summit, Boreal has 37 runs along this 600 foot vertical mountain. Lift lines are usually short, so most of your time is on the slopes. There are the usual mid-week and beginner packages. The popular Skiwee Program for children, four years of age to twelve years, is staffed by specially trained and qualified instructors.

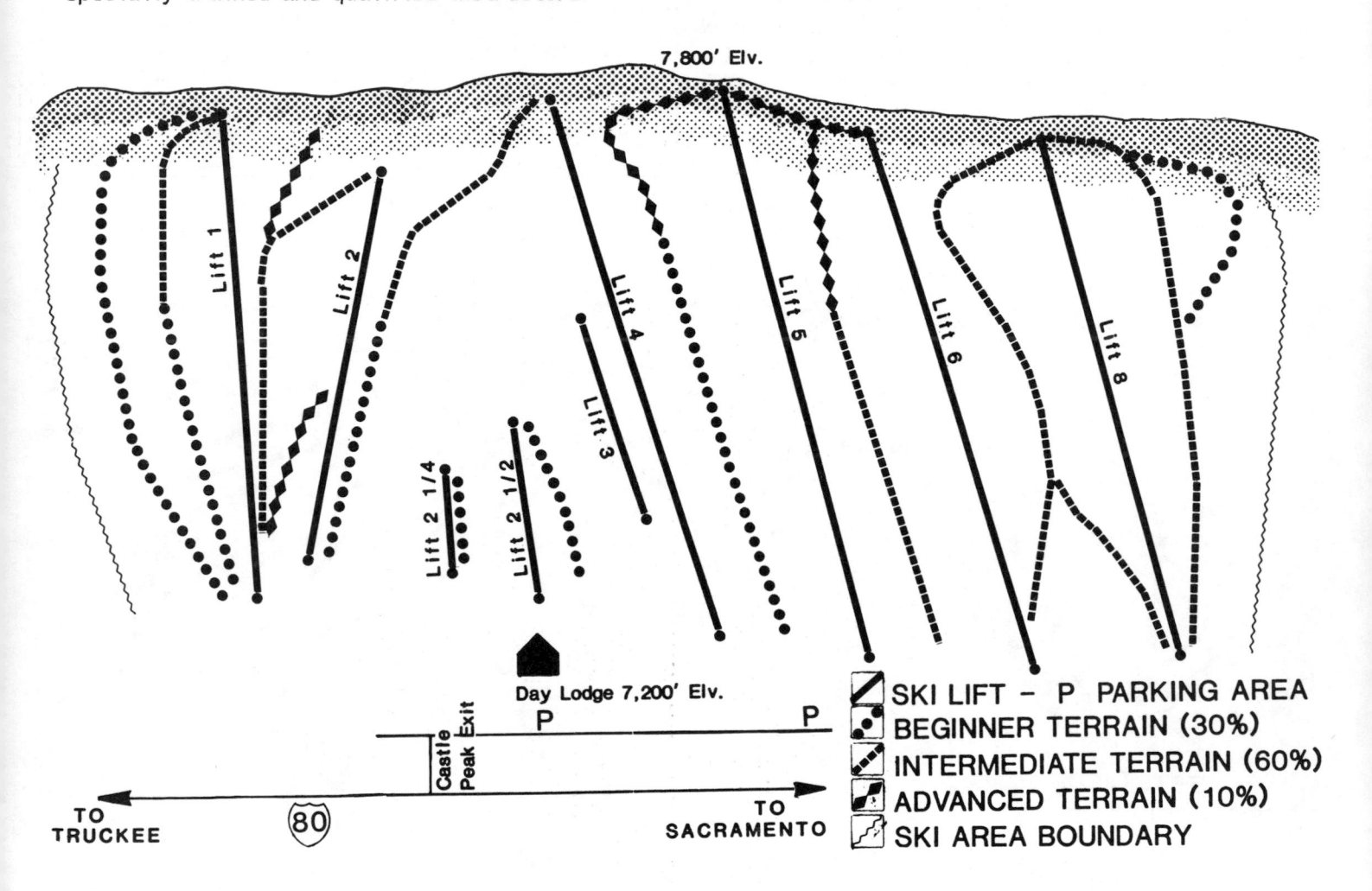

7,800' Elv.

Lift 1
Lift 2
Lift 2 1/4
Lift 2 1/2
Lift 3
Lift 4
Lift 5
Lift 6
Lift 8

Day Lodge 7,200' Elv.

Castle Peak Exit

P   P

TO TRUCKEE   (80)   TO SACRAMENTO

SKI LIFT - P PARKING AREA
BEGINNER TERRAIN (30%)
INTERMEDIATE TERRAIN (60%)
ADVANCED TERRAIN (10%)
SKI AREA BOUNDARY

INFORMATION: Boreal Ski Area, P.O.Box 39, Truckee 95734, Ph: 916-426-3666

SKIING	RENTALS & LESSONS	RECREATION	ACCOMMODATIONS
Alpine: 　9 Chairlifts 　Fees: Adult, 　Senior & Children's 　Rates - Full Day & 　Night, Half Day or 　Night Only - 　Varies from $7-$18 　Group Discounts Normal Season: 　Early November to 　Late April	Ski School: 　Group Lessons: 　All Day - $21 　Half Day - $14 　Private: $27/hour 　Learn to Ski 　Package: $27 　Skiwee-All Day-$35 Rental Ski Equipment: 　$14 ALL FEES SUBJECT TO 　CHANGE	Snow Boarding & Rentals Nearby: 　Cross Country 　Skiing & Rentals 　Snow Play Areas 　Snowmobile Rentals 　ORV Trails 　Casinos 　Live Entertainment	Cafeteria & Lounge Ski Shop & Repairs Western America Ski 　Museum Boreal Village Condos 　Ph: 916-426-3211 Boreal Motel 　Ph: 916-426-3666 Other Lodging in Truckee & North Lake Tahoe Area

SUGAR BOWL

Sugar Bowl has one of the heaviest snow packs in the Sierras. There are 39 runs off the 1,500 vertical drop down Mt. Lincoln. Beginner, intermediate and many advanced runs are regularly groomed. This area offers 1,000 acres of skiable terrain. This unique modern facility has been in operation since 1939 when it was the site of California's first chairlift. Sugar Bowl is reached today by a gondola from an enclosed parking garage. The original main lodge offers all the conveniences including special "Mountain Escape" packages providing lodging, meals, lift tickets and lessons. There will be a new quad-chairlift, Silver Belt, replacing Lincoln Two. A new mid-mountain lodge is in the planning stage.

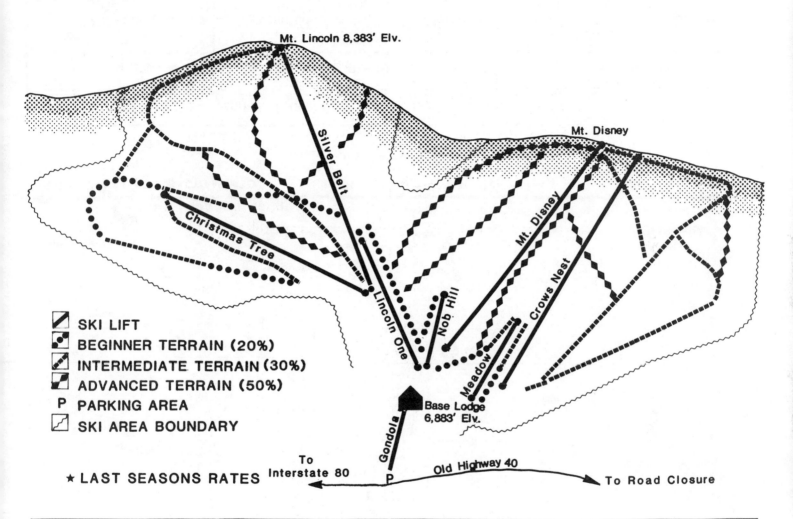

- ⬚ SKI LIFT
- ⬚ BEGINNER TERRAIN (20%)
- ⬚ INTERMEDIATE TERRAIN (30%)
- ⬚ ADVANCED TERRAIN (50%)
- P PARKING AREA
- ⬚ SKI AREA BOUNDARY

★ LAST SEASONS RATES

INFORMATION: Sugar Bowl, P. O. Box 5, Norden 95724, Ph: 916-426-3651

SKIING	RENTALS & LESSONS	RECREATION	ACCOMMODATIONS
Alpine: 　7 Chairlifts 　1 Access Gondola 　1 Access Chair Fees:* Adults–$15–$23 Children–$10–$12 Night Skiing: 　Saturday & Tuesday Season: November 　through April	Ski School:* 　Group Lessons 　Half Day – $14 　Full Day – $20 　Private – $26 Hr. 　Racing Clinic: 　　Sat. p.m.–$14 Rentals:* 　Adults: $13.50 　Children: $8.50 　New Demo Skis: $20 　Nordic Equipment	Nearby: 　Cross Country 　Skiing, Rentals & 　Lessons 　Ski Touring 　Snowmobiling 　Snow Play Areas 　Casinos	Ski Shop: Equipment Repairs & Accessories Dining Room: Dress 　Requirements @ 6pm Cafeteria & Snack Bar Cocktail Lounges Garage & Parking Gift Shop Ski/Lodging Packages 　by Reservation

CLAIR TAPPAAN LODGE

Clair Tappaan Lodge has been owned and operated by the Sierra Club for over 50 years. This facility is open to the public for an additional $2 fee. Reservations are required. Located on Donner Summit near a variety of alpine and nordic resorts, this large rustic mountain lodge provides dormitory style accommodations which include good family style meals. There is a nordic ski school offering trail and downhill lessons. Nordic ski equipment and snowshoes are available to rent. There are 7 miles of groomed nordic trails leading to Lytton Lake. These trails are free to Sierra Club members. Others are requested to make a $4 donation to the Club.

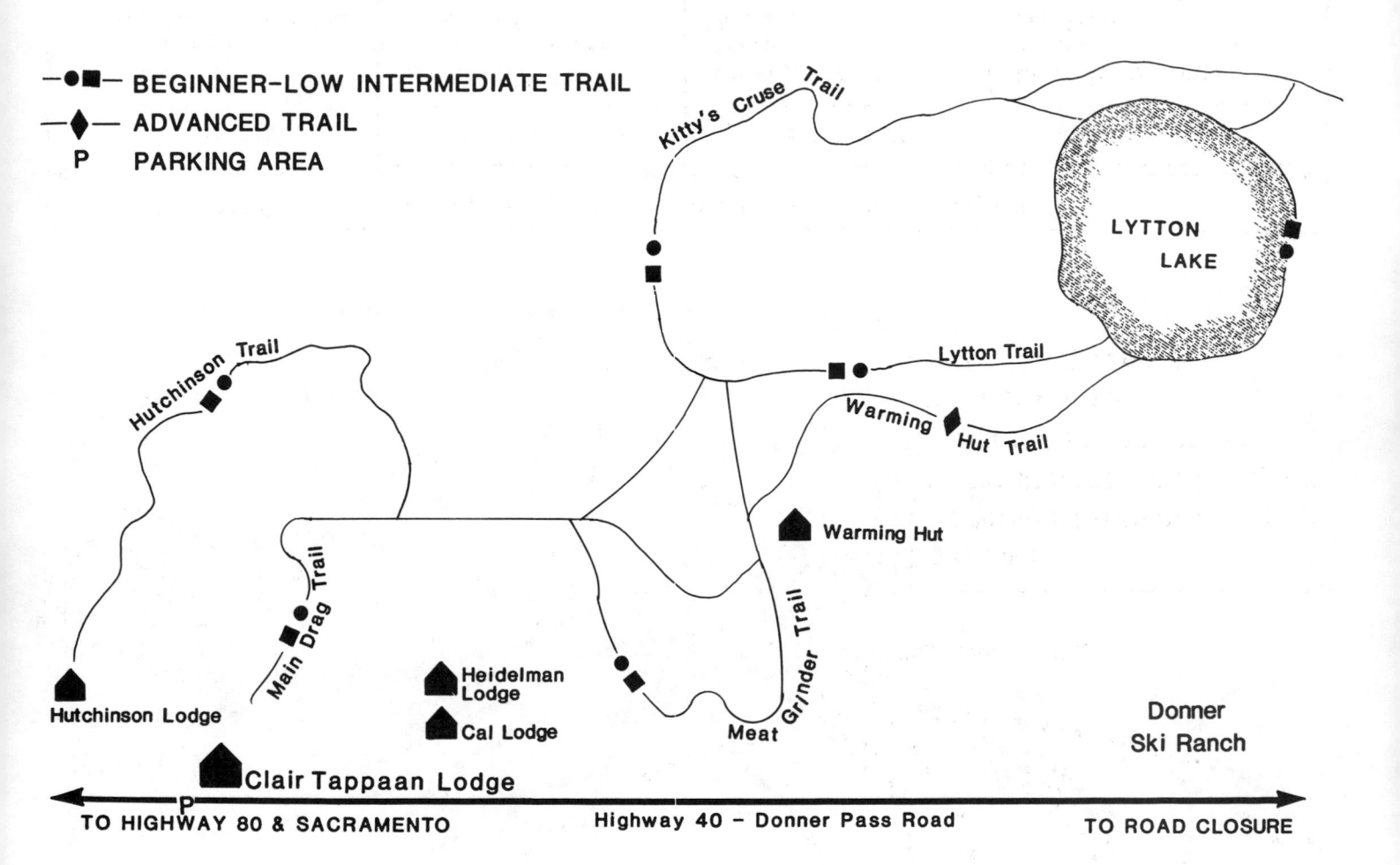

─●■─ BEGINNER-LOW INTERMEDIATE TRAIL

─◆─ ADVANCED TRAIL

P   PARKING AREA

Kitty's Cruse Trail

LYTTON LAKE

Hutchinson Trail

Lytton Trail

Warming Hut Trail

Warming Hut

Main Drag Trail

Meat Grinder Trail

Heidelman Lodge

Cal Lodge

Hutchinson Lodge

Clair Tappaan Lodge

Donner Ski Ranch

P

TO HIGHWAY 80 & SACRAMENTO   Highway 40 – Donner Pass Road   TO ROAD CLOSURE

INFORMATION: Clair Tappaan Lodge, P. O. Box 36, Norden 95724, Ph: 916-426-3632

SKIING	RENTALS & LESSONS	RECREATION	ACCOMMODATIONS

Nordic:
  7 Miles of Groomed Trails
  No Fee for Sierra Club Members
  $4 Donation for Others
 	
Season: Mid November to Mid-April
	Ski School:
	  Group Lessons in Track & Telemark Techniques
	  2 Hrs. – $10
	Rentals:
	  Combinations (Skis, Boots & Poles):
	  Midweek – $7
	  Weekend – $9
	  1/2 Day – $4
	  Snowshoes – $6
		Nearby:
		  Alpine Skiing, Lessons & Rentals
		  Ski Touring
		  Snow Camping
		  Snow Play Areas
		  Snowmobiling
		  Casinos
			Lodge:
			  2 Person Cubicles
			  Family Bunkrooms
			  Gender Dorms
			  Dining Room
			  (Meals Included)
			  Social Room
			Fees: Sierra Club Members –
			Adult – $25.50 Day
			12 & Under – $20.50
			Non-Members Add $2

DONNER SKI RANCH

Donner Ski Ranch was one of the first ski resorts on the West Coast. This friendly Alpine facility offers over 350 acres of skiable terrain. From well-groomed trails to unpacked powder, the varied slopes attract skiers of all levels of ability. There are over 40 runs down the 720 foot vertical. Donner Ski Ranch operating in conjunction with the Alpine Skills Institute, is the forerunner in the revival of the nordic telemark downhill technique which is called "Norpine Skiing". The Ski School offers lessons in Alpine and "Norpine" skiing and individualized attention for young skiers ages 3 to 7. This ski area offers all the amenities including lodging, meals and service.

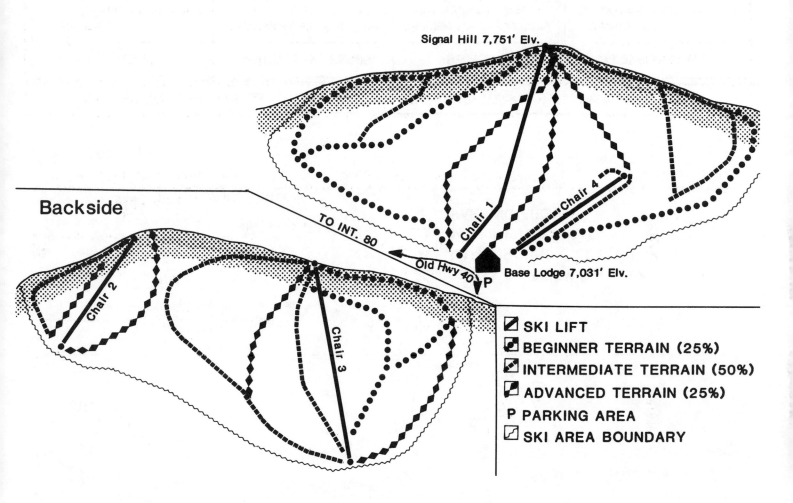

SKI LIFT
BEGINNER TERRAIN (25%)
INTERMEDIATE TERRAIN (50%)
ADVANCED TERRAIN (25%)
P PARKING AREA
SKI AREA BOUNDARY

INFORMATION: Donner Ski Ranch, P. O. Box 66, Norden 95724, Ph: 916-426-3635

SKIING	RENTALS & LESSONS	RECREATION	ACCOMMODATIONS

Alpine:
    4 Chairlifts
Fees: Adults-$12-$18
Children & Seniors –
    $8 – $9
Over 70 – Free
Season: Late November
    through April
Snow Phone:
    916-426-3635
	Ski School: Alpine
	    Group Lessons:
	    $11/1.5 hrs.
	    Private-$22/hr.
	    Kid's Special – $14
	Ski School: Norpine
	    Group-$11/1.5 hr.
	    Private-$22/hr.
	Rentals:
	    Combination: $13
	    Demo Combin: $20
		Special Events &
		Races
		Nearby:
		    Cross Country
		    Skiing, Lessons,
		    Rentals & Tours
		    Snow Play Areas
		    ORV Trails
			Cafe, Restaurant,
			2 Bars
			Ski Shop:
			    Rentals & Repairs
			Group Packages
			Lodging Includes
			Meals & Lift Tickets
			    Rooms: Reservations
			        Required
			    Dorms: Reservations
			        Required

Located at 5,963 feet elevation, this was the site of the Donner Party's winter camp. There are 3 miles of cross-country ski trails, some of which border beautiful Donner Lake. Snowfalls are often heavy in this area and the scenery is spectacular. Tahoe National Forest offers cross-country skiers virtually unlimited trails to try their skills. The State Park is steeped in California history and winter time presents an opportunity to imagine the ordeals of early pioneers.

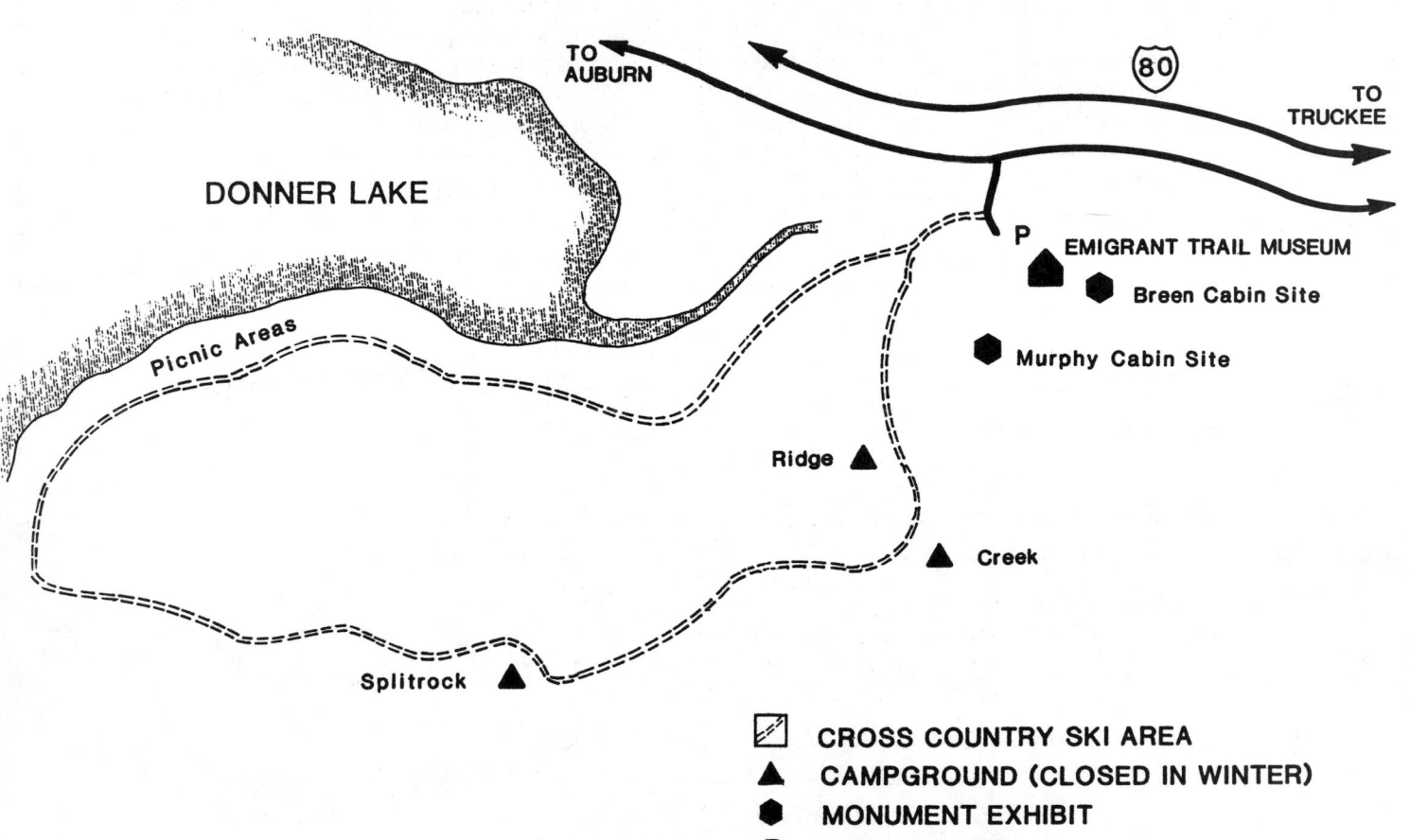

INFORMATION: Donner Memorial State Park , P.O. Box 9210, Truckee 95737 Ph: 916-587-3841			
SKIING	RENTALS & LESSONS	RECREATION	ACCOMMODATIONS

Nordic:
  Beginner and
  Intermediate, 3
  Miles of Marked
  Trails
No Fees
	Not Available at Site	Guided Cross-Country
		Tours, Check Museum
		for Schedule
		Nearby:
		  Downhill Skiing
		  Snow Play Areas
		  Snowmobiling
			Parking: No Fee
			No Dogs Permitted on
			Trails

TAHOE DONNER CROSS COUNTRY SKI AREA

The Tahoe Donner Cross Country Ski Area provides the nordic skier with a variety of opportunities. There are 3,000 acres of scenic wilderness and open slopes along the 50 kilometers of groomed track. The 21 marked trails are being increased with the addition of a new beginners trail and a new advanced trail. The professionally staffed ski school offers a variety of lessons for specific skills such as downhill turns, skate and telemark. The new Kids Ski School is open to children aged 3 to 6 years on Saturday and Sunday mornings at 10:30 a.m. There are several major races scheduled as well as night races, a special telemark camp and a snow camping–backcountry skiing clinic.

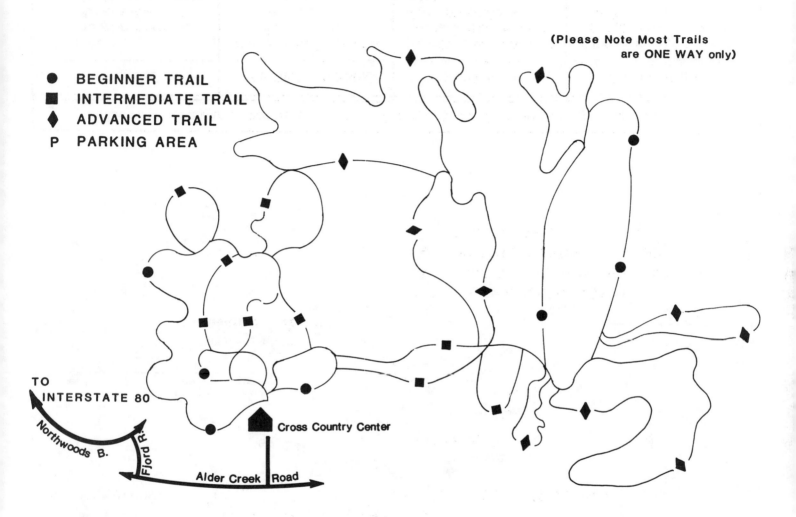

(Please Note Most Trails are ONE WAY only)

● BEGINNER TRAIL
■ INTERMEDIATE TRAIL
♦ ADVANCED TRAIL
P PARKING AREA

TO INTERSTATE 80
Northwoods B.
Fjord R.
Alder Creek Road
Cross Country Center

INFORMATION: Tahoe Donner Cross Country Ski Area, P.O.Box 758, Truckee 95734, Ph: 916–587–7005

SKIING	RENTALS & LESSONS	RECREATION	ACCOMMODATIONS
Nordic: 21 Cross Country Trails – 50 Kilometers of Groomed Track 1 Warming Hut Fees: Adults $3–$9 Seniors $2–$7 Children $2–$5 Wed–Sat: Nights Also Season: November 15 – April 15	Ski School: Lessons & Trail Pass – $10 to $21 Telemark Lesson & Tahoe Donner Lift Ticket – $25 Private – $25/hr. Rentals: $4 to $10 Demos: $10 – $15 Telemark/Skate: $10 – $15	Nearby: Downhill Skiing Ski Tourting Snowmobiling ORV Trails Snow Play Areas Casinos	Lodge & Restaurant Ski Shop Condo Rentals: Ph: 916–587–2310 Other Accommodations: Tahoe North Visitors & Convention Bureau: Ph: 916–583–3494 CA: 800–822–5959 Other:800–824–8557

Northstar at Tahoe offers a complete Nordic Skiing Center in addition to its Alpine skiing and extensive destination resort facilities. Located near the downhill runs off the gondola at mid-mountain, the Nordic Center provides a complete ski shop, equipment rentals, guided tours and a ski school. There are over 40 kilometers, 25 miles, of well-groomed wilderness trails for all levels of cross-country skiing ability. The telemark enthusiast will find the varied terrain of the alpine runs an inviting and open challenge. The ski school offers group and private lessons for both track and telemark skiing.

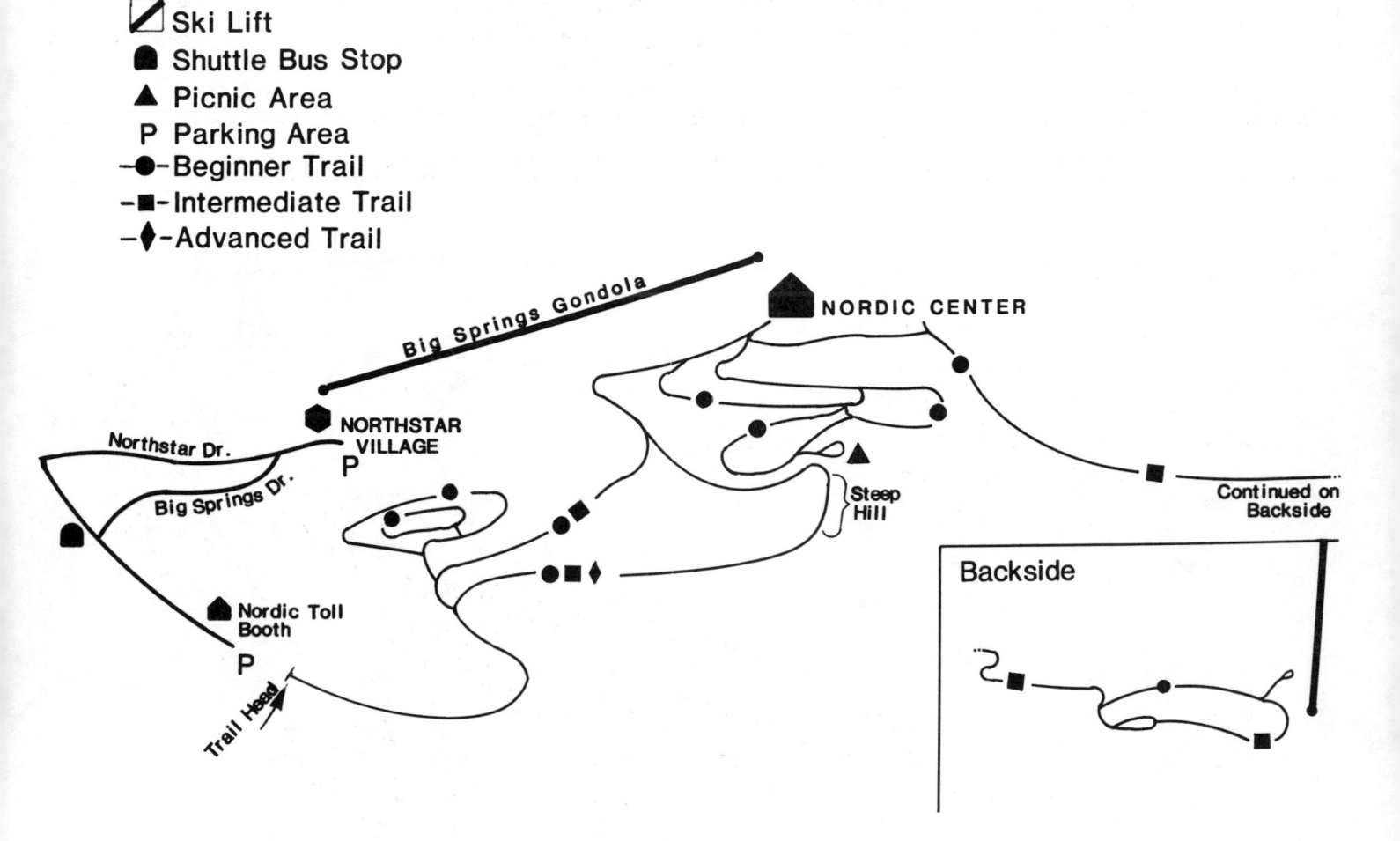

Ski Lift
Shuttle Bus Stop
Picnic Area
P Parking Area
-●-Beginner Trail
-■-Intermediate Trail
-♦-Advanced Trail

Big Springs Gondola

NORDIC CENTER

Northstar Dr.

NORTHSTAR VILLAGE

Big Springs Dr.

P

Steep Hill

Continued on Backside

Nordic Toll Booth

P

Trail Head

Backside

INFORMATION: Northstar Nordic Center, P.O. Box 129, Truckee 95734, Ph: 916-562-1010

SKIING	RENTALS & LESSONS	RECREATION	ACCOMMODATIONS

Nordic:
  40 Kilometers of
  Marked Trails
  Trail Fee Including
  Use of Gondola:
  Adults: $4-$7
  Under 12: $2-$5
Season: Late November
  through April
	Nordic Ski School:
	  Group Lessons:
	  1.5 Hours
	  Adults: $14
	  Children: $8
	  Private: $25/hr.
	  Telemark: $15
	Nordic Rentals:
	  $5 to $11
	  Telemarking: $15
		Alpine Skiing, Lessons
		  & Rentals
		Special Nordic Events
		  & Clinics
		
		Nearby:
		  Snowmobile Rentals
		  ORV Trails
		  Snow Play Areas
		  Casinos
			3 Restaurants, 3 Bars,
			Deli, Pizza Parlor,
			Wine & Cheese House,
			General Store
			Childcare Center
			Recreation Center
			Conference Facilities
			On-Site Shuttle
			Condominiums
			Lodging Information:
			  CA: 800-822-5987
			  USA: 800-824-8516

NORTHSTAR AT TAHOE

Northstar at Tahoe is a complete modern destination resort providing an abundance of support facilities. Downhill skiers of all levels will find a vast variety terrain down the 2,200 foot vertical off Mt. Pluto. There are 48 runs on 1,700 skiable acres at this resort. Lift passes are limited, so lines are relatively short. Early skiing is enhanced by snowmaking equipment on the lower 1,000 foot vertical of the mountain. The Ski School includes a wide range of programs from the Childrens' Skiwee Program to improvement clinics for the advanced skier. BLUESTAR, a dual slalom, and NASTAR, national recreation racing, provide strong racing programs. Northstar has all the amenities.

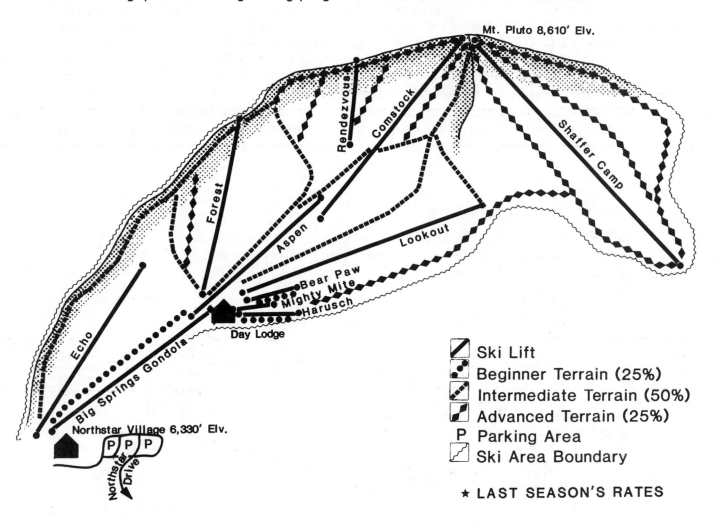

◨ Ski Lift
⋮ Beginner Terrain (25%)
◨ Intermediate Terrain (50%)
◨ Advanced Terrain (25%)
P Parking Area
◨ Ski Area Boundary

★ LAST SEASON'S RATES

INFORMATION: Northstar at Tahoe, P.O. Box 2499, Truckee 95734, Ph: 916-562-1113

SKIING	RENTALS & LESSONS	RECREATION	ACCOMMODATIONS
Alpine: 　1 Gondola 　8 Chairlifts 　2 Surface Lifts Fees:* Adults-$16-$24 　Children-$9-$16 BLUESTAR Dual Slalom NASTAR National 　Racing Program Season: Late November 　Through April Snow Ph: 916-562-1330	Alpine Ski School: 　Groups-Adults & 　Children: $19-$22 　3-Day Learn to Ski 　3-Hour Race Clinic 　Private: $38 　Skiwee-5-12 yr:$40 Rental Equipment: 　Alpine: $9-$15 　Nordic: $7-$11	Cross Country Skiing, Rentals & Lessons (See Previous Page) Special Nordic Events & Clinics Nearby: 　Snowmobile Rentals 　Snow Play Areas 　ORV Trails 　Casinos	3 Restaurants, 3 Bars, Deli, Pizza Parlor, Wine & Cheese House, General Store Childcare Center Recreation Center Conference Facilities On-Site Shuttle Condominiums Lodging Information: 　CA: 800-822-5987 　USA: 800-824-8516

TAHOE DONNER SKI AREA

The Tahoe Donner Ski Area is part of a private resort community. Although primarily used by residents who ski at half price, this small downhill area is open to the public at reasonable rates. There are 120 skiable acres with three trails and two open bowls. The meticulously groomed runs are down a 600 foot vertical drop. Beginner and intermediate skiers will find these wide open runs a compatible environment for developing their skills. Lift lines are short, so relatively uninterrupted skiing is the norm. Recreational races are scheduled for beginners every Thursday, and family fun events are held throughout the season.

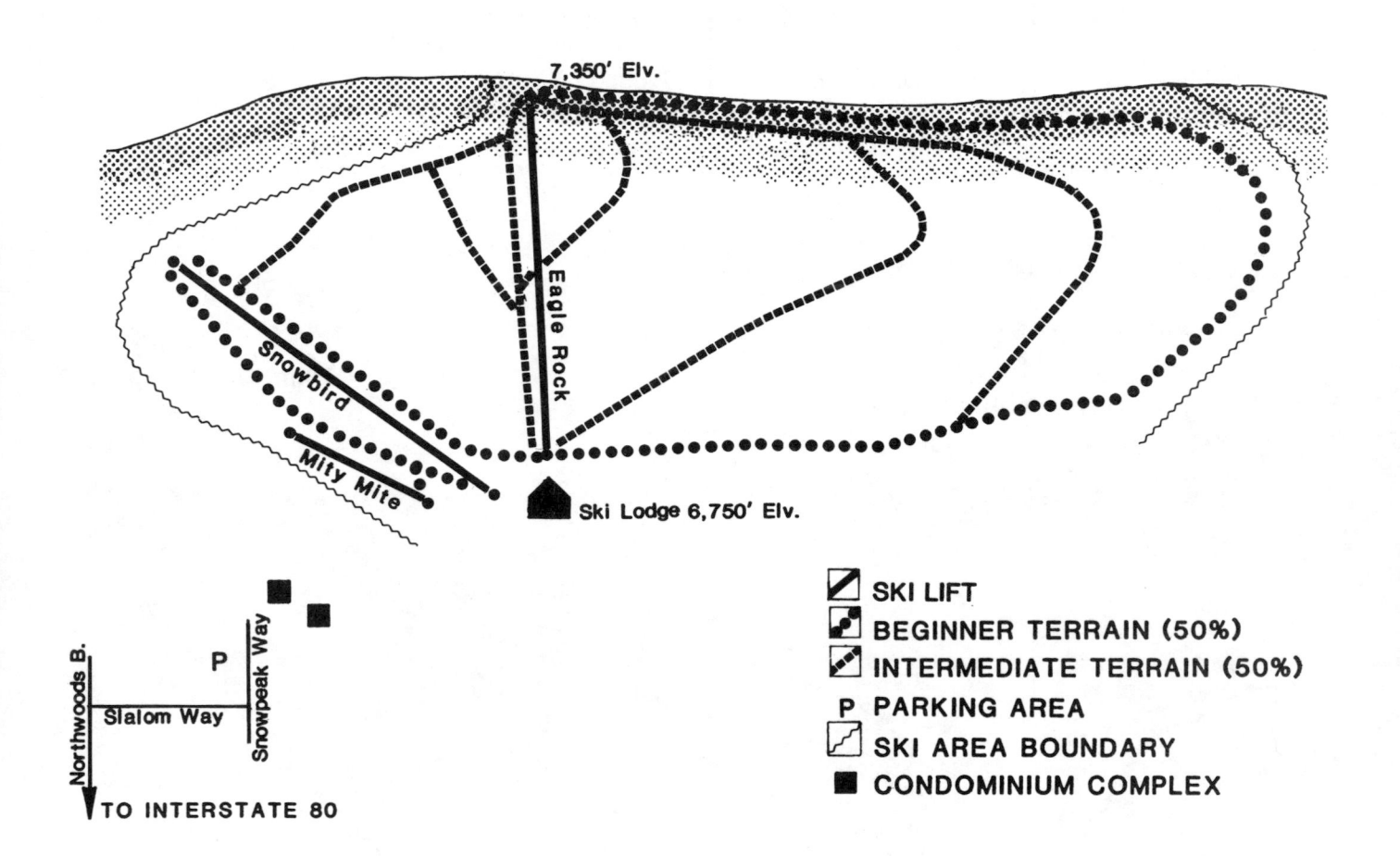

7,350' Elv.

Eagle Rock

Snowbird

Mity Mite

Ski Lodge 6,750' Elv.

P

Snowpeak Way

Northwoods B.

Slalom Way

TO INTERSTATE 80

▨	**SKI LIFT**
▨	**BEGINNER TERRAIN (50%)**
▨	**INTERMEDIATE TERRAIN (50%)**
P	**PARKING AREA**
▨	**SKI AREA BOUNDARY**
■	**CONDOMINIUM COMPLEX**

INFORMATION: Tahoe Donner Ski Area, P.O.Box TDR #45, Truckee 95734, Ph: 916-587-9400 or 9444

SKIING	RENTALS & LESSONS	RECREATION	ACCOMMODATIONS

Alpine:
   2 Chairlifts
   1 Rope Tow
 Fees: Adults–$14
   Children–$8
 Season: Thanksgiving
   through Easter
	Ski School:
	   Group Lessons: $12
	   Private: $24
	   Special Pre-School:
	   $24
	 Rentals:
	   Adults – $11–$13
	   Children – $9–$11
	 Special Package:
	   All Day Lift,
	   Lesson & Equipment:
	   $29.50 Midweek
		Nearby:
		   Cross Country
		   Skiing, Lessons &
		   Rentals
		   Ski Touring
		   Snow Play Areas
		   Snowmobiling
		   Casinos
			Cafeteria & Bar
			 Ski Shop & Store
			 Condo Rentals:
			   Ph: 916-587-2310
			 Other Accommodations:
			   Tahoe North
			   Visitors &
			   Convention Bureau
			   Ph: 916-583-3494
			   or CA-800-822-5959
			   Other-800-824-8557

NORTH TAHOE REGIONAL PARK

The North Tahoe Regional Park Nordic Ski Area has 11.5 kilometers of groomed trails and a snowmobile track. This Park was opened during the 1985/1986 winter season under the direction of Parks and Recreation Department. The North Tahoe Public Utilities District wants public input on how to improve and develop this winter sports facility. Although fees are not charged, contributions are accepted which help defray the costs of trail preparation. The trails are not patrolled, therefore, caution is advised and users are responsible for their own safety.

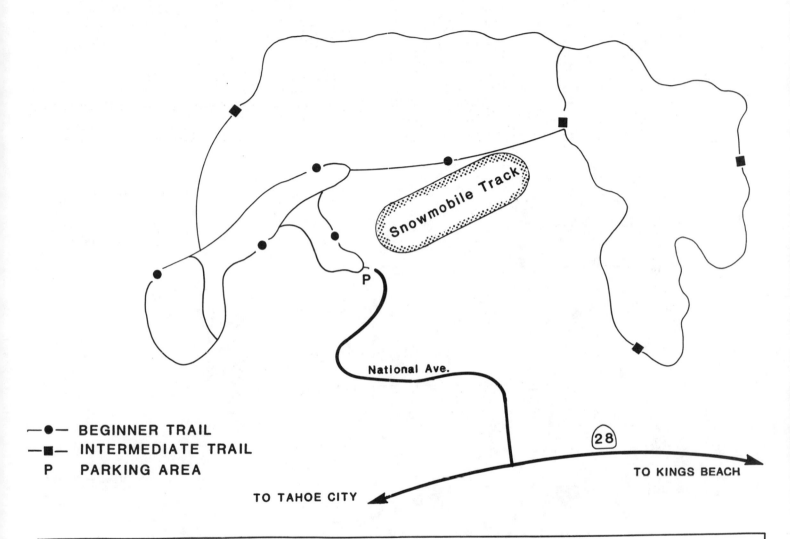

—●— BEGINNER TRAIL
—■— INTERMEDIATE TRAIL
P   PARKING AREA

INFORMATION: NTPUD, P. O. Box 139, Tahoe Vista 95732, Ph: 916-546-7248

SKIING	RENTALS & LESSONS	RECREATION	ACCOMMODATIONS
Nordic: 11.5 Kilometers Marked Trails No Fee, But Contributions Gratefully Accepted	Available Nearby	Snowmobile Track Nearby: Alpine & Nordic Ski Resorts Ski Touring Snow Camping Snow Play Areas Live Entertainment Dancing Casinos	Restrooms Iron Ranger: Comments & Contributions Full Facilities in Surrounding Communities Check with the North Tahoe Visitors Bureau

The Big Chief Nordic Center is the oldest cross country ski resort in the Tahoe Area. Located in the beautiful country off Highway 89 beside the Truckee River, this Nordic Center provides 25 kilometers of marked, groomed trails running along the river, into nearby meadows and mountains. The professional staff specializes in backcountry wilderness travel and snow camping. As a part of this experience, day trips are offered which provide all the equipment, instructions on survival and ski technique plus lunch and a day ending cocktail. In addition, overnight trips and ice climbing seminars are available on request. The rustic lodge offers a hearty meal, drinks and cabins.

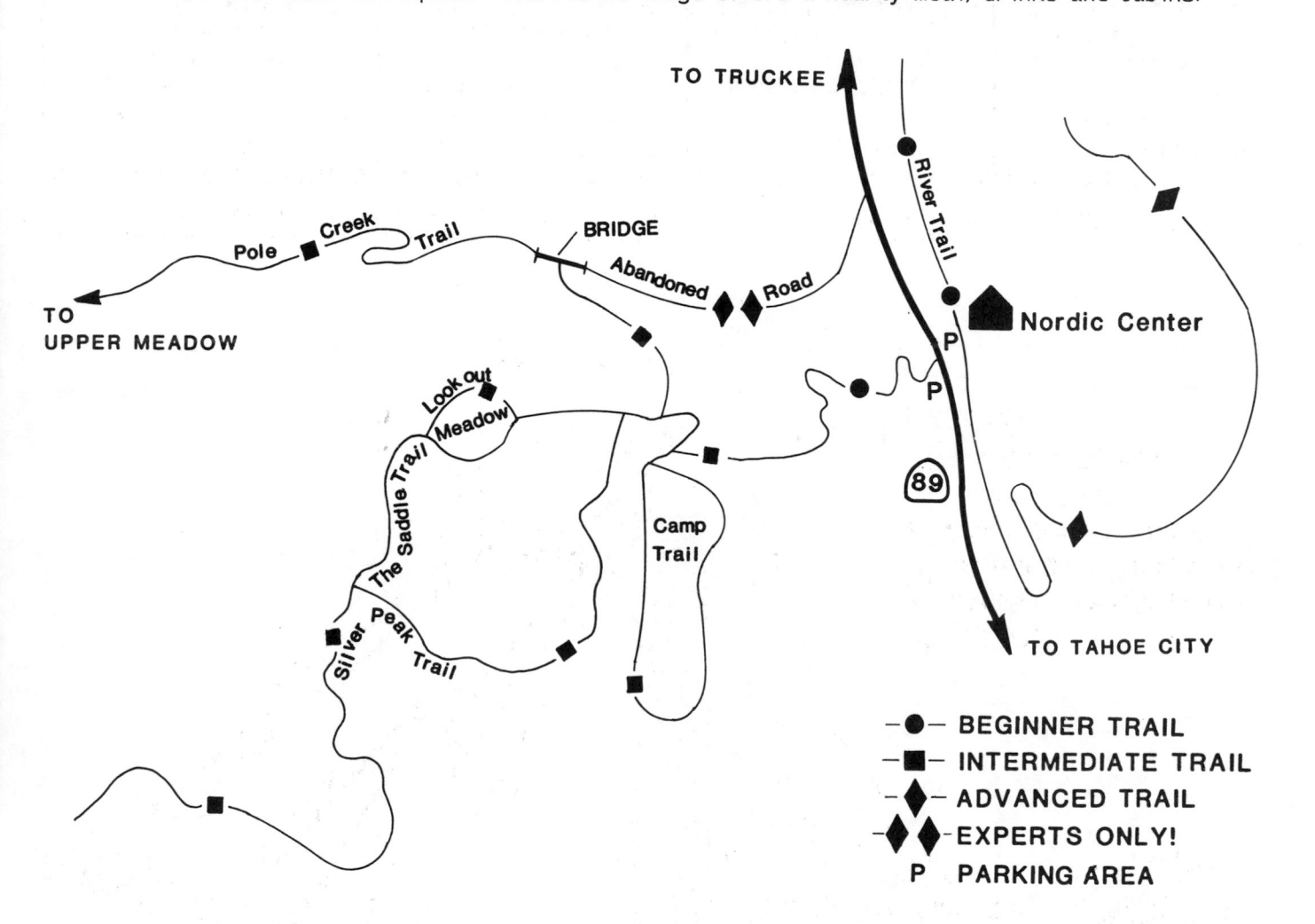

INFORMATION: Big Chief Nordic Center, Box 6717, Tahoe City 95730, Ph: 916-587-8794			
SKIING	**RENTALS & LESSONS**	**RECREATION**	**ACCOMMODATIONS**
Nordic: 25 Kilometers of Groomed Trails Ski Touring – Day and Overnight Trips Season: November to April	Ski School: Group Lessons – $10 per Hour Private Lessons – $15 per Hour Rentals: Combinations – $6.50 – $9 Weekends: $17 Week: $45	Ice Climbing Nearby: Alpine Skiing Snowmobile Rentals ORV Trails Snow Play Areas Casinos	Day Lodge Restaurant Cabins For Other Facilities & Accommodations: Tahoe North Visitors & Convention Bureau Ph: 916-583-3494 CA: 800-822-5959 USA: 800-824-8557

SQUAW VALLEY USA

Squaw Valley USA, site of the 1960 VIII Winter Olympics, is a world class ski resort offering 8,300 acres of varied terrain. There is a 2,700 foot vertical drop off Squaw Peak which is the highest of the six Sierra peaks within the area. From the challenge of world famous K22 to the moderate beginner slopes of Cable Car or Gondola, skiers will find an abundance of runs geared to their level of ability. The 27 lifts are able to accommodate up to 39,500 skiers per hour. An extensive nightly grooming program enhances its 400 plus inches of annual snowfall per year. The Ski School has 150 instructors who provide lessons for skiers of all levels. There is a Junior Ski School and a Toddlers' Snow School. Squaw Valley lives up to its billing as the "Resort of the 21st Century" by providing modern facilities and all the amenities.

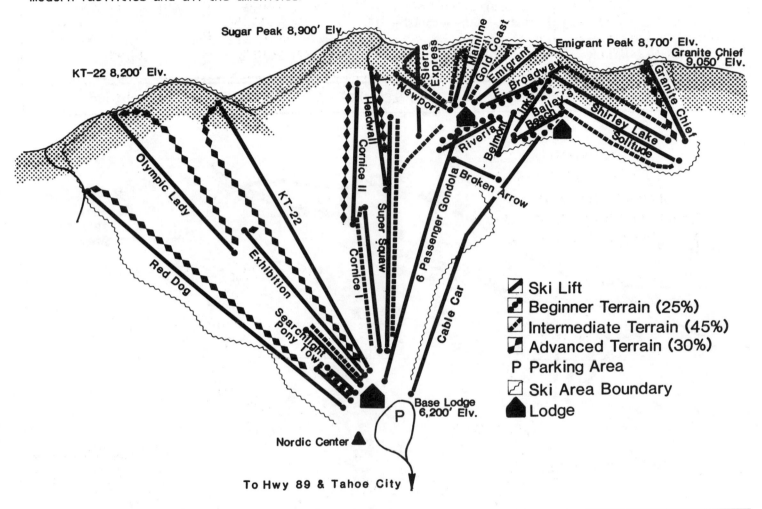

Legend:
- Ski Lift
- Beginner Terrain (25%)
- Intermediate Terrain (45%)
- Advanced Terrain (30%)
- P Parking Area
- Ski Area Boundary
- Lodge

INFORMATION: Squaw Valley USA, P.O. Box 2007, Olympic Valley 95730, Ph: 916-583-6985

SKIING	RENTALS & LESSONS	RECREATION	ACCOMMODATIONS

Alpine:
  1 Cable Car
  1 Gondola
  22 Chairlifts
  2 Pony Tows
Fees: Adults-$19-$27
Children & Seniors: $5
Over 70: Free
2 Race Courses
Season: Late November
  to Early May
Snow Ph: 916-583-6955
	Ski School:
	  Ph: 916-583-0119
	  Group Lessons:
	4 hr. $26, w/Lift $46
	  Jr. Ski School:
	4 hr. $26, w/Lift $30
	Pre Ski(9-11am) $4
	  Private Lessons:
	  $35 per Hour
	Rentals: $6-$15
	High Performance: $20
		Cross Country:
		  Trails, Rentals &
		  Lessons
		Sierra Helicopter Ski:
		  Alpine & Nordic
		  Tours:
		  Ph: 916-587-4573
		Nearby:
		  Snow Play Areas
		  Snowmobile Trails
		  & Tours
		  Casinos
			A Wide Variety of
			Restaurants & Bars
			Ski Shop
			Ten Little Indians
			Snow School-3-5 yrs.
			Day Care- 6 mos-5yrs.
			Bus & Boat Shuttle
			Lodging-Ski Packages:
			  Squaw Valley
			  Central
			  Reservations:
			Calif: 800-545-4350
			USA: 800-824-7954

SQUAW VALLEY NORDIC CENTER

The Squaw Valley Nordic Center offers a complete cross country ski area. Located near the vast Squaw Valley USA Alpine Resort, this popular day use facility provides 25 miles of groomed track and wilderness trails. There is a nordic downhill area with three surface lifts for telemarking. In addition to beginning cross country lessons, the Ski School provides personalized advanced lessons for those skiers wanting to develop the ability to read terrain, technique transitions and advanced skills. Telemark lessons are also given. Races are scheduled throughout the season including the largest winter triathlon in the west. The day lodge houses a cafeteria, the rental shop and ski school.

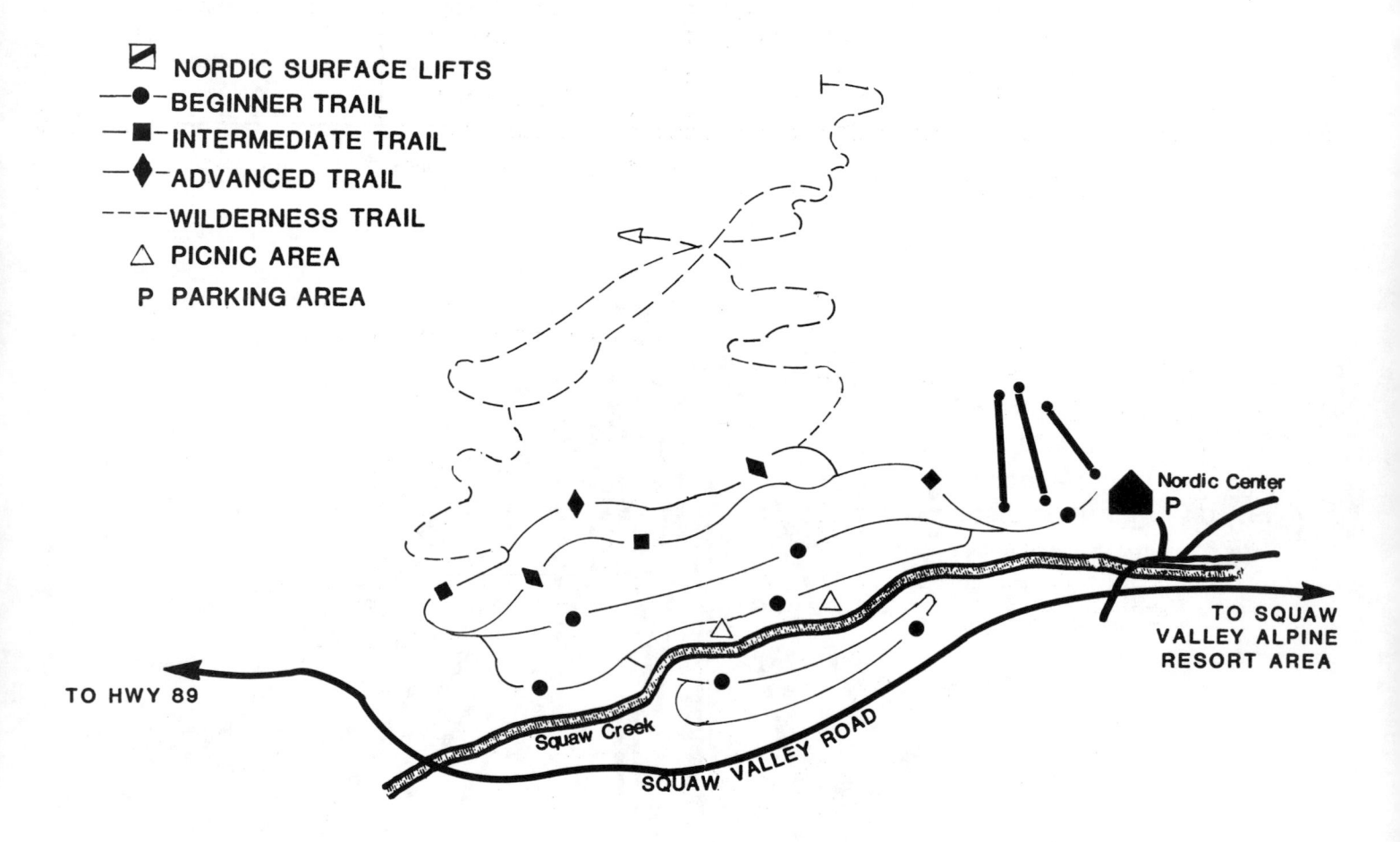

- NORDIC SURFACE LIFTS
- BEGINNER TRAIL
- INTERMEDIATE TRAIL
- ADVANCED TRAIL
- WILDERNESS TRAIL
- △ PICNIC AREA
- P PARKING AREA

Nordic Center
P

TO SQUAW VALLEY ALPINE RESORT AREA

TO HWY 89

Squaw Creek

SQUAW VALLEY ROAD

INFORMATION: Squaw Valley Nordic Center, P.O. Box 2637, Olympic Valley 95730, Ph: 916-583-8951

SKIING	RENTALS & LESSONS	RECREATION	ACCOMMODATIONS

Nordic:
    25 Miles – Groomed
    Trails
    Wilderness Trails
    (Not Patroled)
    3 Nordic Surface
    Lifts
    Fees:
    Adults–$3–$5
    Children–$1.50–$3
Guided Tours & Races
Season: Dec.1 – May 1
	Ski School:
	    Group Lesson –
	    Half Day: $10
	    Private Lesson –
	    1 Hour: $22
	    Telemark –
	    2 Hours: $12
	Rentals:
	    Adult–All Day:$10
	    Half Day: $6
	    Child–All Day: $6
	    Half Day: $4
		Alpine Skiing, Rentals
		& Lessons at Resort
		Moonlight Cross-
		    Country & Fondue
		    Tours
		Nearby:
		    Heli-Skiing
		    Snow Touring
		    Snow Play Areas
		    Snowmobile Rentals
		    ORV Trails
		    Casinos
			Day Lodge, Cafeteria
			Bus & Boat Shuttle
			Full Facilities at
			Squaw Valley USA
			& Nearby Communities
			
			For Information:
			Chamber of Commerce
			Ph: 916-583-2731

Tahoe Nordic is a favorite cross-country ski area for families. An elaborate trail system is machine groomed. Double set tracks, with skating lanes, invite skiers of all levels of ability. The terrain, at 7,000 feet elevation, is varied from meadows to forests and allows for some beautiful views of Lake Tahoe. Certified instructors offer lessons to all levels including telemarking. Moonlight tours are a specialty as well as races and clinics. This is a good facility and an ideal place to be introduced to Nordic skiing.

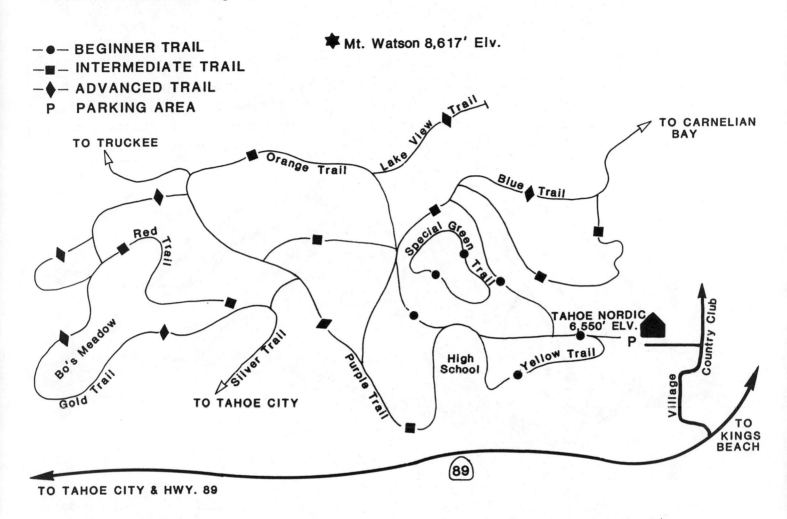

— ● — BEGINNER TRAIL
— ■ — INTERMEDIATE TRAIL
— ◆ — ADVANCED TRAIL
  P   PARKING AREA

★ Mt. Watson 8,617' Elv.

TO TRUCKEE

Orange Trail

Lake View Trail

TO CARNELIAN BAY

Blue Trail

Red Trail

Special Green Trail

TAHOE NORDIC 6,550' ELV.
P

Country Club

Bo's Meadow

Silver Trail

Gold Trail

Purple Trail

High School

Yellow Trail

Village

TO TAHOE CITY

TO KINGS BEACH

89

TO TAHOE CITY & HWY. 89

SKIING	RENTALS & LESSONS	RECREATION	ACCOMMODATIONS
Nordic: Beginner, Intermed, Advanced, Telemark 40 Miles of Trails 25 Miles of Set Tracks Fee:$5	Ski School: Group $15 Downhill X-C $17 Private $17 Kiddies (4-10 yrs.): Weekends & Holidays $11 Packages: Rental, Lesson, Trail Fee: Adults: $22 Children:$15 Rentals: $7-$12	Cross-Country Races Clinics Special Events	Day Lodge Snack Bar Group Discounts

INFORMATION: Tahoe Nordic, P.O. Box 1632, Tahoe City 95730 Ph:916-583-9858

ALPINE MEADOWS

Alpine Meadows claims one of the longest ski seasons in the Tahoe Basin. The season normally runs from early November through Memorial Day. Located on the crest of the Sierras, this resort averages over 350 inches of snow per year. The heavy snowfall is enhanced by extensive snowmaking on 46 acres at the base. Alpine provides some of the best spring skiing in the area.

This Resort has 2,000 acres of skiable terrain down the slopes of Ward and Scott Peak. The vertical off Ward Peak is 1,790 feet to the base. Thirteen lifts provide access to 100 designated runs. From extensive nightly-groomed trails, wide open bowls, steep chutes, timbered runs, and gentle mountain meadows, skiers will find abundant challenges matching their level of ability. The beginner will find gentle, well-groomed slopes off the main trails near the base. There is an abundance of intermediate runs throughout the area while the expert will be challenged on the upper elevations on the face and Sherwood Bowls. There are some spectacular views of Lake Tahoe.

Alpine prides itself as a "low-key family resort". Billing itself as "big mountain skiing with small mountain friendliness", this popular facility offers all the amenities. While most of the facilities are located at the base area, the Chalet Restaurant at mid-mountain provides a warm repast. The excellent Children's Snow School, ages 3 to 6, offers a unique ski/snow experience. In addition to group and private lessons, there are special racing programs including NASTAR. The Kangaroo Racing Arena provides a self-timed course. The retail shop, one of Northern California's largest, features both standard and premium equipment. There is a free shuttle serving the major lodging areas throughout the Tahoe Basin.

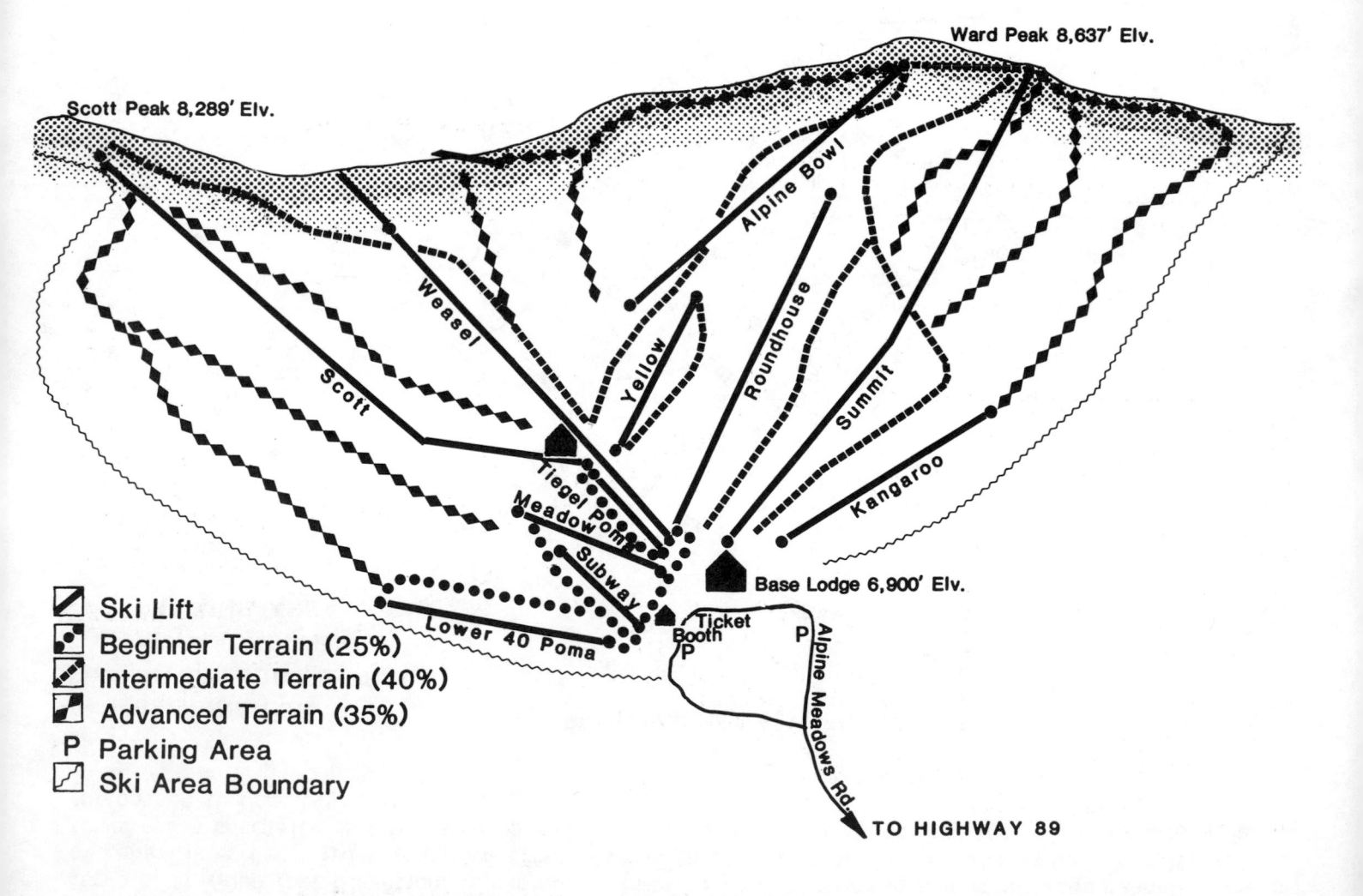

Ski Lift
Beginner Terrain (25%)
Intermediate Terrain (40%)
Advanced Terrain (35%)
P Parking Area
Ski Area Boundary

Continued...

Alpine Meadows Continued...

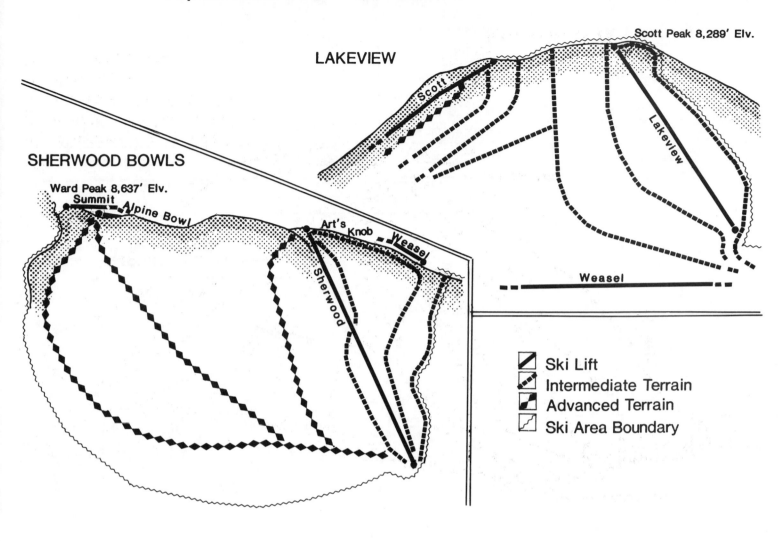

LAKEVIEW

Scott Peak 8,289' Elv.

Scott

Lakeview

SHERWOOD BOWLS

Ward Peak 8,637' Elv.
Summit
Alpine Bowl

Art's Knob   Weasel

Sherwood

Weasel

- ▨ Ski Lift
- ▨ Intermediate Terrain
- ▨ Advanced Terrain
- ▨ Ski Area Boundary

INFORMATION: Alpine Meadows, P.O. Box 5279, Tahoe City 95730, Ph: 916-583-4232			
SKIING	**RENTALS & LESSONS**	**RECREATION**	**ACCOMMODATIONS**
Alpine: 　11 Chairlifts 　2 Poma Lifts Fees: Adults-$18-$26 　Children-$8-$11 　Seniors(65-70)-$18 　Over 70-Free NASTAR Program, Self- Timed Race Course & Race Programs Season: Mid-November 　to Memorial Day	Group Lessons: Beginner thru Expert and Race Clinics 　Fees: $21-$26 Private Lessons: 　Fees: $25-$55 Rentals: Extensive 　Standard & Premium 　Rental Equipment- 　Daily, Multi-Day & 　Seasonal Rates	Nearby: 　Heli-Skiing 　Cross Country 　　Trails & Rentals 　Snow Play Areas 　Snowmobile Rentals 　　& Tours 　Casinos Children's Snow School: 3-6 yrs. All Day - $36 Snow Ph: 916-583-6914	Base Lodge, Cafeteria, Bar, Restaurant, Lounge, Sundeck, Live Bands-Weekends Free Shuttle Buses Infant Care Nearby Lodging: Contact Tahoe North Visitor & Convention Bureau: Ph: 800-822-5959

47

GRANLIBAKKEN SKI RESORT

Granlibakken is the first ski resort established at Lake Tahoe. Named after the Norwegian word meaning "hillside sheltered by fir trees", this four season resort has a tiny hill, 280 feet vertical drop, for beginning and intermediate skiers. Although there are two lifts, the T Bar is only used when crowded, which is seldom. An 8 kilometer Nordic course covers Granlibakken's surrounding wooded acreage, and unlimited virgin cross-country terrain is adjacent to the Resort at Page Meadows. There is also a snow play area on the hill for saucers and sleds. This is a nice family resort with good lodging and facilities for both overnight and day use.

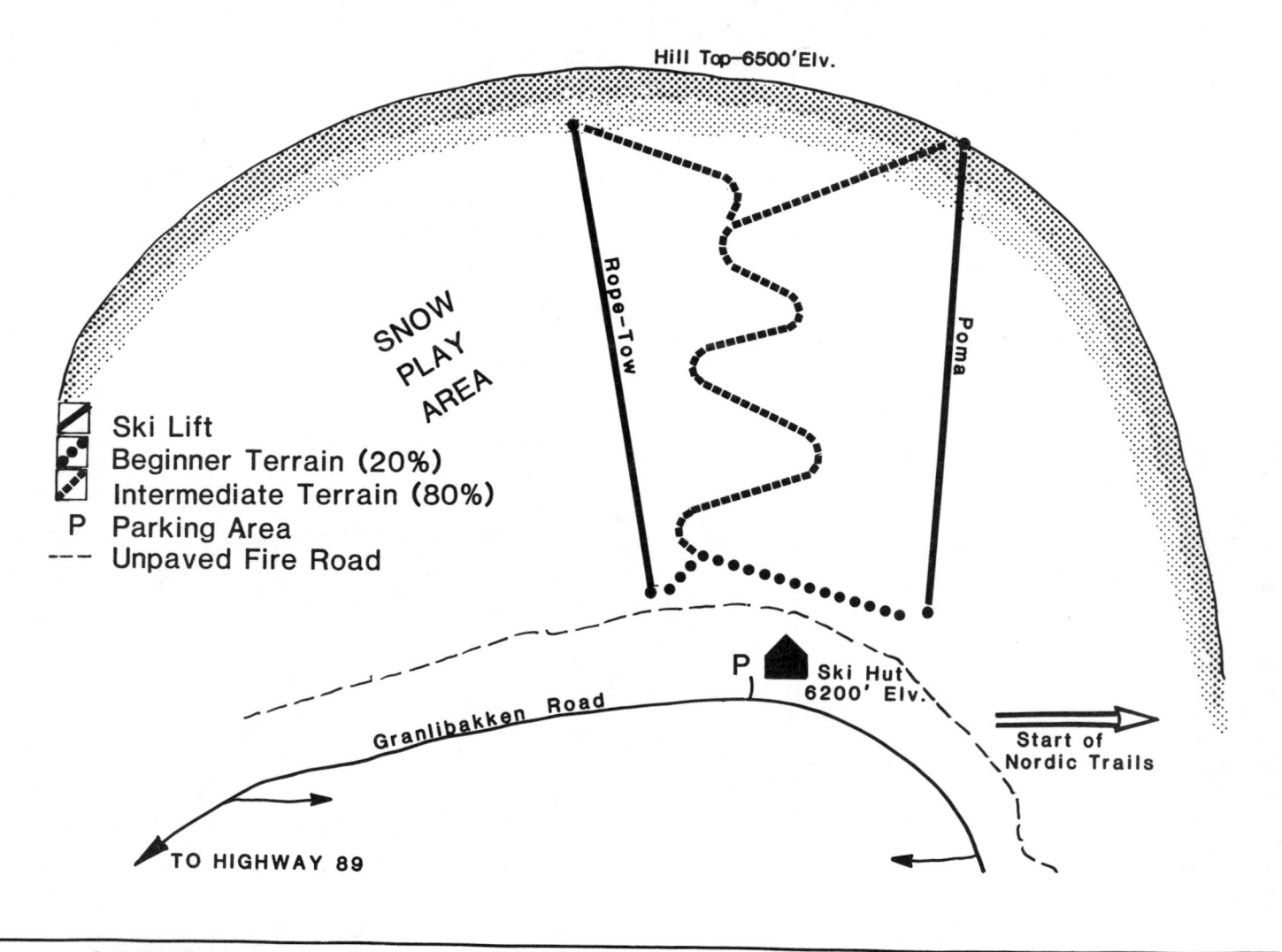

Hill Top–6500' Elv.

SNOW PLAY AREA

Rope-Tow

Poma

Ski Lift
Beginner Terrain (20%)
Intermediate Terrain (80%)
P Parking Area
- - - Unpaved Fire Road

P Ski Hut 6200' Elv.

Granlibakken Road

Start of Nordic Trails

TO HIGHWAY 89

INFORMATION: Granlibakken, P.O. Box 6329, Tahoe City 95730, Ph:916–583–4242

SKIING	RENTALS & LESSONS	RECREATION	ACCOMMODATIONS

Alpine:
  1 Poma
  1 T Bar
Fees:
  Adults: $6 – $10
  Children: $4 – $6
  Lodge Guests: Free
Cross Country:
  8 K Trail & Tours
Normal Season:
  Thanksgiving to
  Easter
	Alpine & Cross
	Country
	Ski School:
	  Group Lessons:
	  1 Hour – $10
	  Private Lessons:
	  1 Hour – $20
	Nordic & Alpine:
	  Full Equipment: $14
	  Saucers & Sleds
		At Resort:
		  Snow Play Area
		Nearby:
		  Other Alpine
		  Resorts
		  Cross Country
		  Snow Play Areas
		  Snowmobile Rentals
		  ORV Trails
		  Casinos
		  Live Entertainment
			Lodge: Suites, Studios,
			  1 Bedroom
			Condos: 1 to 4
			  Bedrooms
			Call for Fees &
			  Reservations
			Breakfast Included
			Ski Hut: Snacks, Hot
			  Drinks, Beer & Wine
			Sun Deck, Hot Spa &
			  Sauna
			Shuttles

BLACKWOOD CANYON SNO-PARK SITE

This area is ideal for cross-country skiing and snowmobiles. The Sno-Park Site for 30 vehicles is located just off Highway 89 on Blackwood Canyon Road. Skiers have miles of open meadows through the Canyon, but the north side peaks should be avoided due to possible avalanches. The main road covers about 10 miles to Barker Pass and is used by snowmobiles. There are several side roads with gently rolling terrain for the beginning nordic skier. You must have a Sno-Park Permit to use the Parking Area.

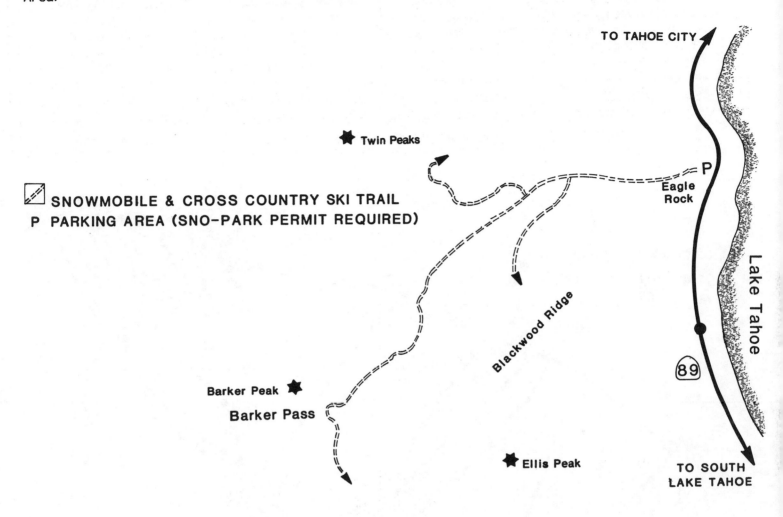

SNOWMOBILE & CROSS COUNTRY SKI TRAIL
P PARKING AREA (SNO-PARK PERMIT REQUIRED)

INFORMATION: Lake Tahoe Basin, USFS, P. O. Box 8465, S. Lake Tahoe 95731, Ph: 916-544-6420			
SKIING	RENTALS & LESSONS	RECREATION	ACCOMMODATIONS

Nordic:
  Beginner,
  Intermediate &
  Advanced Skiers
	Not Available at Site	Snow Play Area
		Snowmobiling
		
		SNO-PARK PERMITS
		ONLY:
		Contact –
		California Sno-Park
		Permit Program
		P. O. Box 2390
		Sacramento 95811
		Ph: 916-322-8993
			Parking: 30 Vehicles
			
			Sno-Park Permit Fees:
			  $2 – Day
			  $10 – Annual
			Must Have Permit in
			  Advance
			
			See Following Pages
			for Lodging
			Information

The Homewood Ski Area with its northern exposure and surrounding mountains provides some of the best ski conditions in the Tahoe area. The 275 acres of well-groomed trails overlooking Lake Tahoe attract skiers of all levels of ability. While some of the more formidable challenges are found on the lower face, most of the skiing is done on the upper part of this 1,650 foot vertical mountain. This complete resort offers many amenities including easy access by car or public transportation from nearby Tahoe City. Homewood is uncrowded since lift tickets are limited to 2,000 skiers. Its mid-week specials make it relatively inexpensive.

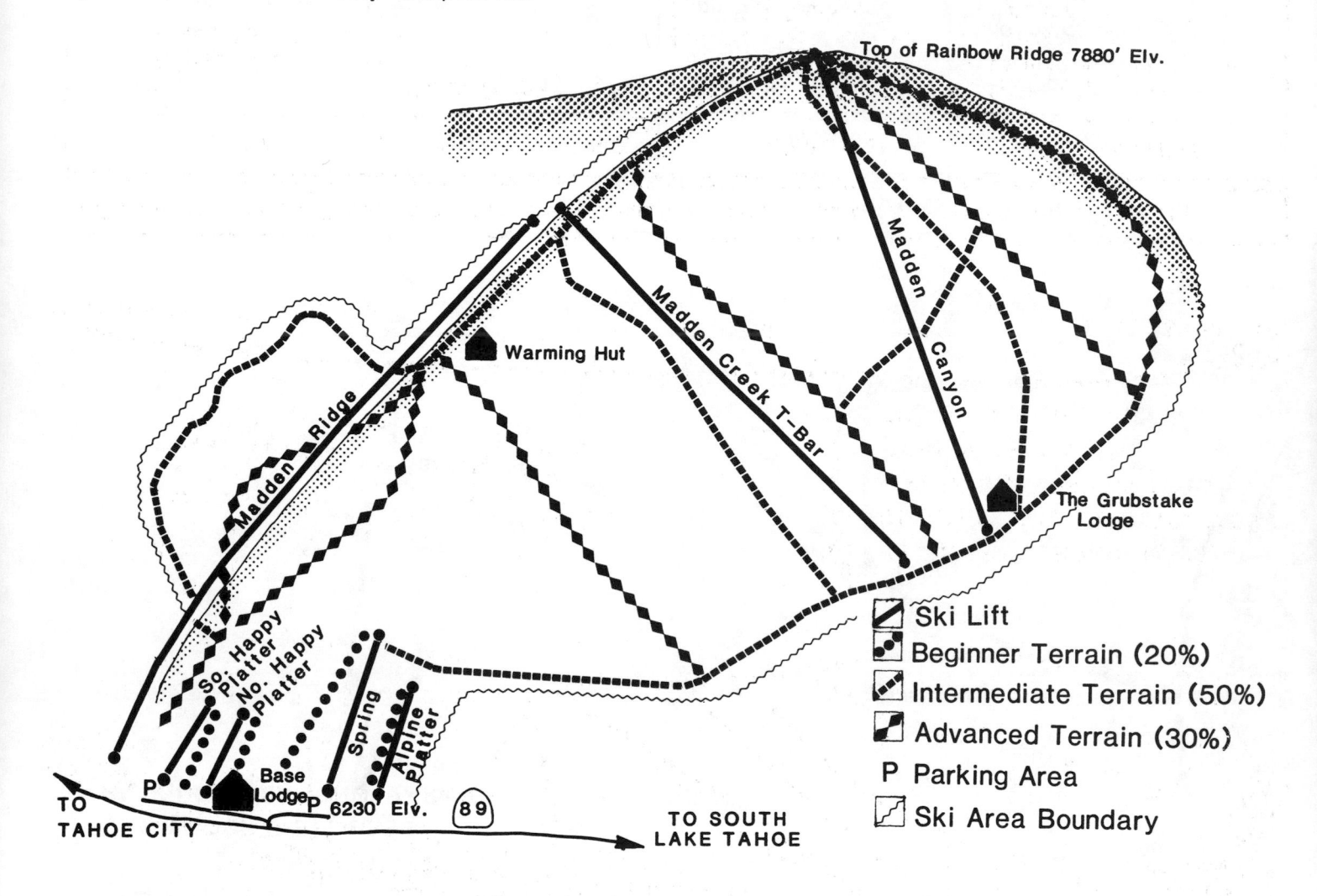

SKIING	RENTALS & LESSONS	RECREATION	ACCOMMODATIONS

Alpine:24 Groom.Trails
  3 Chairlifts
  3 Poma Lifts
  1 T Bar
Fees: Adults-$10-$12
  Juniors-$7-$10
  Under 12-$3-$5
  Seniors-$8
  Specials Mid-Week
Normal Season:
  Thanksgiving to
  Easter
	Ski School:
	  Private-$28 hour
	  Group-$14-$28
	  Pre-School-$6
	  Beginner Packages
	    Available
	Ski & Equipment
	Rentals at Main Lodge
		Nearby:
		  Cross Country
		  Snowmobile Rentals
		  ORV Trails
		  Snow Play Areas
		  Casinos
		  Live Entertainment
			Hof Brau Cafeteria
			Snack Bar & Lounge
			Sport Shop & Repairs
			For Other Information:
			  Tahoe North
			  Visitors &
			  Convention Bureau
			  P.O. Box 5578
			  Tahoe City 95730
			  Ph: 916-583-3494
			  or 800-583-3494

INFORMATION: Homewood Ski Area, P.O. Box 165, Homewood 95718, Ph: 916-525-7256

Tahoe Ski Bowl is a modern, well designed facility. There are 442 acres of skiable terrain with snowmaking when necessary. The vertical drop off the mountain is 1,750 feet. There are a total of 24 runs with some offering spectacular views of Lake Tahoe. A ridge is shared with Homewood. Tahoe Ski Bowl offers some of the finest intermediate skiing in the Tahoe Basin. There is a relatively new base lodge with cafeteria, ski shop and bar. Unfortunately, it is questionable if or when this ski area will reopen. Contact the Tahoe North Convention and Visitors Bureau for the current status before planning a trip to this resort.

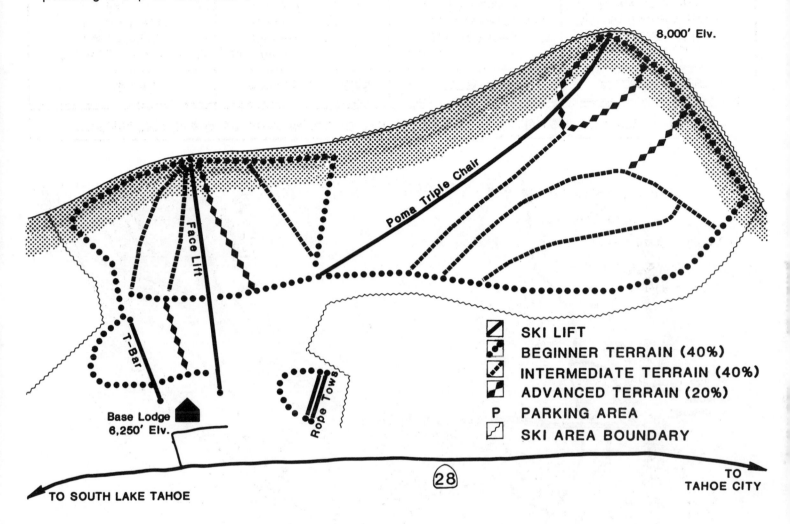

8,000' Elv.

Poma Triple Chair

Face Lift

T-Bar

Rope Tows

Base Lodge
6,250' Elv.

	SKI LIFT
	BEGINNER TERRAIN (40%)
	INTERMEDIATE TERRAIN (40%)
	ADVANCED TERRAIN (20%)
P	PARKING AREA
	SKI AREA BOUNDARY

28

TO SOUTH LAKE TAHOE

TO TAHOE CITY

INFORMATION: Status: Tahoe North Visitors Bureau, Box 5578, Tahoe City 95730, Ph: 916-583-3494

SKIING	RENTALS & LESSONS	RECREATION	ACCOMMODATIONS

Alpine:
  2 Chairlifts
  3 Surface Lifts
	Check Current Status	Nearby:
		  Cross Country
		  Skiing & Rentals
		  Ski Touring
		  Snowmobile Rentals
		  Snow Play Areas
		  ORV Trails
		  Casinos
			Base Lodge
			Cafeteria, Beer & Wine
			Ski Shop
			Nursery
			Lodging Information:
			  Tahoe Visitors &
			  Convention Bureau
			  CA 800-822-5959
			  Other 800-824-8557

SUGAR PINE POINT STATE PARK

Sugar Pine Point State Park on the west side of Lake Tahoe is open to winter camping and cross country skiing. There are four nordic trails on both sides of Highway 89. The longest and most difficult of these is a moderate trail that follows General Creek 3 miles up from the cross-country ski parking lot. There are also three short beginner trails; one within the campground and two on the lake side. The campground is open during the winter with heated restrooms, but the showers are closed. Parking spaces are cleared of snow. Be prepared for cold weather and snow storms.

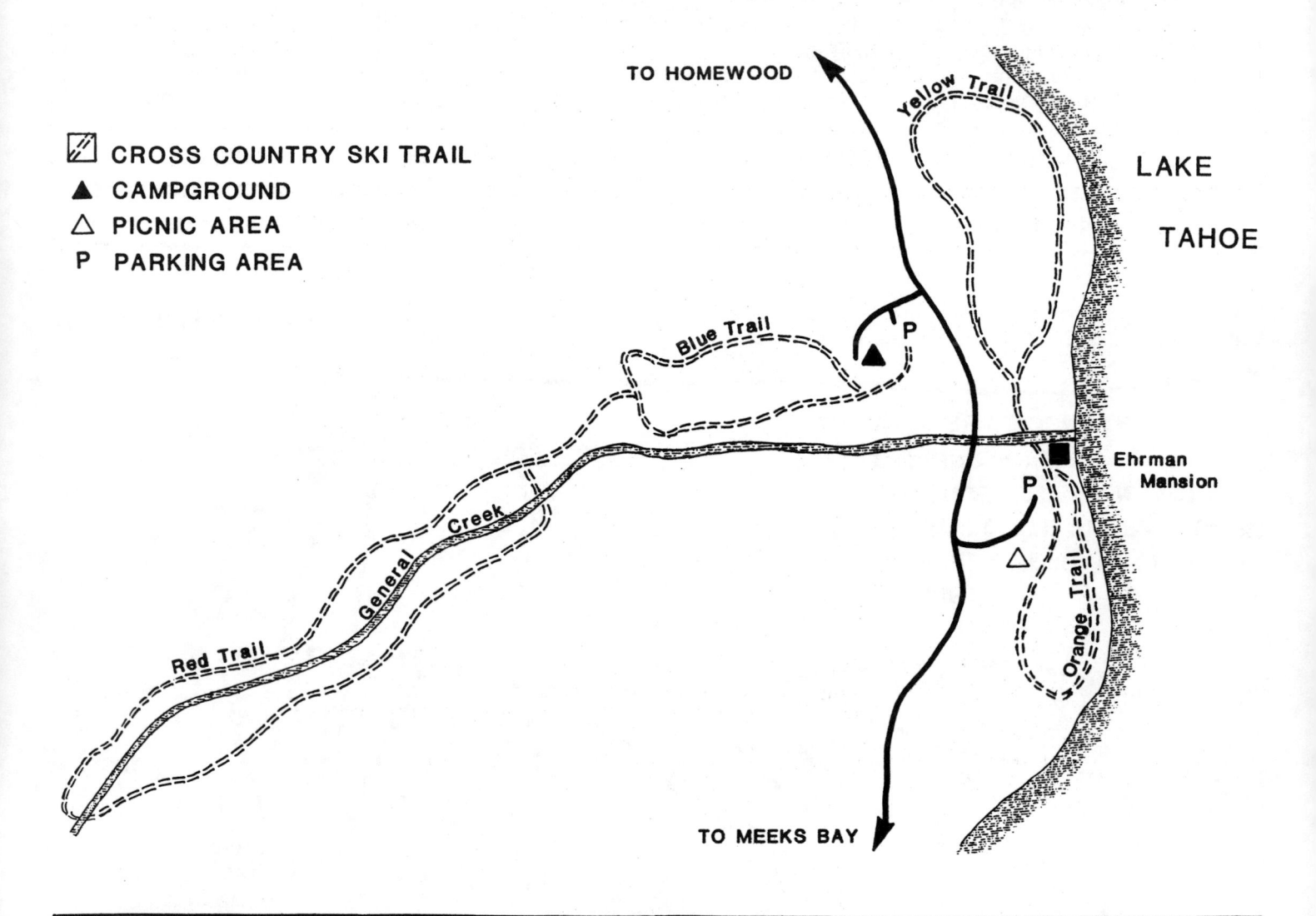

INFORMATION: Sugar Pine Point State Park, P. O. Box 266, Tahoma 94733, Ph: 916-525-7982 or 7232

SKIING	RENTALS & LESSONS	RECREATION	ACCOMMODATIONS

Nordic:
   11.3 Miles of
   Marked Trails
	Not Available at Site	Nearby:
		   Alpine Skiing
		   Ski Touring
		   Nordic Resorts
		   Snow Play Areas
		   Snowmobiling
		   Snow Camping
		   Casinos
			Campground:
			   16 Tent/R.V. Sites
			      to 30 feet long
			   Heated Restrooms
			   Cleared Parking

Season: Mid-November to April			Full Facilities in Nearby Communities

LAKE TAHOE VISITOR CENTER
SNO-PARK SITE

Located along the shores of Lake Tahoe off Highway 89, the Visitor Center Sno-Park offers an excellent route for beginning cross-country skiing through the old Estates of the Tallac Historic Site. Although snow can be scarce, this is one of the loveliest scenic spots in the Tahoe basin for snow play. Motorized vehicles are not permitted outside the parking lot, and the actual Visitor Center is closed in the winter. Visitors are to stay away from the marked wintering areas for the bald eagle. Be certain to have a Sno-Park Permit in your vehicle.

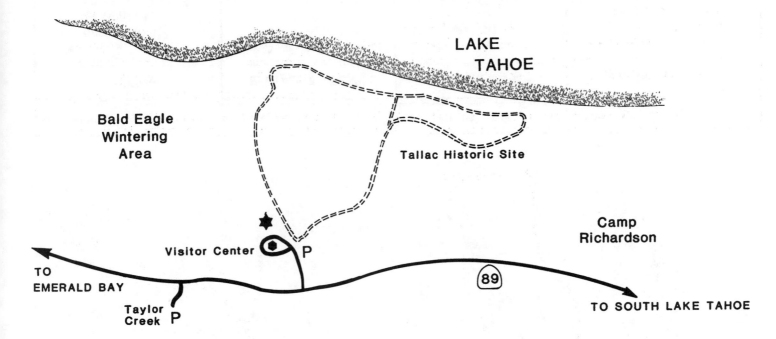

- ◩ CROSS COUNTRY SKI TRAIL
- P PARKING AREA (SNO-PARK PERMIT REQUIRED)
- ✶ SNOW PLAY AREA

INFORMATION: Lake Tahoe Basin, USFS, P. O. Box 8465, S. Lake Tahoe 95731, Ph: 916-544-6420

SKIING	RENTALS & LESSONS	RECREATION	ACCOMMODATIONS
Nordic: Beginners - 1-1/2 Miles of Marked Trail	Not Available at Site	Snow Play Area SNO-PARK PERMITS ONLY: Contact - California Sno-Park Permit Program P. O. Box 2390 Sacramento 95811 Ph: 916-322-8993	Parking: 100 Vehicles Sno-Park Permit Fees: $2 - Day $10 - Annual Must Have Permit in Advance See Following Pages for Lodging Information

A part of the California Sno-Park Permit Program, the Taylor Creek/Fallen Leaf area provides excellent, marked trails for the cross-country skier. The scenery is spectacular through meadows and forests, and snow is usually present late in the season. In addition, experienced skiers and snowshoers have access to Desolation Wilderness, permits required. A popular 3-mile route is up Cathedral Ridge to Floating Island Lake climbing 950 feet in elevation. Adjacent to the parking lot is a nice snow play area for supervised children. Snowmobiles are permitted only on the south side of Highway 89.

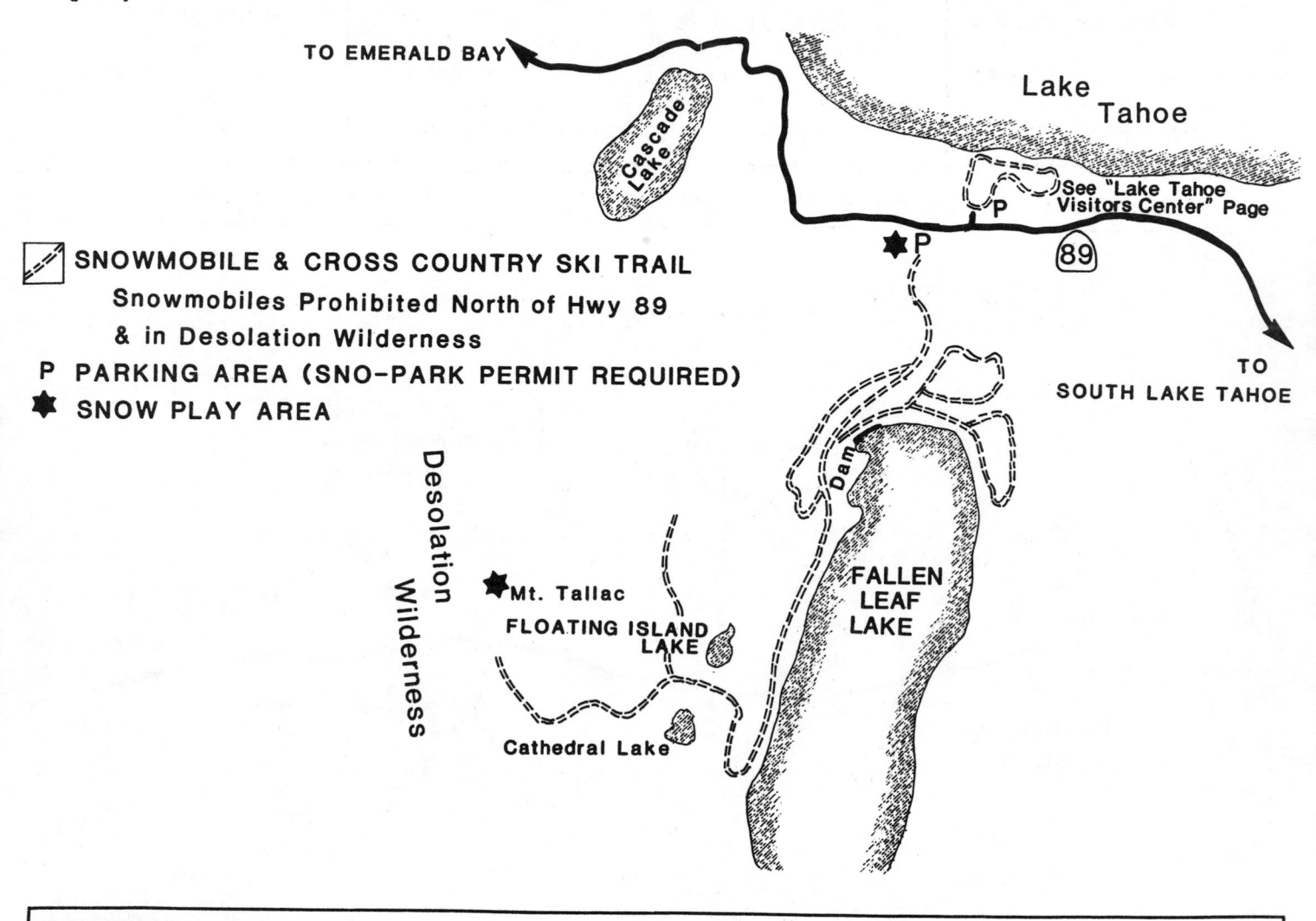

SNOWMOBILE & CROSS COUNTRY SKI TRAIL

Snowmobiles Prohibited North of Hwy 89

& in Desolation Wilderness

P PARKING AREA (SNO-PARK PERMIT REQUIRED)

✹ SNOW PLAY AREA

INFORMATION: Lake Tahoe Basin, USFS, P. O. Box 8465, S. Lake Tahoe 95731, Ph: 916-544-6420

SKIING	RENTALS & LESSONS	RECREATION	ACCOMMODATIONS

Nordic:
  Marked Trails for
  Beginners
  Entry to Desolation
  Wilderness for
  Experienced Skiers
    Permit Required
	Not Available at Site	Snow Play Areas
		Snowmobiling
		
		SNO-PARK PERMITS
		ONLY:
		Contact -
		California Sno-Park
		Permit Program
		P. O. Box 2390
		Sacramento 95811
		Ph: 916-322-8993
			Parking: 50 Vehicles
			
			Sno-Park Permit Fees:
			  $2 - Day
			  $10 - Annual
			Must Have Permit in
			Advance
			
			See Following Pages
			for Lodging
			Information

SPOONER LAKE CROSS COUNTRY SKI AREA

The Spooner Lake Cross Country Ski Area is within the Lake Tahoe Nevada State Park atop Spooner Summit. This popular nordic area offers 40 kilometers of well-groomed trails throughout the meadows around Spooner Lake and up into Snow Valley and Marlette Lake. The Ski School offers lessons and tours for all levels of ability including private lessons for backcountry telemarking. There are free scheduled moonlight tours where a warm fire, hot cider and good fellowship await at the meadow shelter. The races at Spooner Lake are designed for everybody, and the trails are specially groomed flat with a track to the side for diagonal skiing. Located near the intersection of Highway 28 and Highway 50, this area is easily reached from both North and South Lake Tahoe.

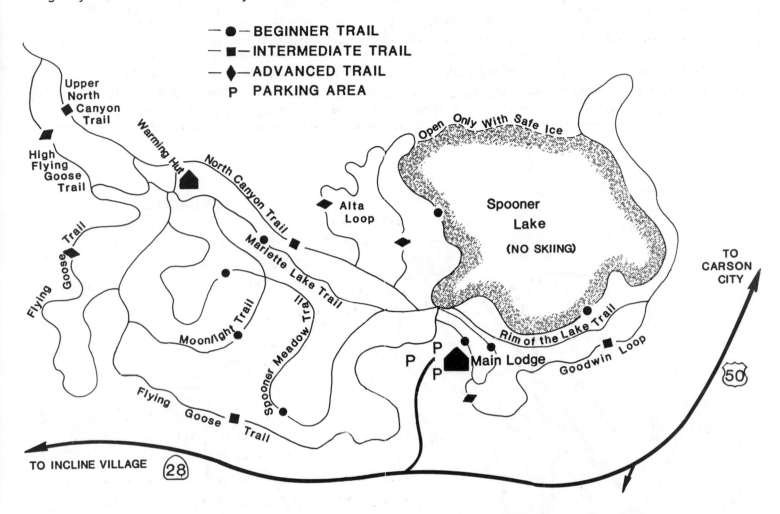

INFORMATION: Spooner Lake, P. O. Box 5329, Incline Village, NV 89450, Ph: 702-749-5349

SKIING	RENTALS & LESSONS	RECREATION	ACCOMMODATIONS

Nordic:
  40 Kilometers of
  Marked, Groomed
  and Wilderness
  Trails
Trail Fees:
  Adults – $5
  Seniors –1/2 Price
  Children – $3.50
  Under 5 – Free
  Moonlight Tours
  Special Races
	Ski School:
	Package – Rental &
	Pass – $14.50
	+ Lesson–$22 (2 hr.)
	Lesson Only–$17
	By Appt. Only–
	Full Day Int/Adv.Tour
	Package–$35
	Lesson Only – $28
	Private/Backcountry
	Telemarking – $25 hr
	Rentals: $6 – $10
		Nearby:
		  Downhill Skiing
		  Ski Touring
		  Snow Play Areas
		  Snowmobile Rentals
		  ORV Trails
		  Casinos
			Warming Hut
			
			Lodging and Other
			Accommodations at
			South and North Lake
			Tahoe

SKI INCLINE

Ski Incline offers relaxed recreational skiing for the entire family. This compact ski area has 120 acres of varied terrain down a vertical of 900 feet. The 22 runs vary in challenge from beginner to expert. Nightly groomed slopes are enhanced by the most extensive snowmaking in the Sierras. Located on the Nevada side of Lake Tahoe's north shore, Snowflake Lodge, on top of the mountain provides a spectacular vista of the surrounding area and the lake below. The resort has all the amenities from snacks to repairs. There are lessons for skiers of all levels, and a Skiwee learning program for children. The "Super-Skier" program offers an economical ski package for the entire family.

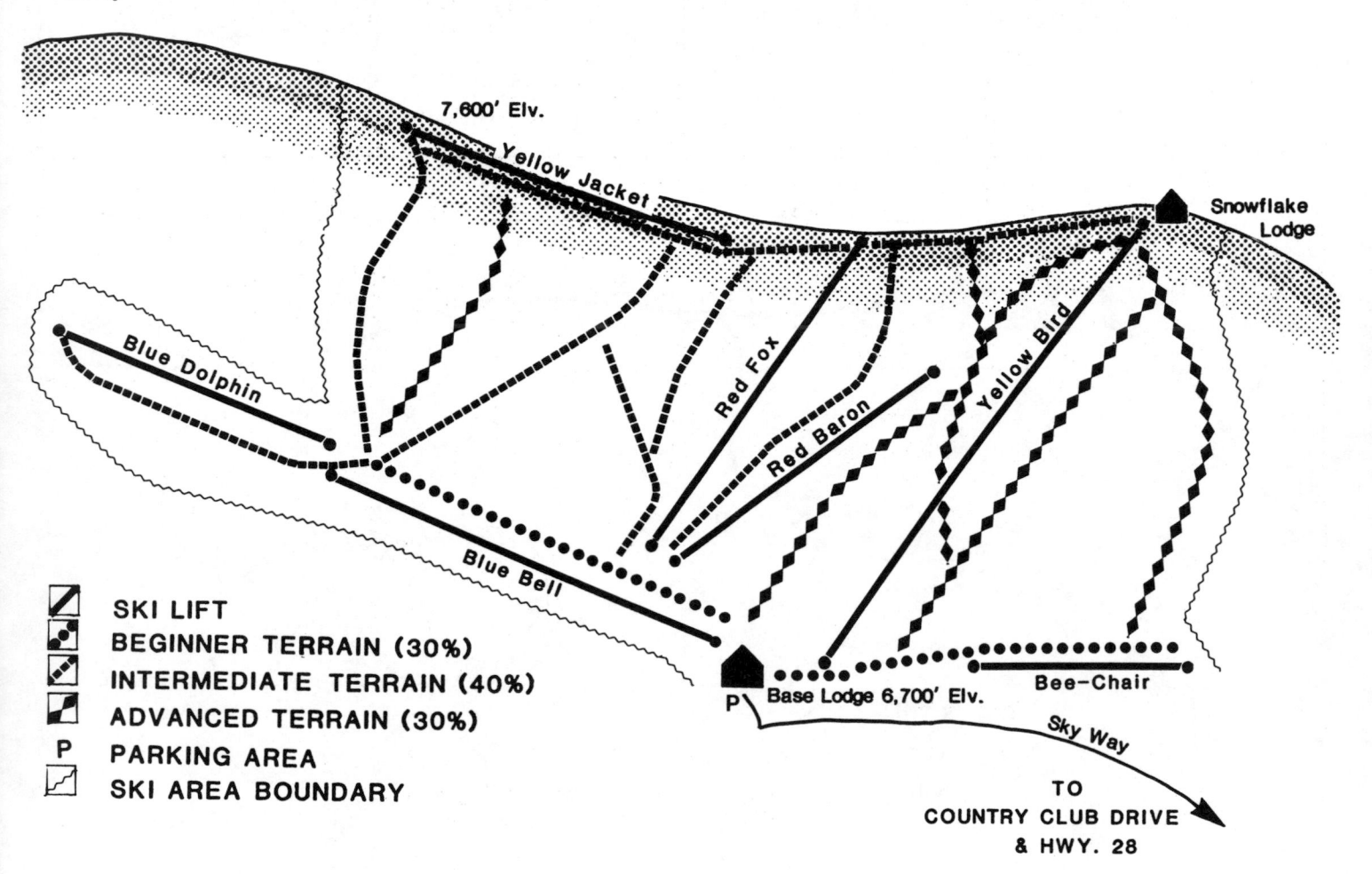

SKI LIFT
BEGINNER TERRAIN (30%)
INTERMEDIATE TERRAIN (40%)
ADVANCED TERRAIN (30%)
P PARKING AREA
SKI AREA BOUNDARY

INFORMATION: Ski Incline, P. O. Drawer AL, Incline Village, NV 89450, Ph: 702-832-1177

SKIING	RENTALS & LESSONS	RECREATION	ACCOMMODATIONS

Alpine:
   7 Chairlifts
Fees: Adults-$14-$20
Seniors & Children -
   $11 - $14
Children Under 5 Free
Family Super Skier
Fares: $39 Weekdays
$49 Weekends for
Family of Four
Season: Late November
   to Mid April
Snow Ph: 702-831-3211
	Ski School:
	Group Lessons:
	   All Day - $22
	   Half Day - $15
	Private:
	   One Hour - $30
	Skiwee Program:
	   Ages 5 - 12
	   All Day - $36
	Rentals:
	   Combinations:
	   $10 - $20
		Nearby:
		   Cross Country
		   Trails, Lessons &
		   Rentals
		   Ski Touring
		   Snowmobile Rentals
		   ORV Trails
		   Snow Play Areas
		   Casinos
			Summit Lodge-Snacks
			Base Lodge-Cafeteria,
			   Cocktail Lounge &
			   Sundeck
			Ski Shop & Repairs
			Family Packages
			Free Shuttle Bus
			Condominiums
			Lodging & Ski
			Packages:
			CA 800-242-SNOW
			USA 800-257-SNOW

TAHOE MEADOWS CROSS COUNTRY SKIING

Tahoe Meadows is at an elevation of 8,600 feet atop the summit of Mt. Rose Highway. Located within the Toiyabe National Forest, this area provides an excellent opportunity for novice cross-country skiers. The 1.8 mile marked trail travels through open meadows and gently rolling hills. There is also a snowmobile track alongside the trail. These trails offer some excellent views of the Lake and the Tahoe Basin. Beginning and early season tourers find the surrounding area attractive because of the abundance of relatively easy skiing and early snow. Be aware that Mt. Rose's slopes are avalanche prone and often cold. There is a snow play area just up the highway from Tahoe Meadows.

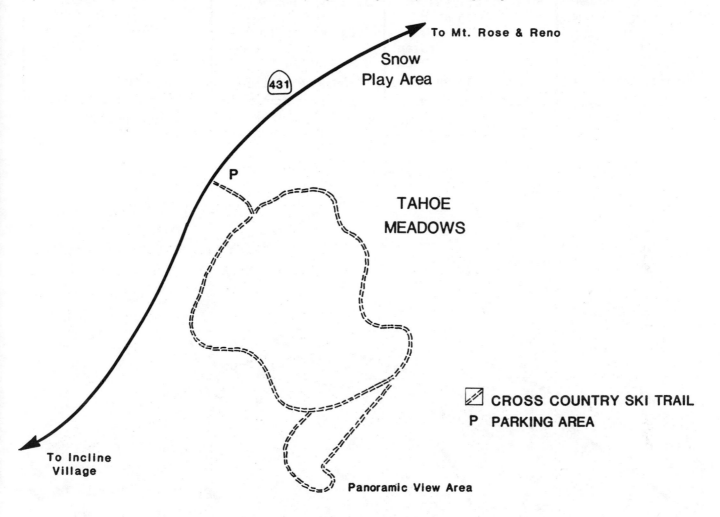

INFORMATION: Carson Ranger District, 1536 S. Carson St., Carson City, NV 89701, Ph: 702-882-9211

SKIING	RENTALS & LESSONS	RECREATION	ACCOMMODATIONS

Nordic:
   1.8 Miles of Marked
     Trail
Ski Touring
 	
Season: Late November
   to May
	Rentals & Lessons in
	North Lake Tahoe or
	Incline Village
		Snowmobiling
		Snow Play Area
		
		Nearby:
		   Alpine Skiing
		   Casinos
			Full Facilities in
			North Lake Tahoe,
			Incline Village &
			Reno
			Lodging Information:
			   Tahoe North
			   Visitors &
			   Convention Bureau
			   P. O. Box 5578
			   Tahoe City 95730
			   CA 800-822-5959
			   Other 800-824-8557

The Mt. Rose Ski Resort has some of the best snow in the Sierras. Its high base elevation, 8,260 feet, and close proximity to the Nevada desert has created an abundant drier snow pack. This, along with quality grooming virtually guarantees good conditions. There are excellent beginner and intermediate runs, and the advanced skier will enjoy cruising down the 1,400 foot vertical of Northwest Passage. The Day Lodge provides all the services including food and drink, sport shop and rentals. There are special lift, lesson and rental packages including mid-week specials and first-timer packages. The Rosebuds is a good children's' ski school program.

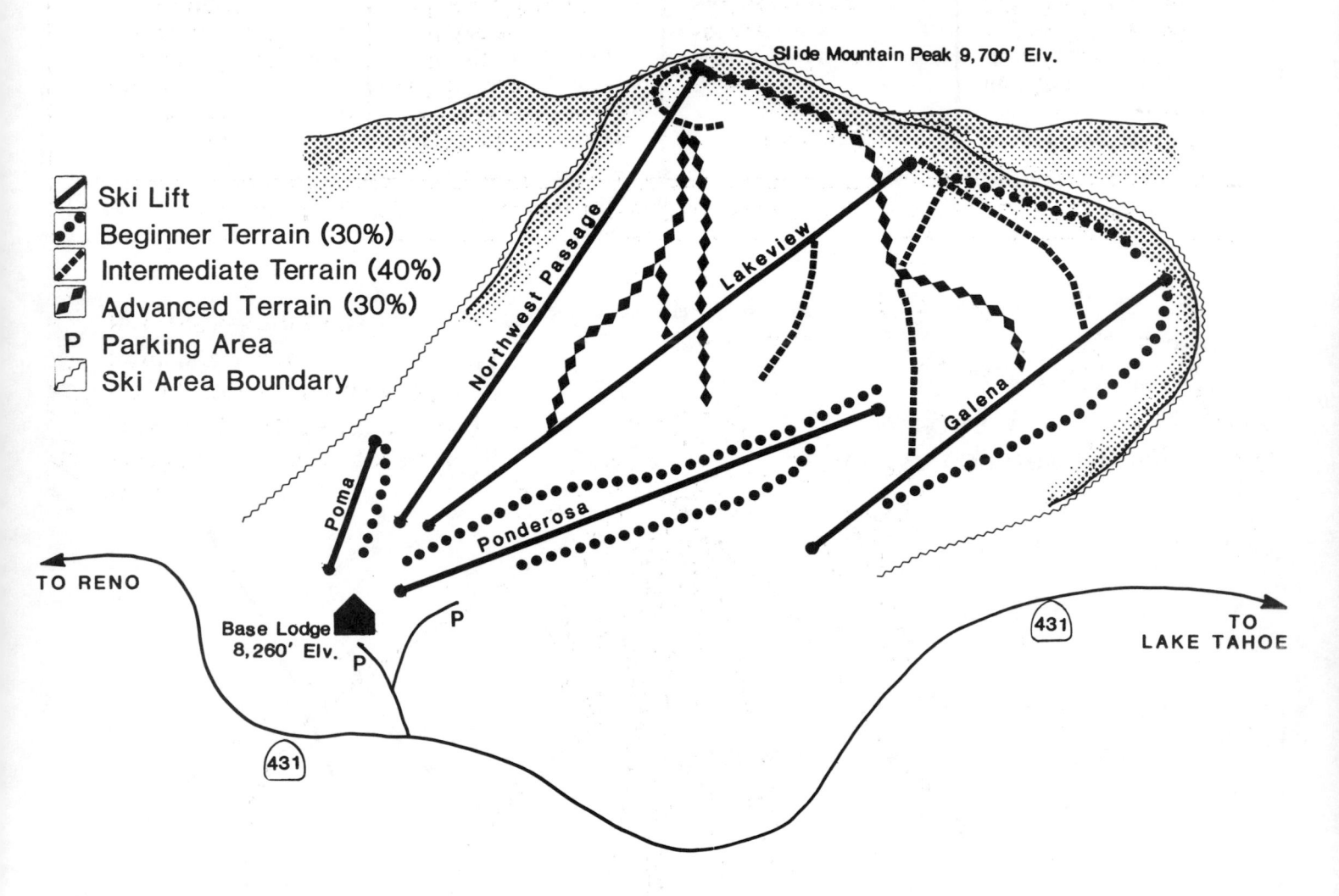

Ski Lift
Beginner Terrain (30%)
Intermediate Terrain (40%)
Advanced Terrain (30%)
P Parking Area
Ski Area Boundary

Slide Mountain Peak 9,700' Elv.

Northwest Passage

Lakeview

Galena

Poma

Ponderosa

TO RENO

Base Lodge 8,260' Elv.

P

431

431

TO LAKE TAHOE

INFORMATION: Mount Rose Ski Resort, P.O.Box 2406, Reno, NV 89505, Ph:702-849-0704

SKIING	RENTALS & LESSONS	RECREATION	ACCOMMODATIONS

Alpine:
  4 Chairlifts
  1 Poma
Lift Fees:
  Adults – $14-$20
  Under 6 – $7-$10
  Seniors – Half
  Price
Season: Mid-November
  to Late April
Snow Phone:
  702-849-0706
	Ski School:
	  Group Lesson: $14
	  Private: $28
	  Rosebuds–Age 3-7:
	  Half Day: $20
	  Full Day: $35
	Equipment Rentals:
	  $10 – $13.50
	Special Packages
		Nearby:
		
		Cross Country
		  Skiing & Rentals
		Snow Play Areas
		Snowmobile Rentals
		  & Tours
		ORV Trails
			Cafeteria & Deli
			Cocktail Lounge
			Sport & Repair Shop
			Medical Clinic
			Shuttle Buses to Reno
			  & Lake Tahoe
			Lodging & Packages:
			  Reno: 800-367-7366
			  Northshore:
			    800-822-5959

SLIDE MOUNTAIN

Slide Mountain is a small day use area on the eastern slopes of Mt. Rose with whom they share a common ridge. This relatively quiet facility is used mainly by local skiers from the Reno area. Slide Mountain is said to offer the best day powder due to its proximity to the Nevada Desert. Although there is a small, separate beginner's slope, this mountain is known for its steep runs down a vertical of 1,450 feet that challenge the experienced intermediate to advanced skier. There are 10 groomed trails. There is a small day lodge with cafeteria, bar, ski shop and ski school. Always check, in advance, for current status as to when Slide Mountain will be open.

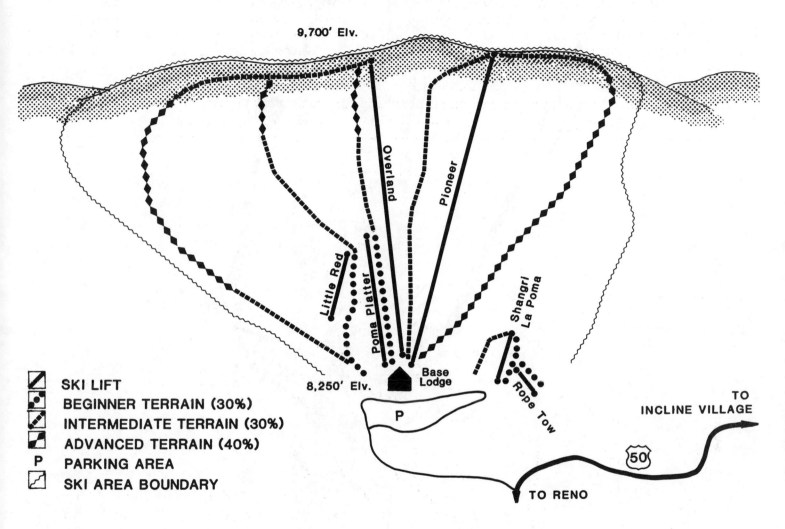

SKI LIFT
BEGINNER TERRAIN (30%)
INTERMEDIATE TERRAIN (30%)
ADVANCED TERRAIN (40%)
P PARKING AREA
SKI AREA BOUNDARY

INFORMATION: Slide Mountain P.O. Box 11156, Reno, Nv. 89510, Ph:702-849-0303

SKIING	RENTALS & LESSONS	RECREATION	ACCOMMODATIONS

Alpine:
  2 Chairlifts
  2 Poma Lifts
  1 Platter
Fee: $14
Season: Nov.–April
	Ski School:
	  Group
	  Private
	  Race Clinics
	Rentals:
	  Combo Package
		Skiboarding
		Telemark Skiing
		Nearby:
		  Cross-Country
		   Skiing
		  Snow Play
		  Ski Touring
		  Snowmobiling
		  Live Entertainment
		  Casinos
			Day Lodge
			  Cafeteria, Bar
			  Ski Shop & Repairs
			Full Facilities in
			Reno and N. Lake
			Tahoe

ADDITIONAL CROSS—COUNTRY TRAILS

For additional cross–country ski trails in the Lake Tahoe Area
contact:

The U.S. Forest Service
Lake Tahoe Basin Management Area
Head Office
P.O. Box 8465
870 Emerald Bay Rd.
South Lake Tahoe   95731
Ph: 916–544–6420

LAKE TAHOE GENERAL INFORMATION

Lodging and accommodations are extensive throughout the Lake Tahoe Area. The casinos at South Shore offer luxurious hotel rooms with full facilities. Condominiums, cabins and houses are also available for rent around the lake. An enormous variety of motel rooms and inns also offer lodging. Many offer ski packages in conjunction with nearby resorts.

For Full Information and Reservations Contact:

Tahoe North Visitors and Convention Bureau
Toll Free: 800-822-5959 (California)
          800-824-8557 (all other states)

South Lake Tahoe Visitors Bureau:
Toll Free: 800-822-5922 (California)
          800-824-5150 (all other states)

Chamber of Commerce:
     South Lake Tahoe Area: 916-541-5255
     North Lake Tahoe Area: 916-583-2371
     Reno Area: 702-329-3558

LAKE TAHOE AREA CAMPGROUNDS
AND R.V. SITES

KOA Campground
P.O. Box 11552
Tahoe Paradise 95708
Ph: 916-577-3693
Hwy 50 West of Myers, R.V. Sites, Open Year Round

Lakeside Mobile Home Park
P.O. Box 4493
South Lake Tahoe 95729
Ph: 916-544-4704
3 Blocks to Casinos at Stateline, off Hwy 50 on Cedar Ave.,
R.V. Sites,Open Year Round

Zephyr Cove Resort
P.O. Box 830
Zephyr Cove, NV 89448
Ph: 702-588-6644
1-1/2 Miles North of Zephyr Cove on Hwy 50, 6 R.V. Sites,
Snowmobile Tours and Rentals, Open Year Round

Sugar Pine Point State Park
P.O. Box 266
Tahoma 95733
Ph: 916-525-7982
10 Miles South of Tahoe City on Hwy 89, Campground with
R.V. Sites, Open Year Round

LAKE TAHOE AREA SNOWMOBILING

RECOMMENDED AREAS FOR SNOWMOBILES

There are a variety of snowmobile trails throughout the Tahoe National Forest. The following areas are recommended when there are six or more inches of snow on the ground:

Blue Lakes Road in Hope Valley
Genoa Peak Road
North Shore (designated trails)
Blackwood Canyon Road
Portion of Tahoe Meadows near Mt. Rose
McKinney-Rubicon Road

AREAS PROHIBITED TO SNOWMOBILES

The following areas are closed to snowmobiles, three wheeled vehicles or other motorized vehicles at all times:

All of Desolation Wilderness
The Area North of Highway 89 between Pope and Baldwin Beaches
(Camp Richardson, Estates, Kiva and Visitor Center Areas, inclusive)
The Echo Lakes Area
Meiss Country, including Grass Lake

The Area North of Trout Creek to Heavenly Valley, California and Nevada
From Skunk Harbor to Marlette Creek
The Meeks Bay and General Creek Drainages
Paige Meadows Area
All State Park Properties, Nevada and California
The Snow Play Area across from Black Bart and Pioneer Trail

For more detailed information and maps contact the Lake Tahoe Basin Management Area Head Office at P.O. Box 8465, 870 Emerald Bay Rd., South Lake Tahoe 95731; Ph: 916-544-6420.

Southern
Lake Tahoe Area

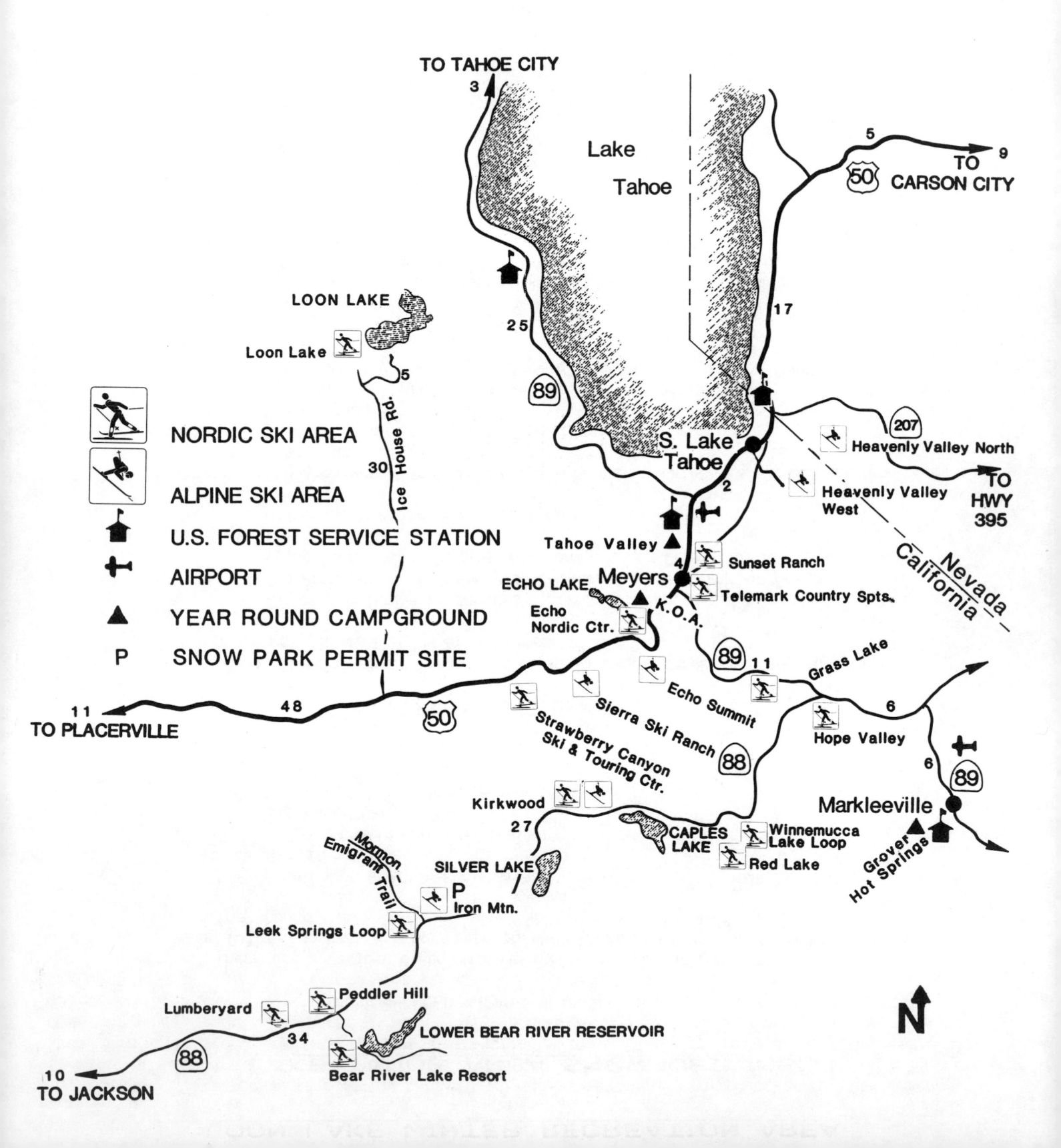

TO TAHOE CITY

3

Lake
Tahoe

5

TO
CARSON CITY

9

50

LOON LAKE

Loon Lake

25

17

89

207

S. Lake
Tahoe

Heavenly Valley North

NORDIC SKI AREA

5

Ice House Rd.

ALPINE SKI AREA

30

2

Heavenly Valley
West

TO
HWY
395

U.S. FOREST SERVICE STATION

Tahoe Valley

AIRPORT

4

Sunset Ranch

Nevada

YEAR ROUND CAMPGROUND

ECHO LAKE   Meyers

Telemark Country Spts.

California

P   SNOW PARK PERMIT SITE

Echo
Nordic Ctr.

K.O.A.

89   11

Grass Lake

11

48

50

Echo Summit

6

TO PLACERVILLE

Sierra Ski Ranch

Hope Valley

Strawberry Canyon
Ski & Touring Ctr.

88

Kirkwood

27

CAPLES
LAKE

Winnemucca
Lake Loop

Markleeville

6

89

Mormon
Emigrant Trail

SILVER LAKE

P
Iron Mtn.

Red Lake

Grover
Hot Springs

Leek Springs Loop

Lumberyard

Peddler Hill

34

LOWER BEAR RIVER RESERVOIR

88

Bear River Lake Resort

10
TO JACKSON

N

LOON LAKE WINTER RECREATION AREA

This area is spectacular for winter sports enthusiasts wanting a remote backcountry experience. 11 miles of rated trails cover a wide range of terrain as well as access to the Desolation Wilderness Area, permit required. The snow conditions are often excellent but extreme caution is advised due to changing weather and avalanches. This area is reached via Ice House Road, which is plowed only on weekdays, so be prepared for possible closure. Only skiers with a good background of wilderness travel are advised to venture into Loon Lake during winter months.

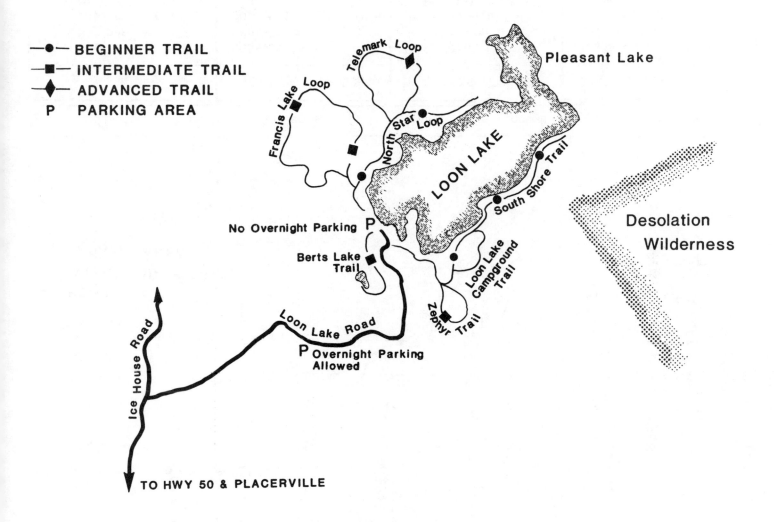

INFORMATION: Pacific Ranger District, Star Rte. 3, Pioneer 95666, Ph: 209-295-4251			
SKIING	RENTALS & LESSONS	RECREATION	ACCOMMODATIONS

Nordic:
   Beginner,
   Intermediate &
   Advanced –
   Marked Trails
   11 Miles – Not
   Groomed
 	
Expert Ski
   Mountaineers
	Not Available at Site	Ski Touring
		Snow Play
		Snow Camping
		
		Access to Desolation
		   Wilderness – Permit
		   Required for Day
		   Use and Overnight
		   Camping
			No Facilities
			
			Remote Area:
			   30 Miles to
			   Highway 50
			   45 Miles to
			   Placerville

STRAWBERRY CANYON

Within the El Dorado National Forest, the Strawberry Canyon and Strawberry Lodge offer a wonderful opportunity for cross-country skiers. Beginner and intermediate skiers can enjoy the 12 miles of marked trails within the Canyon. More advanced skiers can take part in one of the Cody Hut Ski Treks into remote meadows at high elevations, spending the night in a rustic cabin, meals included, returning the following day via a route excellent for telemark practice. In addition there are learning treks for a full day which stop at hot springs in the spectacular back country of this area.

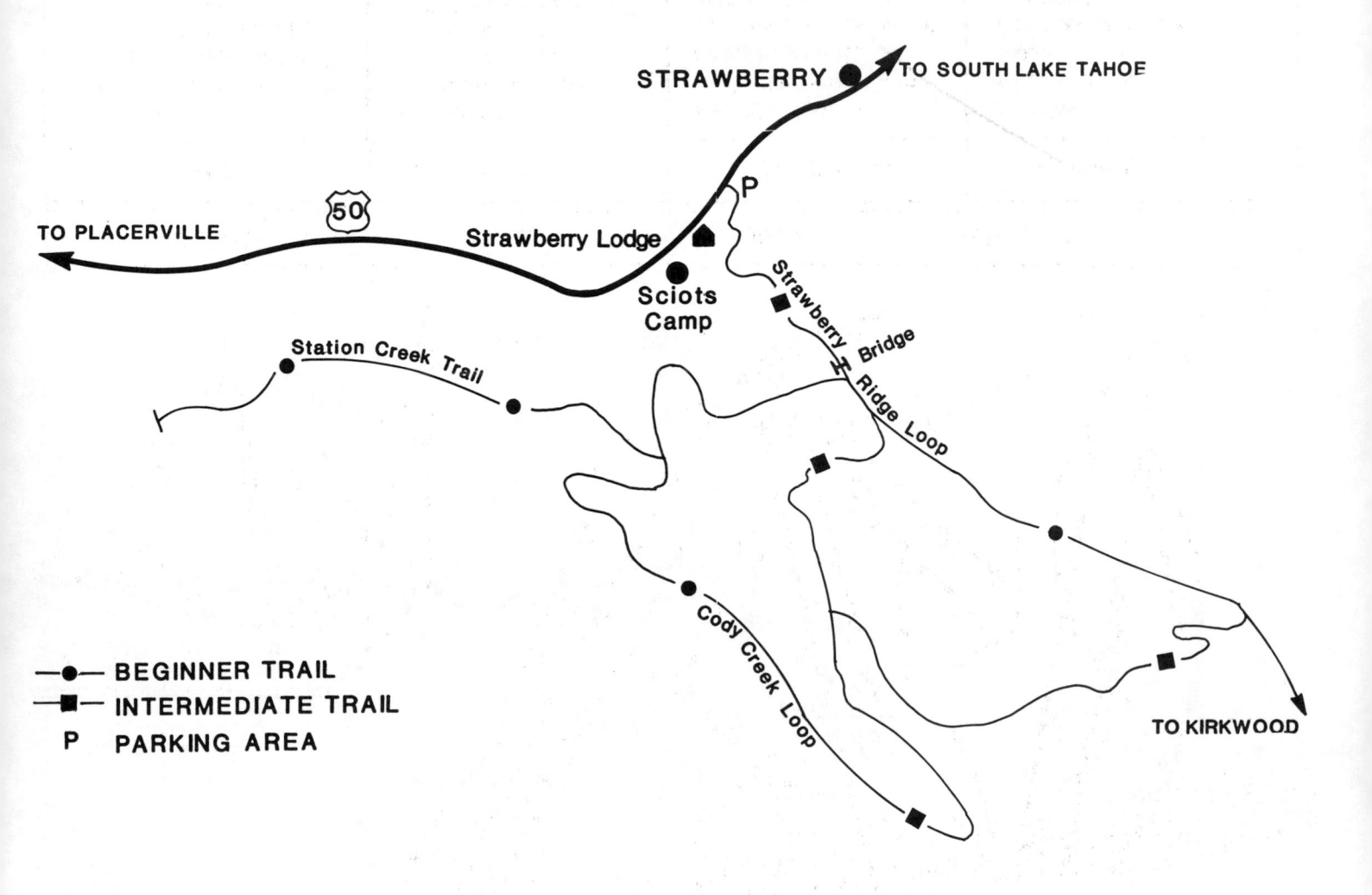

INFORMATION: Strawberry Ski Center, P.O. Box 14184, S. Lake Tahoe 95702, Ph: (916) 659-7585			
SKIING	**RENTALS & LESSONS**	**RECREATION**	**ACCOMMODATIONS**

Nordic:
  Beginner &
  Intermediate 12
  Miles of Marked
  Trails, Ungroomed
	Lessons $9
	Rentals $9
	Mountain Touring Skis
	$12
		Cody Hut Ski Treks
		  3520 Forni Rd.
		  Placerville 95667
		  Ph:(916) 626-5097
		Wilderness Tours
		  From Strawberry
		  Lodge to Cody Hut
		  (Sleeps 10
		  Dormitory Style)
		  Exper. Skiers Only
		  $100 ea.-2 Days
		Snowshoeing
			Rooms: Dormitory and
			  Private-$33-$60
			  Ph:(916) 659-7200
			Restaurant & Bar
			Ski Shop

SIERRA SKI RANCH

The Sierra Ski Ranch has been hosting downhill skiers for over 40 years. After moving uphill in 1968, this area has expanded to 2,000 acres of skiable terrain. There are three different skiing areas, each unique to itself. Every level of skier will find an interesting run down the 2,212 foot vertical drop off Huckleberry Mountain. There is an annual snowfall of over 450 inches. The 65 instructors offer both group and private lessons, and specially selected instructors create a funfilled environment for youngsters. Ample modern support facilities are found at the two base and one mountaintop lodges. Although there are no overnight accommodations, there are a variety of lodging packages available at South Shore where a shuttle bus will transport skiers to and from this ski area.

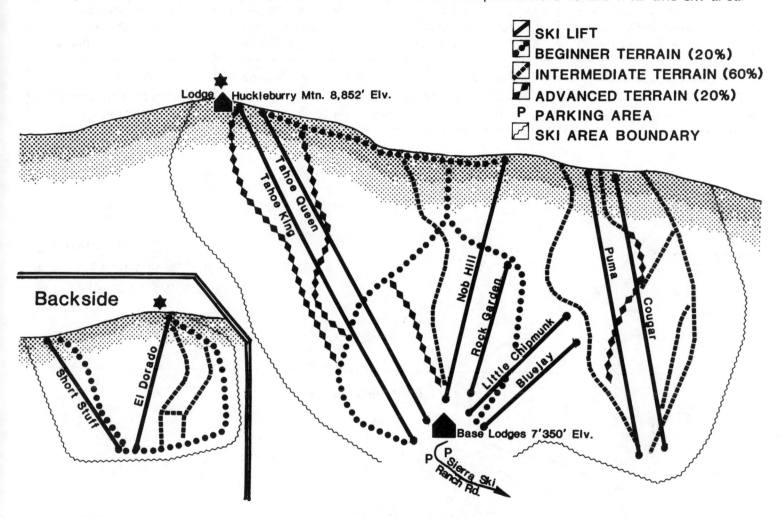

| SKI LIFT |
| BEGINNER TERRAIN (20%) |
| INTERMEDIATE TERRAIN (60%) |
| ADVANCED TERRAIN (20%) |
| P PARKING AREA |
| SKI AREA BOUNDARY |

Lodge   Huckleburry Mtn. 8,852' Elv.

Tahoe Queen
Tahoe King
Nob Hill
Rock Garden
Little Chipmunk
Bluejay
Puma
Cougar

Backside
Short Stuff
El Dorado

Base Lodges 7'350' Elv.
P P Sierra Ski Ranch Rd.

INFORMATION: Sierra Ski Ranch, Box 3501, Twin Bridges 95735, Ph: 916-659-7519

SKIING	RENTALS & LESSONS	RECREATION	ACCOMMODATIONS
Alpine: 　10 Chairlifts Fees: Adults–$21–$15 Children & Seniors – 　$12 – $8 Season: November to 　End of April Snow Ph: 916-659-7475	Ski School: 　Group Lessons: 　Single – $15 　Double – $23 　Private Lessons: 　1 Hour – $30 Rentals: 　Adults: $13 　Children: $10	Shuttle Bus to 　South Lake Tahoe Special Events: So. Lake Tahoe Winter Carnival St. Patrick's Day Event Easter Week Kid's Events	2 Lodges 3 Cafeterias 1 Deli 4 Sundecks – 2 with Barbecues – Weather Permitting Ski Shop – Repairs Lodging & Packages: 　South Lake Tahoe 　Visitors Bureau 　Ph: 800-822-5922

ECHO SUMMIT NORDIC CENTER

The Echo Summit Nordic Center is a part of the Echo Summit Ski Resort. Located in the beautiful high Sierras just eight miles from South Lake Tahoe, this resort provides both downhill and cross country skiing at one location. Telemark downhill is just a short walk from the Nordic Center. There are 25 kilometers of marked, groomed trails into the meadows, forest and lakes of this majestic area. There is a Nordic Ski School offering both group and private lessons as well as a special learn-to-tour package. Nordic equipment rentals, including high performance Telemark skis, are available. The Center also offers guided Tours.

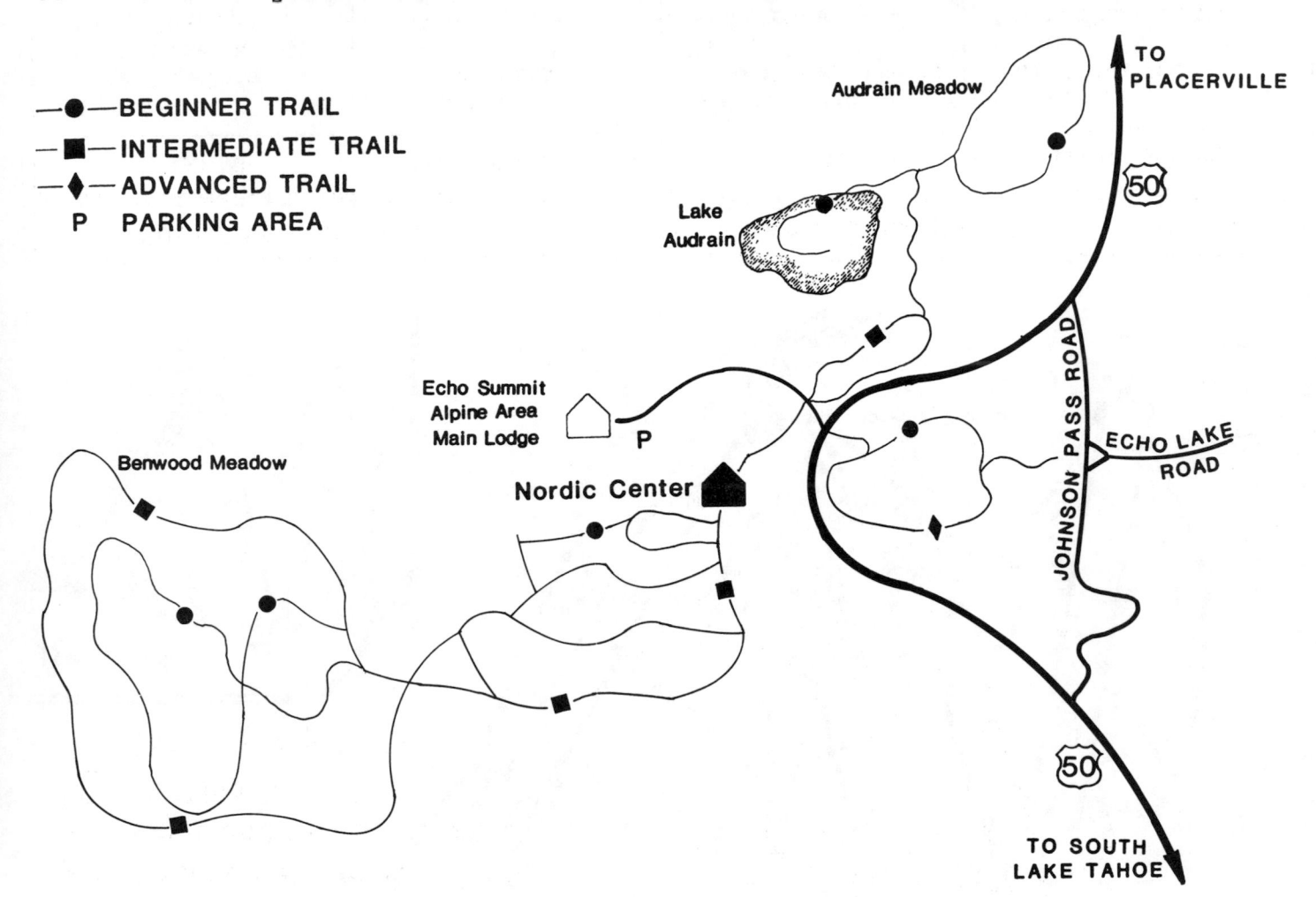

- ● —BEGINNER TRAIL
- ■ —INTERMEDIATE TRAIL
- ◆ —ADVANCED TRAIL
- P   PARKING AREA

INFORMATION: Echo Summit Nordic Center, P.O.Box 8955, South Lake Tahoe 95731, Ph: 916-659-7154

SKIING	RENTALS & LESSONS	RECREATION	ACCOMMODATIONS
Nordic: 25 Kilometers of Marked Groomed Trails Guided Tours Telemark Trail Fees: Adults – $6 Seniors & Children – $4	Ski School: Group Lesson – 1-1/2 hr. – $9 Private – $25 hr. Learn To Tour: Trail Fee, Rental Equipment & Group Lesson–$18.50 Rentals: Adults: $10 Seniors & Children: $6 Telemark Skis	Alpine Skiing, Lifts Lessons & Rentals Nearby: Ski Touring Snowmobile Rentals ORV Trails Snow Play Areas Casinos	Cafeteria Beer & Wine Bar Ski Shop Free Shuttle to South Lake Tahoe Lodging – Contact: South Lake Tahoe Visitors Bureau Ph: 800-822-5922

ECHO SUMMIT SKI AREA

Echo Summit is one of the Tahoe Area's newest ski resorts. Located high above the Tahoe Basin off Highway 50, this small family-oriented resort offers reasonable prices and a nice day lodge, cafeteria, bar and ski shop. There is a good ski school offering lessons to all levels of ability. The children are offered the popular Skiwee learn-to-ski program. Lift ticket sales are limited, so lines are minimal. There is a separate beginner's area, Tortilla Flats, away from the major runs. At the present time, there is a total of 75 skiable acres down a 550 foot vertical drop. Plans are to add a new chair lift and another 150 acres to the ski area.

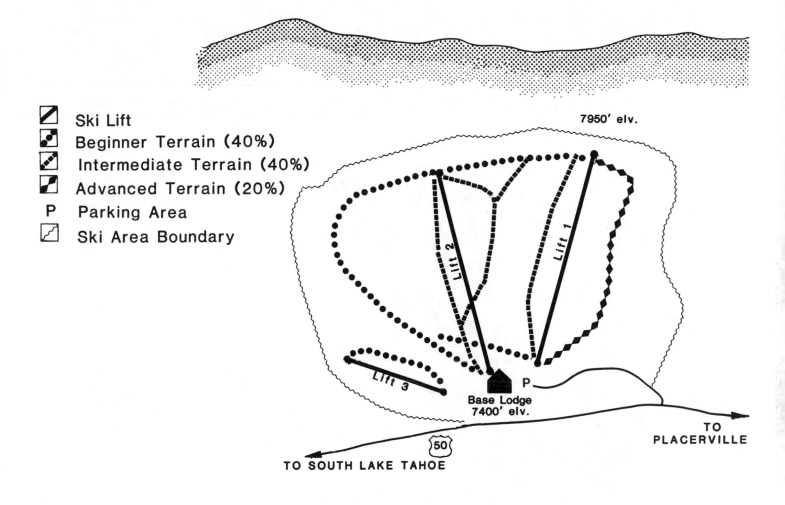

Ski Lift
Beginner Terrain (40%)
Intermediate Terrain (40%)
Advanced Terrain (20%)
P   Parking Area
Ski Area Boundary

7950' elv.

Lift 2   Lift 1   Lift 3

Base Lodge
7400' elv.

P

TO SOUTH LAKE TAHOE

50

TO PLACERVILLE

INFORMATION: Echo Summit Ski Area, P.O. Box 8955, South Lake Tahoe 95731, Ph: 916-659-7154

SKIING	RENTALS & LESSONS	RECREATION	ACCOMMODATIONS

Alpine:
  2 Chairlifts
  1 Rope Tow
Fees: Chairs –
  Adults – All Day
  $15, Half Day $12.
  Seniors $9,
  Children $8
  Rope Tow – $10
  Season: Nov.–April
Snow Phone:
  916-659-SNOW
	Ski School:
	  Group Lessons –
	  2 hr. $13
	  4 hr. $20
	  Private – $25/hr.
	  Skiwee – Age 7–12:
	  Day Lift,
	  Lesson,Lunch –$32
	Rentals:
	  Combinations –
	  Adults $13,
	  Children $9
		Nordic Skiing, Trails,
		  Rentals & Lessons
		Nearby:
		  Ski Touring
		  Snowmobile Rentals
		  ORV Trails
		  Snow Play Areas
		  Casinos
			Cafeteria
			Wine & Beer Bar
			Ski Shop
			Group Discounts by
			  Reservation
			Free Shuttle Bus to
			  South Lake Tahoe
			Lodging – Contact:
			  South Lake Tahoe
			  Visitors Bureau
			  Ph: 800-822-5922

Heavenly Valley is one of America's largest and most complete Alpine Resorts with over twenty square miles of varied terrain. The California or West side of this vast two-State complex provides runs of every description ranging from the imposing drop down the face of Gunbarrel to the gentle slope of Maggie's Trail. The skier will find the advanced runs near the bottom, the beginner in the middle, and the intermediate at the top and into the Nevada side. The Nevada side can be reached via the Sky Chairlift then by the Skyline Trail into Nevada. This full service Resort is supported by an abundance of other recreational opportunities and facilities at nearby South Lake Tahoe.

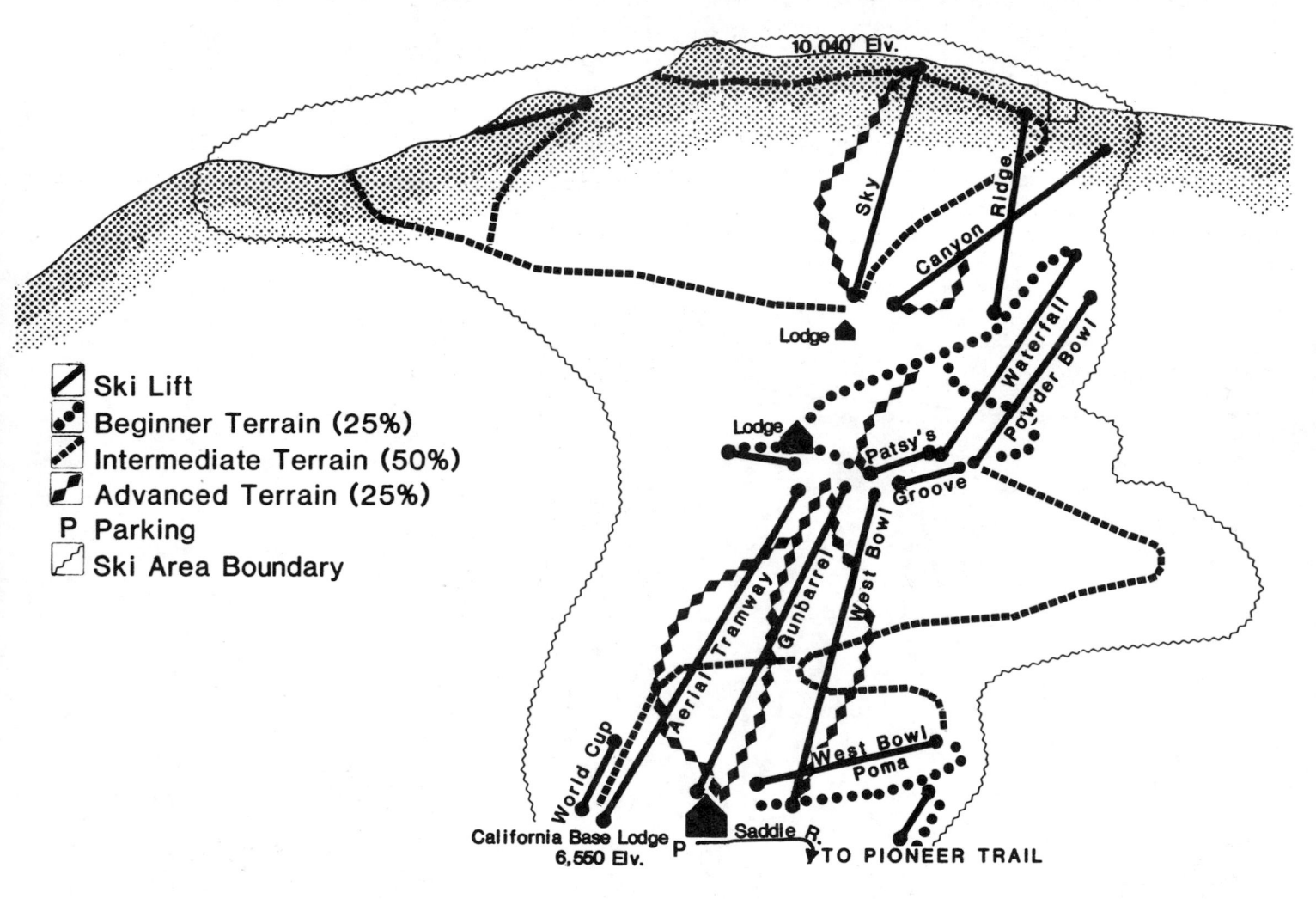

Ski Lift
Beginner Terrain (25%)
Intermediate Terrain (50%)
Advanced Terrain (25%)
P Parking
Ski Area Boundary

INFORMATION: Heavenly Valley–California, Box AT, South Lake Tahoe 95705, Ph:916–541–1330			
SKIING	**RENTALS & LESSONS**	**RECREATION**	**ACCOMMODATIONS**

Alpine:
  1 Aerial Tramway
  2 Poma Lifts
  10 Chairlifts
  Fees: To $26
  Pay To Race Course
  NASTAR Program
  Custom Races
Season: Mid-November
  to Mid-May
Snow Phone:
  916-541-SKII
	Ski School:
	  Children and Adults
	  Every Level Skier
	  Group: $16–23
	  Private: $38–$190
	  Children's Skiwee
	  Program, Ages 4–12;
	  Includes Lesson,
	  Lifts, Lunch
	  and Fun! $45
	Ski Rentals at Base
	Lodge
		Nearby:
		  Cross Country
		  Snowmobile Rentals
		  Snow Play Areas
		  ORV Trails
		  Casinos
		Heavenly Central
		  Reservations:
		  Complete 4-day-
		  plus Ski Vacations
		  Fly-Ski Packages
		  Ph: 702-588-4584
			Restaurant, Cafeteria,
			Snackbar, Sundecks,
			Barbecues, Cocktails
			Full Service Ski Shop
			Group Programs
			Free Shuttle Buses:
			  Ph: 916-544-2266
			Full Facilities Nearby
			  Contact South Lake
			  Tahoe Visitors
			  Bureau:
			  Ph: 800-822-5922

HEAVENLY VALLEY — NEVADA

The Nevada Side of Heavenly Valley offers an equally abundant variety of Alpine opportunites as the California Side. Numerous groomed slopes, open bowls and timbered areas of unpacked powder provide a challenge to skiers of all abilities. Even the "super expert" will find Mott Canyon an unforgettable experience with its 2,000 foot vertical drop through unimproved terrain. This is accessible only through designated gates, and caution is always advised when skiing in this unstable area. Snowcats shuttle Mott Canyon skiers back to the Perimeter Run Area. The Nevada side is often less crowded although usually easily reached from the South Shore area.

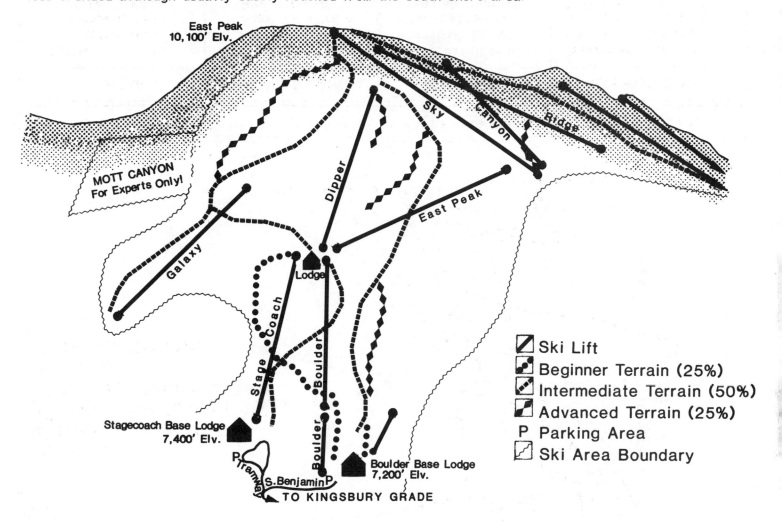

SKIING	RENTALS & LESSONS	RECREATION	ACCOMMODATIONS
Alpine: 　6 Chairlifts 　Fees: $26 　Snow Cat Shuttle 　to Mott Canyon 　Pay-to-Race Course Normal Season: 　Mid-November to 　Mid-May Snow Phone 　916-541-SKII	Ski School: 　Children and Adults 　Every Level Skier 　Group: $16 - $23 　Private: $38 - $190 　Children's Skiwee 　Program, Ages 4-12; 　Includes: Lesson, 　Lunch, Lifts 　and Fun! $45 Ski Rentals at Base Lodge & Throughout South Lake Tahoe	Nearby: 　Cross Country 　Snowmobile Rentals 　Snow Play Areas 　ORV Trails 　Four World Class 　Hotel/Casinos Heavenly Central Reservations: 　Ph:(702) 588-4584 　Special Fly-Ski 　Packages	3 Cafeterias, Wine & Cheese Bar, Sundecks, Barbecues, Cocktails Full Service Ski Shop Group Programs Free Shuttle Buses: 　Ph: 916-541-1330 Full Facilities Nearby 　Ph: 800-822-5922

INFORMATION: Heavenly Valley, P. O. Box 2180, Stateline, NV 89449, Ph: 916-541-1330

TELEMARK COUNTRY SPORTS

Located at the base of Echo Summit, this unique Nordic Shop has its own winter trails on the Tahoe Paradise Golf Course for lessons and telemarking practice. Several trips are offered including a day tour in the El Dorado National Forest. Custom tours can accommodate small groups for overnight trips into the back country staying at a rustic cabin located at Meiss Meadow. A winter survival course is also offered for those wanting to learn the safety techniques for winter travel in remote areas.

 CROSS COUONTRY SKI TRAIL
P PARKING AREA

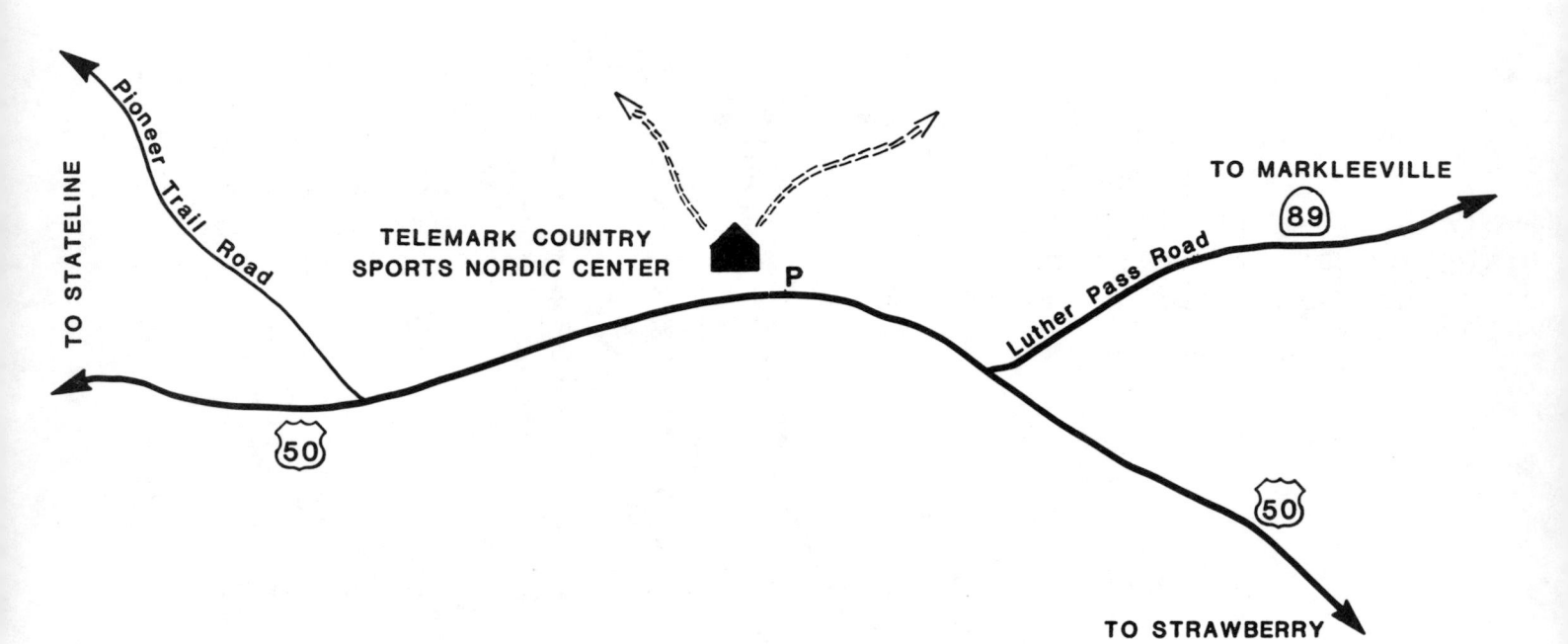

INFORMATION: Telemark Country Sports, P.O. Box 11975, Tahoe Paradise 95808, Ph: 916-577-6811

SKIING	RENTALS & LESSONS	RECREATION	ACCOMMODATIONS

Nordic:
  5 Kilometers of
  Groomed Trails
  Telemark Hill
	Ski School:
	  Private – $20 Hr.
	  Group – Lesson &
	  Trail Fee – $10
	  Lesson/Rental– $16
	  Mini Tours – 4 or
	  More People–$25 ea
	  Telemarking Clinics
	Rentals:
	Cross Country–$9–$12
	Snowshoes – $6
	Downhill Combo – $12
		Remote Back Country
		Cabin Tour Includes
		Meals – $75 per
		Person per Day – By
		Reservation Only
		
		Winter Survival
		Course
		
		Snow Camping
			Restaurant
			Ski & Backpacking
			  Shop

GRASS LAKE SNO-PARK SITE

Up to 50 vehicles with Sno-Park Permits can park along the wide shoulders of Highway 89. This Site is for day use only, and all off-road vehicles are prohibited. Grass Lake Area is a combination of open meadows and old logging roads excellent for beginning cross-country skiing and snow play. This is a good spot to try moonlight skiing. Advanced skiers can proceed north to Tucker Flat and Freel Meadows along the Tahoe Rim Trail. Beware of Grass Lake and do not go near the edges.

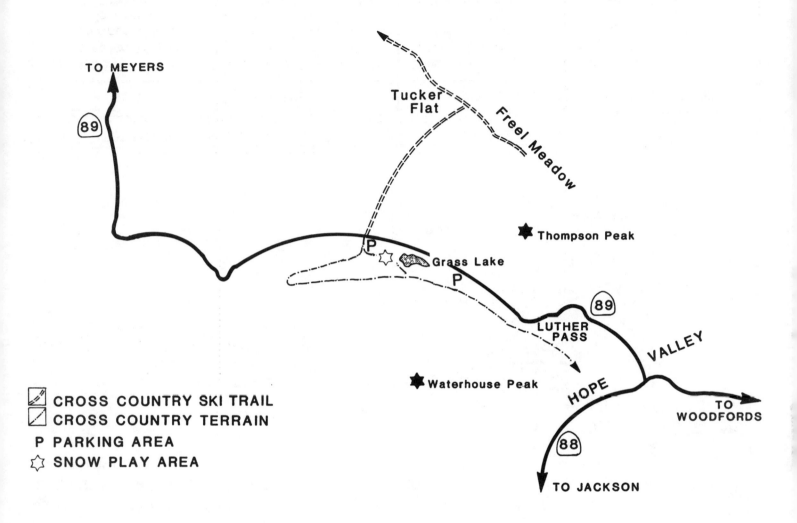

CROSS COUNTRY SKI TRAIL
CROSS COUNTRY TERRAIN
P PARKING AREA
☆ SNOW PLAY AREA

INFORMATION: Lake Tahoe Basin, USFS, P.O. Box 8465, S. Lake Tahoe 95731, Ph: (916) 544-6420			
SKIING	**RENTALS & LESSONS**	**RECREATION**	**ACCOMMODATIONS**

Nordic:
  Beginner,
  Intermediate &
  Advanced
  Terrain
	Not Available at Site	Snow Play
		  No ORV's
		
		SNO-PARK PERMITS
		ONLY: Contact-
		California Sno-Park
		Permit Program
		P.O. Box 2390
		Sacramento 95811
		Ph: (916) 322-8993
			Parking: 50 Vehicles
			
			Sno-Park Permit Fees:
			  $2 – Day
			  $10 – Annual
			Must Have Permit in
			  Advance

At this Site there is an area for snow play as well as a large meadow to the west. The Winnemucca Lake Loop to the south provides the intermediate and advanced cross-country skier an opportunity to also experience snow camping in beautiful surroundings. The bowls along the trails allows for practicing telemark turns. Beware of avalanches around Elephants Back and Round Top areas. To the north of Highway 88, skiers can climb up to the headwaters of the upper Truckee River, to Meiss Lake and further to Highway 89, which is about a 10-mile trip. A Sno-Park Permit must be in your vehicle for parking at this site.

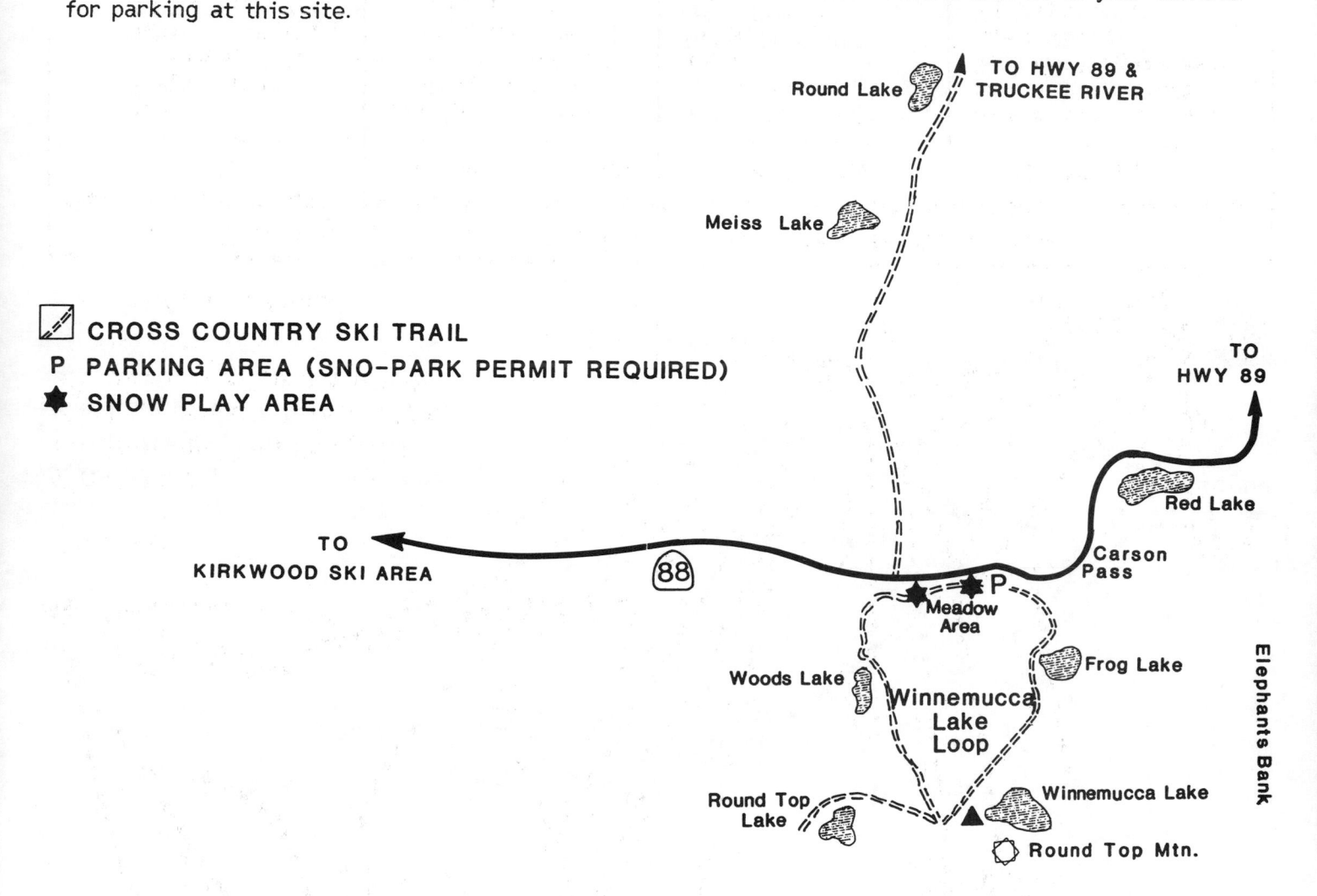

INFORMATION: Amador Ranger Dist., 26820 Silver Dr., Pioneer 95666, Ph: 209-295-4251

SKIING	RENTALS & LESSONS	RECREATION	ACCOMMODATIONS
Nordic: Beginners – Meadow Intermediate & Advanced – Winnemucca Lake Loop	Not Available at Site	Snow Play Snowmobiling: Restricted to Routes – None Nearby SNO-PARK PERMITS ONLY: Contact – California Sno-Park Permit Program P. O. Box 2390 Sacramento 95811 Ph: 916-322-8993	Snow Camping Parking: 40 Vehicles at Sno-Park Site Sno-Park Permit Fees: $2 – Day $10 – Annual Must Have Permit in Advance

KIRKWOOD SKI RESORT

Kirkwood offers some of the most spectacular mountain scenery and diversified skiing in the Sierras. Blessed with an abundant annual snowfall averaging 425 inches, this complete Ski Resort is attractive to skiers of all levels of ability. There are over 2,000 acres of varied terrain from steep chutes and open bowls to well-groomed gentle slopes. The vertical is 2,000 feet. While some of the 68 runs are among the most challenging in the Sierras, the beginner and intermediate skier will also find ample learning opportunities. There is a fine ski school, and Mighty Mountain provides an excellent learning environment for young skiers. Kirkwood has all the amenities of a destination resort including lodging, restaurants and support facilities.

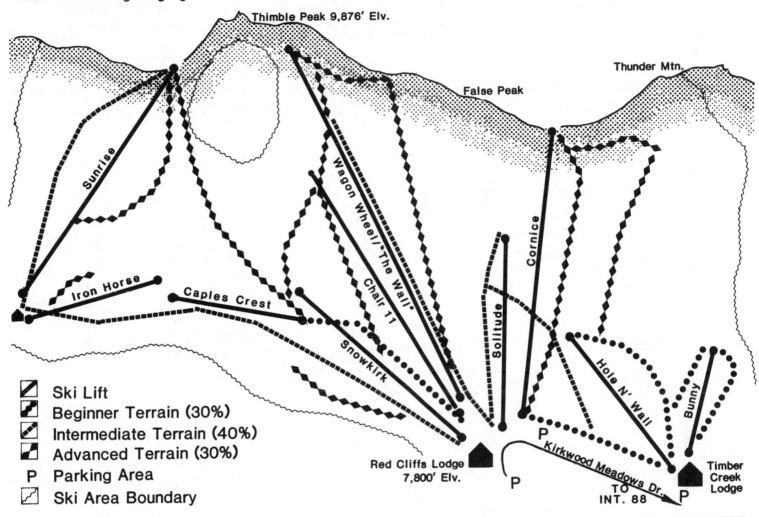

- ◪ Ski Lift
- ◪ Beginner Terrain (30%)
- ◪ Intermediate Terrain (40%)
- ◪ Advanced Terrain (30%)
- P Parking Area
- ◪ Ski Area Boundary

INFORMATION: Kirkwood Ski Resort, P. O. Box 1, Kirkwood 95646, Ph: 209-258-6000

SKIING	RENTALS & LESSONS	RECREATION	ACCOMMODATIONS

Alpine:
  10 Chairlifts
  1 Surface Lift
Fees: Half/Full Day
Adults-$18/$25
Children-$7/$10
Seniors-$7-$10
Race Program:
  1 Run - $2
Season: Mid-November
  through May
Snow Ph: 209-258-3000
	Ski School:
	  Group Lessons:
	  $15, Private-$38
	  Beginner Special:
	  Lesson, Lift &
	  Rental-$30
	  Mighty Mountain-
	  4-12 yrs. old
	  Includes Double
	  Session Lessons,
	  Lift and Lunch $35
	Rentals:-$14-$18
		Nordic Cross Country
		Skiing: Lessons &
		Rentals
		Telemarking
		
		Nearby:
		  Snowmobile Rentals
		  Snow Play Areas
		  ORV Trails
		  Ski Touring
		  Casinos
			Cafeteria, Restaurants
			Bars, General Store,
			Weekend Entertainment
			Sport Shop &
			Equipment Service
			Day Care Center
			Conference Facilities
			Ski Shuttle-S. Tahoe
			Condominiums
			Lodging Reservations:
			  Economy to Luxury
			  Ph: 209-258-7247

The Kirkwood Cross Country Ski Area provides some of the finest Nordic terrain in North America. In addition to this area of fine ski touring along the Sierra Crest, the Kirkwood Area offers 75 kilometers of extensively groomed track within its three interconnected track systems. These diversified trails go across high slopes, through open meadows and forests, challenging skiers of every level. Many special events, clinics and races are held throughout the season. The excellent Nordic School provides clinics and lessons for all levels of skiers including telemark and biathlon. Located near the complete destination resort facilities of Kirkwood, there are special ski/lodging packages at the Resort as well as the nearby resorts listed below.

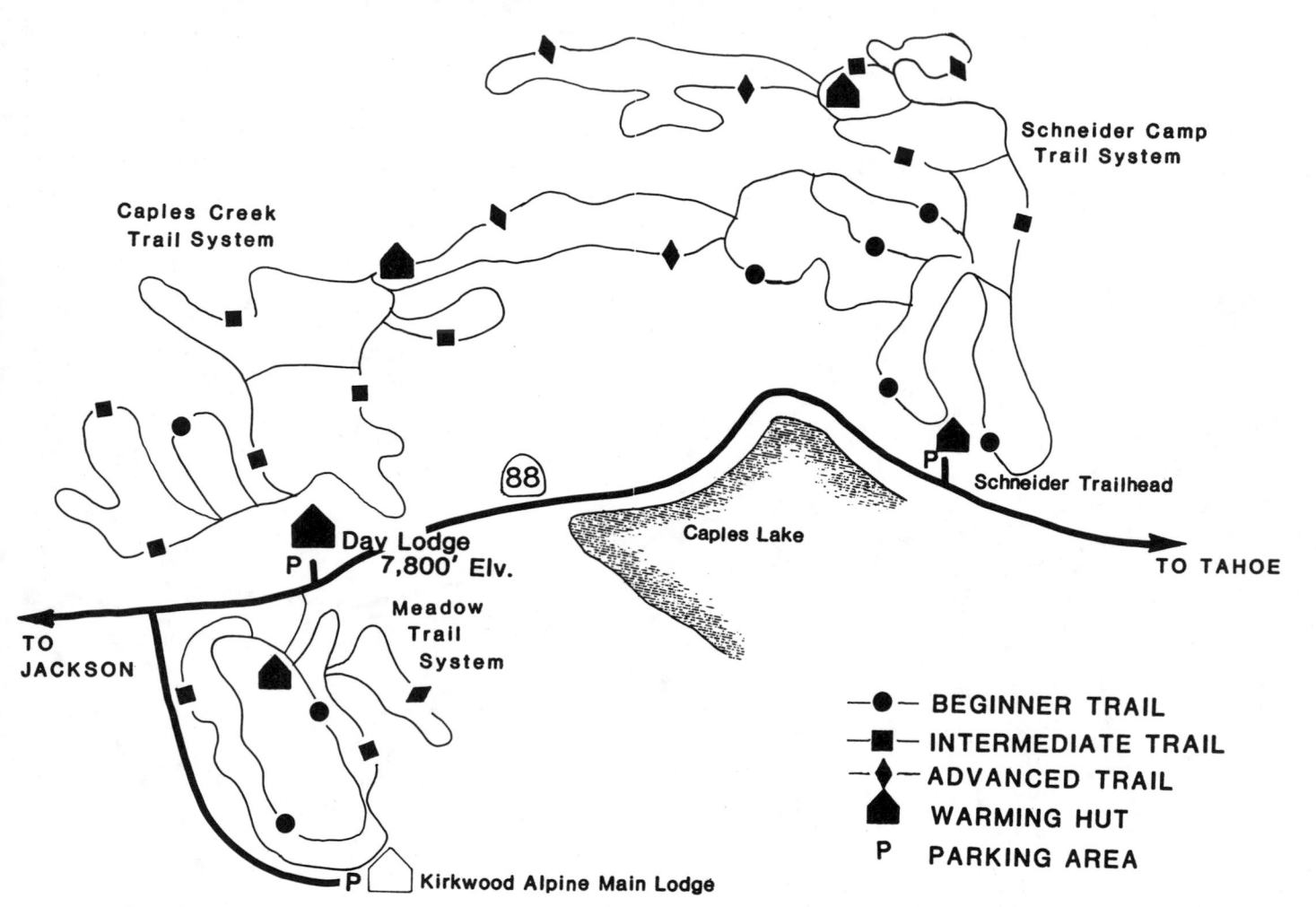

— ● — BEGINNER TRAIL
— ■ — INTERMEDIATE TRAIL
— ◆ — ADVANCED TRAIL
▲ WARMING HUT
P PARKING AREA

INFORMATION: Kirkwood Cross Country, P.O. Box 77, Kirkwood 95646, Ph: 209-258-8864

SKIING	RENTALS & LESSONS	RECREATION	ACCOMMODATIONS

Nordic:
  75 Kilometers of
  Marked Groomed
  Trails
Fees:Adults-$5.50-$10
  Children-$4-$5.50
  Seniors-$6-$7.50
Cross Country Tours &
  Races
Biathlon Races
Snow Ph: 209-258-3000
	Ski School:
	  Groups: $14-$23
	  Includes Trail Pass
	  Private: $22 hr.
	  Basic Downhill,
	  Telemark & Advance
	  Track Lessons
	Rentals: $6-$15
	Package: $14-$25
	  Lesson, Trail Pass
	  & Rental
		Alpine Skiing
		
		Nearby:
		  Snowmobile Rentals
		  Snow Play Areas
		  ORV Trails
		  Ski Touring
		  Casinos
			Complete Facilities at
			  Kirkwood Resort
			Ski Shop & Service
			Lodging & Packages:
			  Kirkwood Resort:
			  Ph: 209-258-7247
			  Caples Lake Resort:
			  Ph: 209-258-8888
			  Sorensen's Resort:
			  Ph: 916-694-2203
			  Woodford's Inn:
			  Ph: 916-694-2410

IRON MOUNTAIN

Iron Mountain is a relatively new resort 12 miles west of Kirkwood off Highway 88. The ski area is downhill from the base lodge so you must ski down to the lifts. There are 20 runs down a vertical of 1,200 feet. The varied terrain is rated 20% beginner, 60% intermediate and 20% expert. The lodge, cafeteria, ski shop and parking are at the top of the hill. There is a chance that this resort will not reopen this season, so check with the Forest Service for current status.

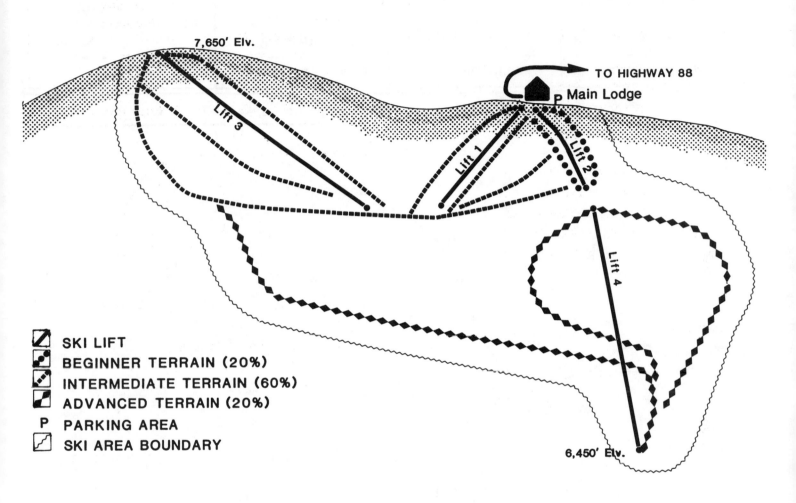

SKI LIFT

BEGINNER TERRAIN (20%)

INTERMEDIATE TERRAIN (60%)

ADVANCED TERRAIN (20%)

P PARKING AREA

SKI AREA BOUNDARY

INFORMATION: Amador Ranger District, 26820 Silver Dr., Star Route #3, Pioneer, Ph: 209-295-4251

SKIING	RENTALS & LESSONS	RECREATION	ACCOMMODATIONS

Alpine:
   5 Chairlifts
	Check Current Status	Nearby:
		   Cross Country
		   Skiing & Rentals
		   Ski Touring
		   Snow Play Areas
		   Snowmobiling
			Day Lodge
			Cafeteria
			Cocktail Lounge
			Snack Bar
			Ski Shop
			Motel & Dormitories

West of the Iron Mountain downhill ski resort, this Sno-Park Site is off Highway 88. Designated snowmobile routes are in process of development throughout this area. The unplowed section of Iron Mountain Road beyond the Parking area continues on to Leek Springs Hill Lookout and is open to snowmobiles. The Leek Springs Loop offers over 10 miles of trails for intermediate to advanced skiers. In addition this Site is the trailhead for many cross-country trails for skiers of all levels.

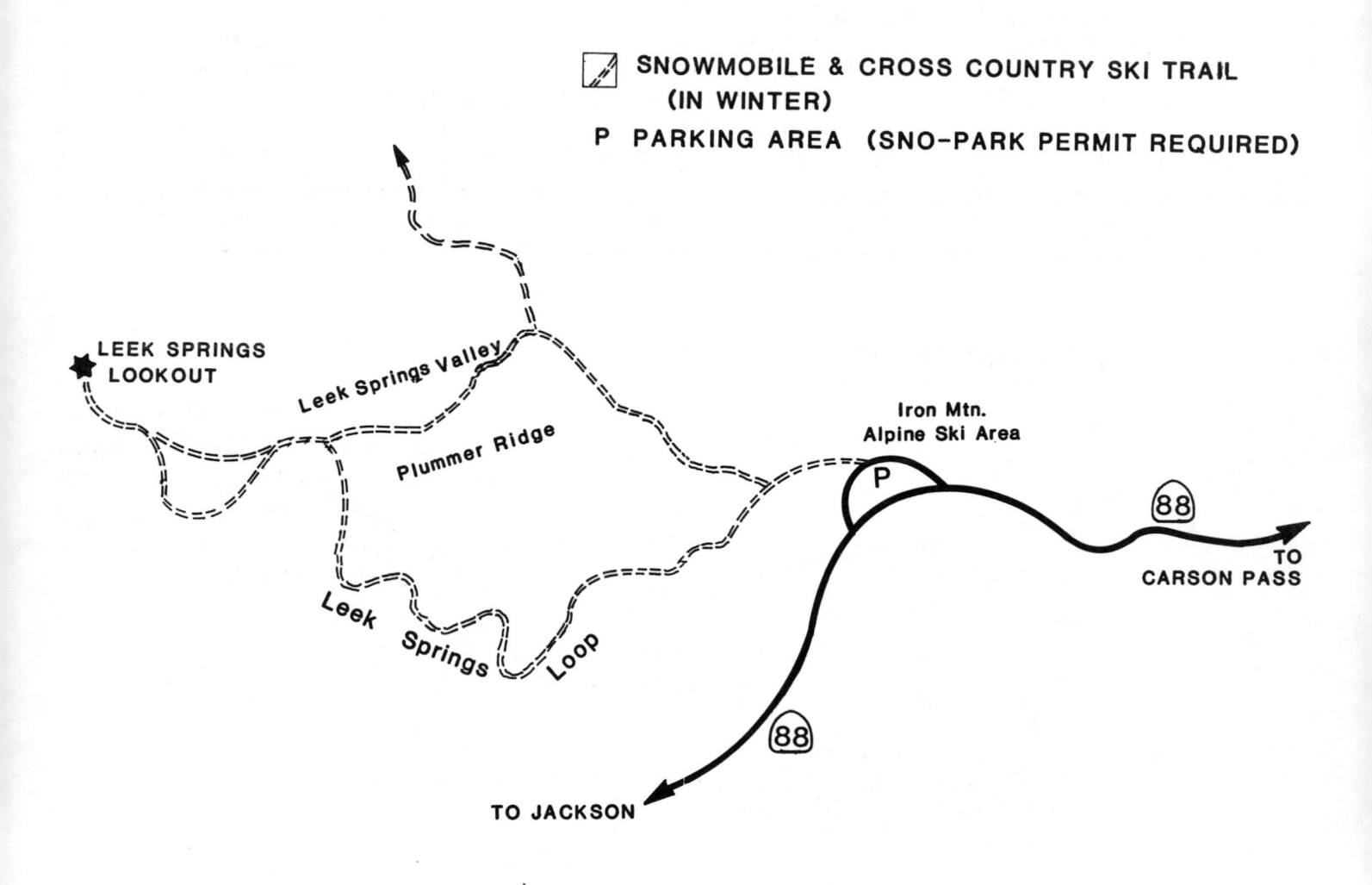

SNOWMOBILE & CROSS COUNTRY SKI TRAIL (IN WINTER)

P PARKING AREA (SNO-PARK PERMIT REQUIRED)

INFORMATION: Sno-Park Permits, P. O. Box 2390, Sacramento 95811, Ph: 916-322-8993

SKIING	RENTALS & LESSONS	RECREATION	ACCOMMODATIONS
Nordic: Leek Springs Loop- 10 miles; Intermediate & Advanced Trails	Not Available at Site	Snow Play Snomobiling	Parking: 20 Vehicles Sno-Park Permit Fees: $2 – Day $10 – Annual Must Have Permit in Advance

Located south of Carson Pass on Highway 88 are two short trails for beginning cross-country skiers. Lumberyard is a 1/2 mile marked trail for practicing techniques. Peddler Hill is an old ski area across from the Bear River Lake Resort. There is a 1 mile marked trail for beginners which is good for nordic downhill practice. The scenery in this area offers beautiful views of the eastern Sierras.

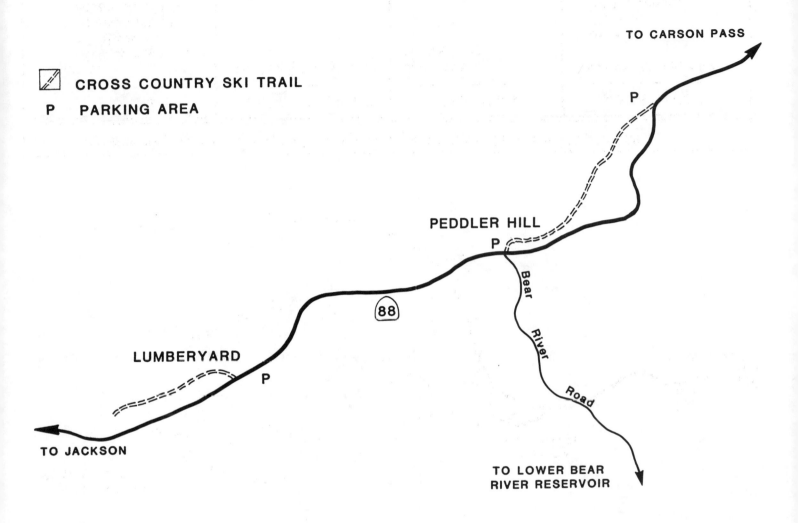

INFORMATION: Amador Ranger Dist., USFS, Star Rte. 3, Pioneer 95666, Ph: 209-295-4251			
SKIING	RENTALS & LESSONS	RECREATION	ACCOMMODATIONS

Nordic:
   Beginner Trails
   3 Kilometers
	Not Available at Site	Nearby:
		   Bear River Lake
		   Resort – See
		   Following Page
		
		   Alpine Skiing
		   Snowmobiling
		   Snow Play Areas
			Limited Parking
			
			Restrooms at
			Lumberyard

Located at 5,840 feet elevation in the beautiful El Dorado National Forest, Bear River Lake Resort is open year around. From this Resort, unplowed roads go 35 miles into the backcountry offering the cross-country skier an opportunity to try new techniques. There are several good areas for sleds and innertubes as well as snowmobile touring. A 50-mile loop from Bear River Lake to Silver Lake primarily for snowmobiles, is in process of development by the Forest Service.

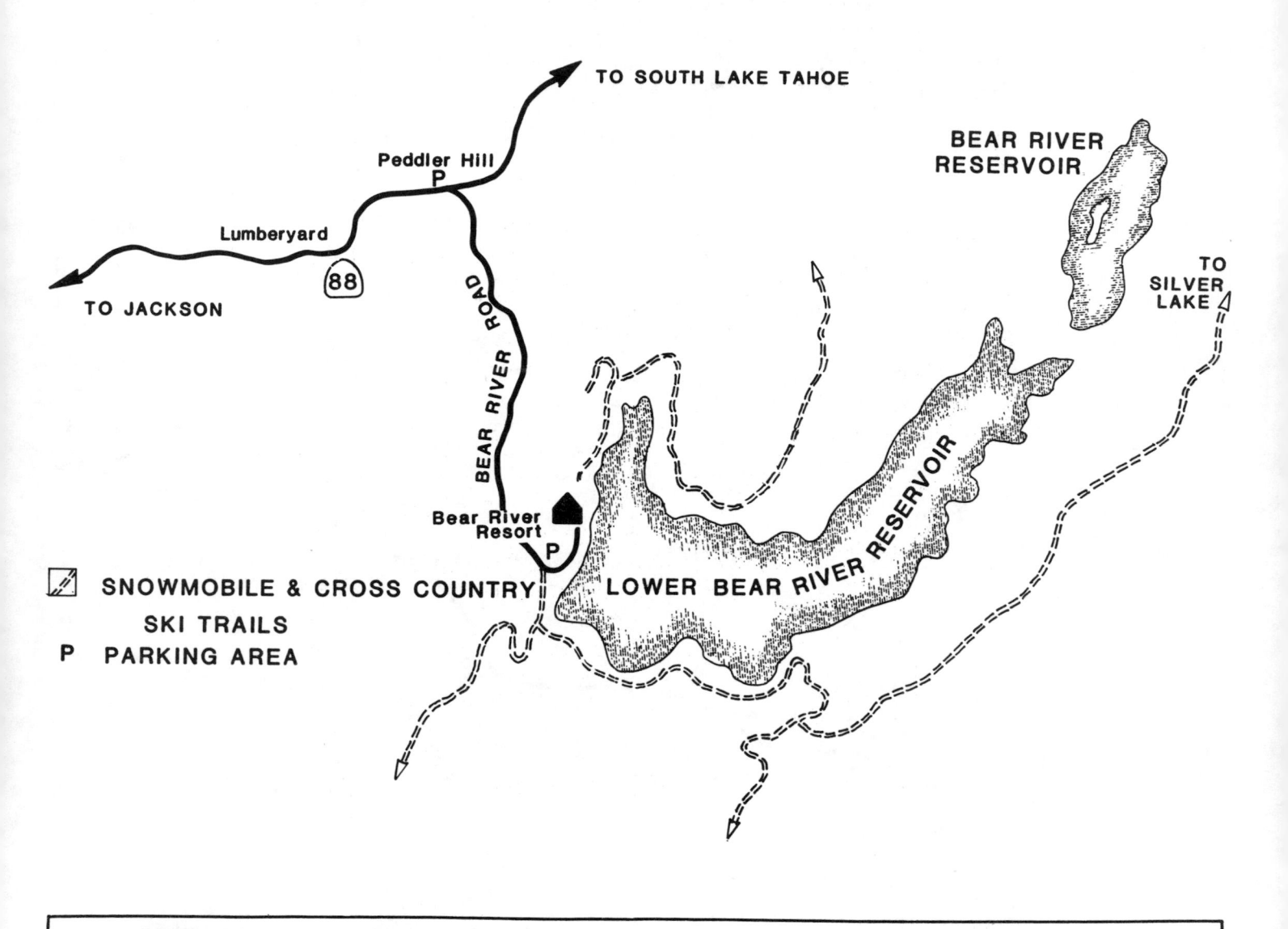

SNOWMOBILE & CROSS COUNTRY SKI TRAILS

P PARKING AREA

INFORMATION: Bear River Lake Resort, 40800 Hwy 88, Pioneer 95666, Ph: 209-295-4868			
SKIING	RENTALS & LESSONS	RECREATION	ACCOMMODATIONS
Nordic: 35 Miles of Groomed Forest Service Roads Miles of Snowmobile Trails	Not Available At Site	Snow Play Areas Snowmobiling Tours (Pending Pemits for '86-87 Season)	Lodging: Fully Equipped House Trailers Snack Bar Beer & Wine

Highway 4 -

Stanislaus
National Forest

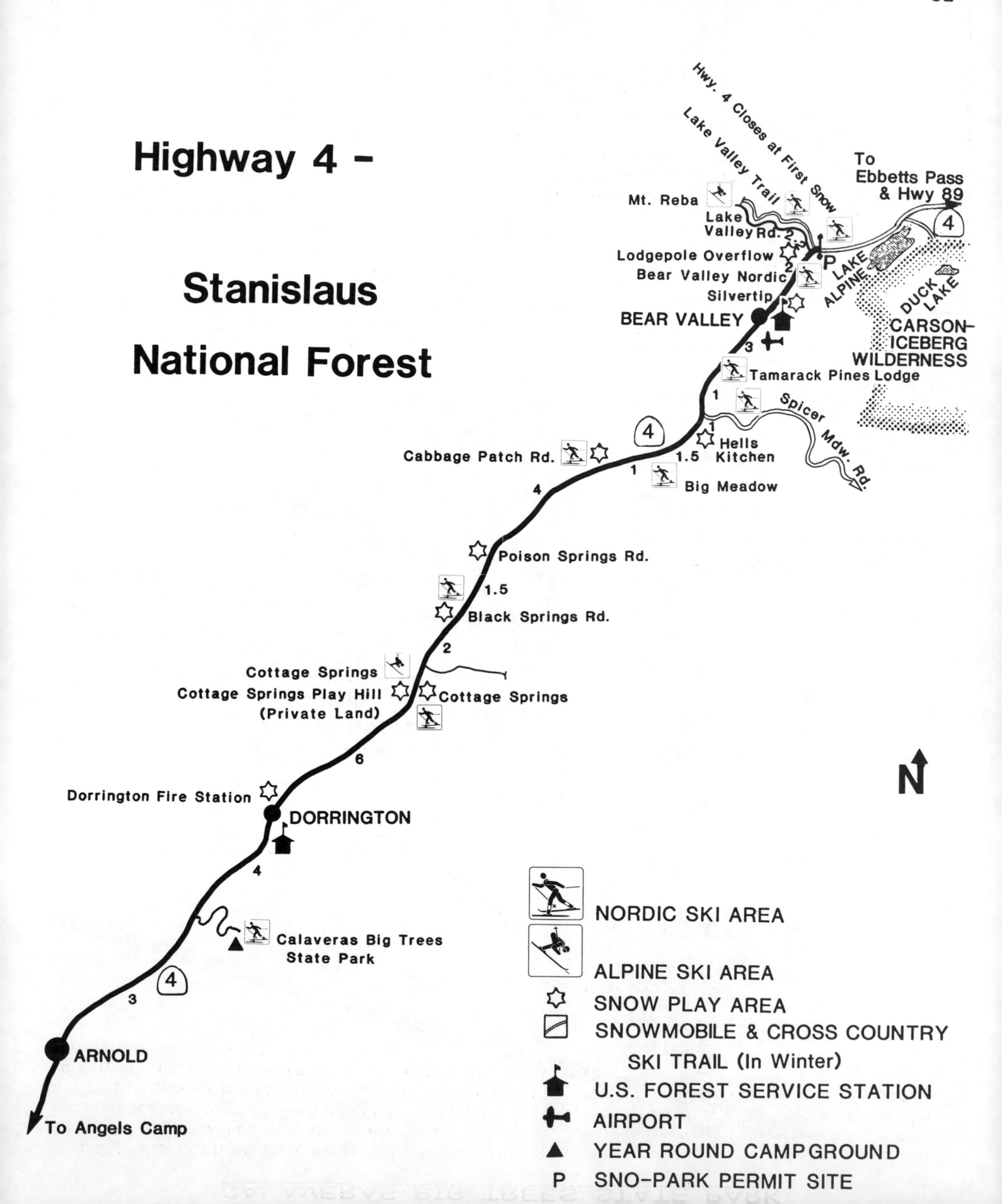

Hwy. 4 Closes at First Snow

Lake Valley Trail

To Ebbetts Pass & Hwy 89

Mt. Reba

Lake Valley Rd.

Lodgepole Overflow

Bear Valley Nordic

Silvertip

BEAR VALLEY

LAKE ALPINE

DUCK LAKE

CARSON-ICEBERG WILDERNESS

Tamarack Pines Lodge

Spicer Mdw. Rd.

Hells Kitchen

1.5

Big Meadow

Cabbage Patch Rd.

4

Poison Springs Rd.

1.5

Black Springs Rd.

2

Cottage Springs

Cottage Springs Play Hill
(Private Land)

Cottage Springs

6

Dorrington Fire Station

DORRINGTON

4

Calaveras Big Trees
State Park

4

3

ARNOLD

To Angels Camp

N

NORDIC SKI AREA

ALPINE SKI AREA

☆ SNOW PLAY AREA

SNOWMOBILE & CROSS COUNTRY
SKI TRAIL (In Winter)

U.S. FOREST SERVICE STATION

AIRPORT

▲ YEAR ROUND CAMPGROUND

P SNO-PARK PERMIT SITE

CALAVERAS BIG TREES STATE PARK

One of the loveliest State Parks in California, this area offers some unique winter activities. At 4,800 feet in elevation, snow is not always present so check before making a trip. Home for the giant sequoias, cross-country skiers can enjoy the nature trail along the outer 3-mile loop as well as the one mile loop near the Parking Area. The North Grove Campground remains open unless there are sub-zero temperatures. Tent campers must carry in their gear about 1/4 of a mile. The Parking Area, however, is available for R.V.s.

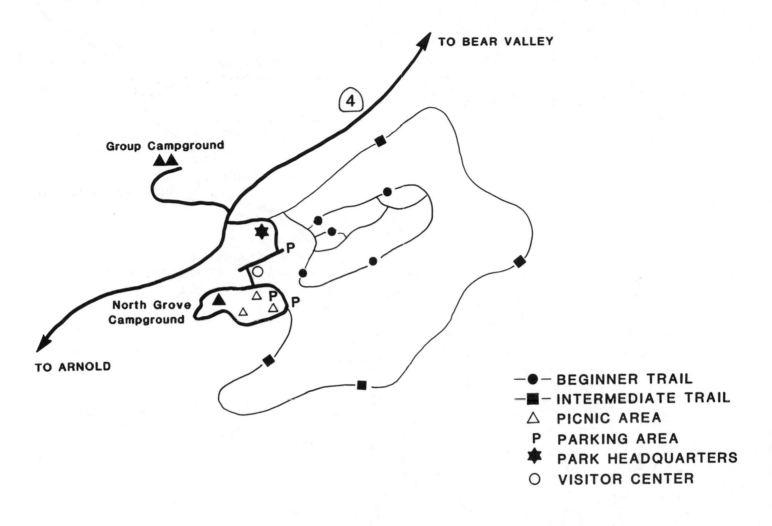

TO BEAR VALLEY

Group Campground

North Grove Campground

TO ARNOLD

—●— BEGINNER TRAIL
—■— INTERMEDIATE TRAIL
△ PICNIC AREA
P PARKING AREA
★ PARK HEADQUARTERS
○ VISITOR CENTER

INFORMATION: Calaveras Big Trees State Park, P.O. Box 120, Arnold 95223, Ph: 209-795-2334			
SKIING	**RENTALS & LESSONS**	**RECREATION**	**ACCOMMODATIONS**
Nordic: 4 Miles of Marked Trails	Not Available at Site	Snowshoeing Snowmobiles Not Permitted within Park Boundaries Visitor Center Open on Weekends: 11:00 a.m. to 3:00 p.m.	North Grove Campground: 12 Tent Sites Parking Area: R.V.s Overnight Day Use Fee: $2 per Car

Cottage Springs is a small alpine resort on Highway 4 seven miles east of Calaveras Big Trees State Park. There are two surface lifts and one chairlift. The vertical down the mountain is 500 feet. This day use facility is primarily a beginner and intermediate mountain with open, groomed slopes. Night skiing is offered on Friday, Saturday and school vacation days until 9:00 p.m. The Ski School offers beginning and private lessons. Cross-country lessons are available by appointment. The rental shop offers both alpine and nordic equipment as well as tube rentals. There is a special hill for tubing away from the ski slopes.

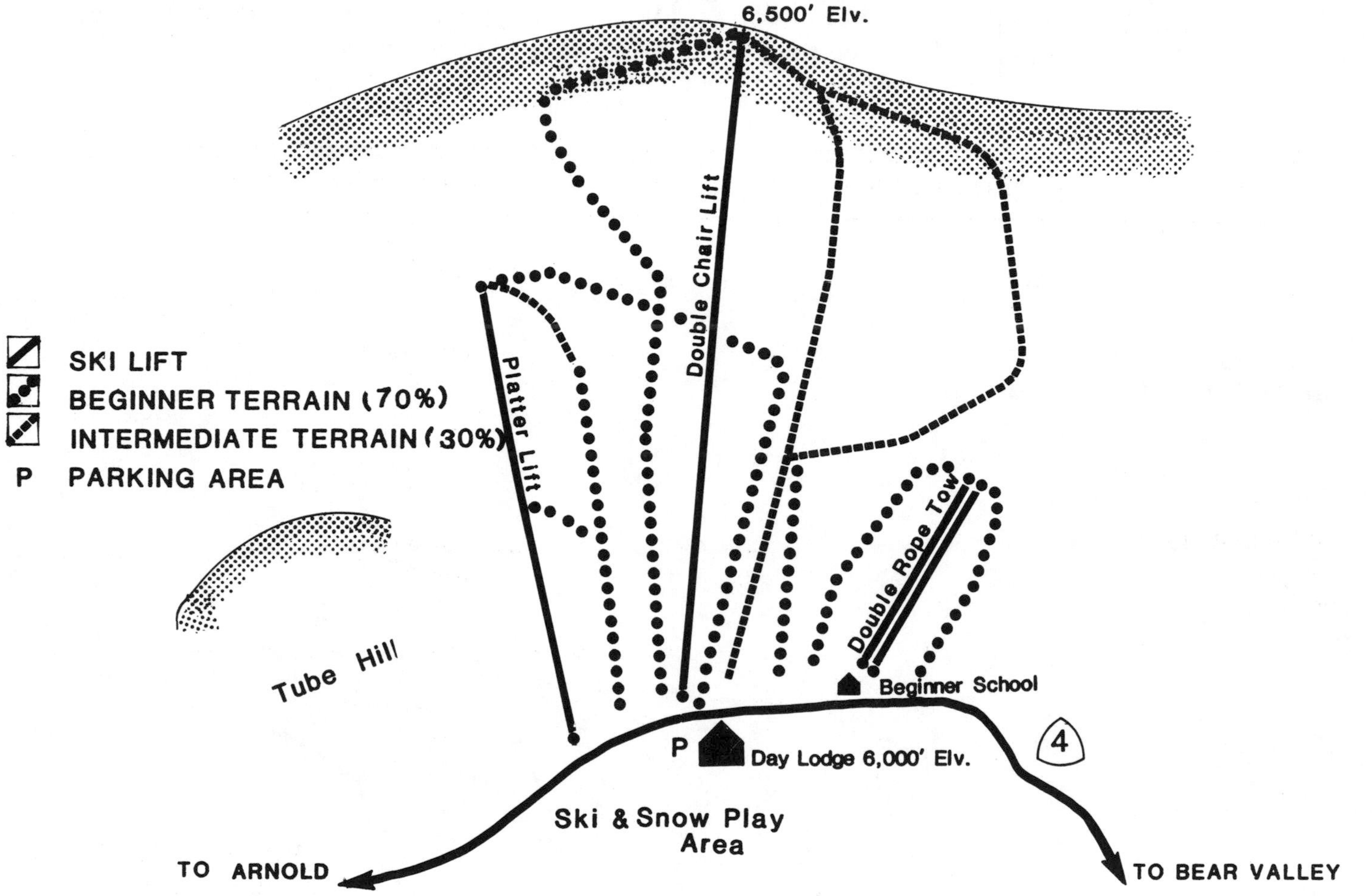

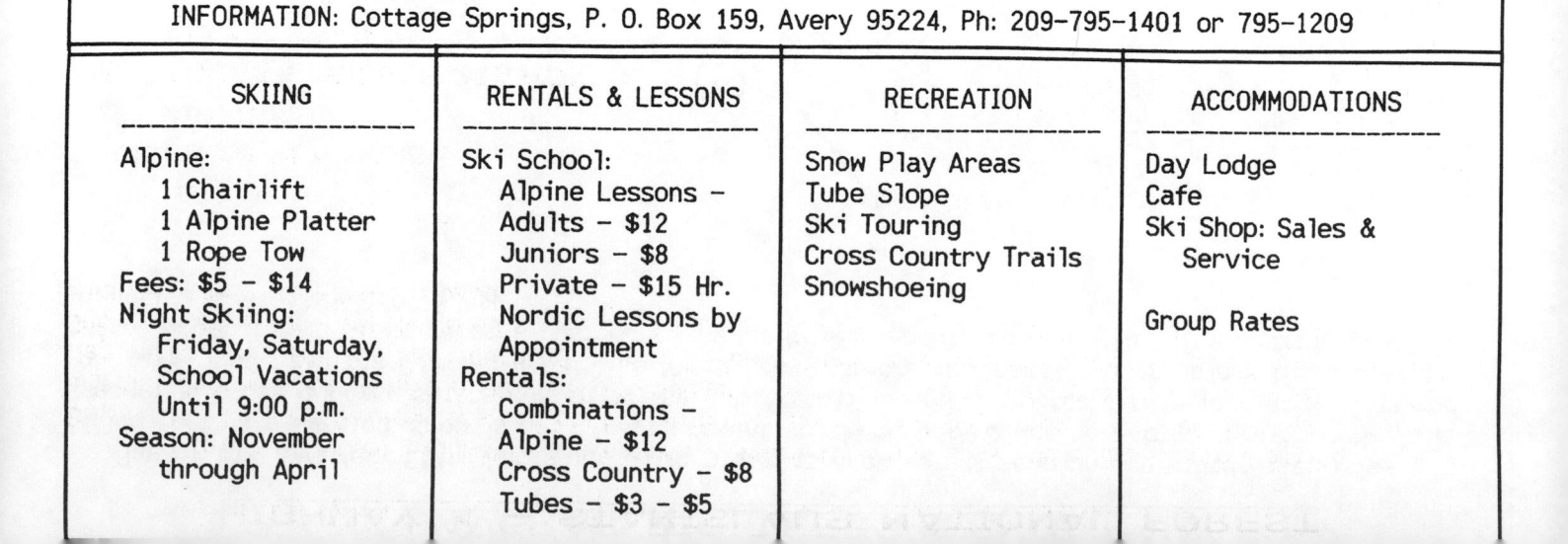

SKI LIFT
BEGINNER TERRAIN (70%)
INTERMEDIATE TERRAIN (30%)
P   PARKING AREA

6,500' Elv.

Double Chair Lift

Platter Lift

Double Rope Tow

Tube Hill

Beginner School

P   Day Lodge 6,000' Elv.

4

Ski & Snow Play Area

TO ARNOLD

TO BEAR VALLEY

INFORMATION: Cottage Springs, P. O. Box 159, Avery 95224, Ph: 209-795-1401 or 795-1209

SKIING	RENTALS & LESSONS	RECREATION	ACCOMMODATIONS

Alpine:
  1 Chairlift
  1 Alpine Platter
  1 Rope Tow
Fees: $5 – $14
Night Skiing:
  Friday, Saturday,
  School Vacations
  Until 9:00 p.m.
Season: November
  through April
	Ski School:
	  Alpine Lessons –
	  Adults – $12
	  Juniors – $8
	  Private – $15 Hr.
	  Nordic Lessons by
	  Appointment
	Rentals:
	  Combinations –
	  Alpine – $12
	  Cross Country – $8
	  Tubes – $3 – $5
		Snow Play Areas
		Tube Slope
		Ski Touring
		Cross Country Trails
		Snowshoeing
			Day Lodge
			Cafe
			Ski Shop: Sales &
			  Service
			
			Group Rates

HIGHWAY 4 — STANISLAUS NATIONAL FOREST

Along this section of Highway 4 are numerous areas for snow play and cross-country skiing. Beyond the Closure Gate skiers can continue on 1/2 day or full day trips to Mosquito Lakes. Trails are not groomed but when the snowfall is adequate, there are numerous Forest Service Roads for beginners, intermediate and advanced skiers. Snowmobilers also use the roads so caution is advised. Snowplay areas are available as shown on the map, but parking is limited along sections of the Highway which have been plowed.

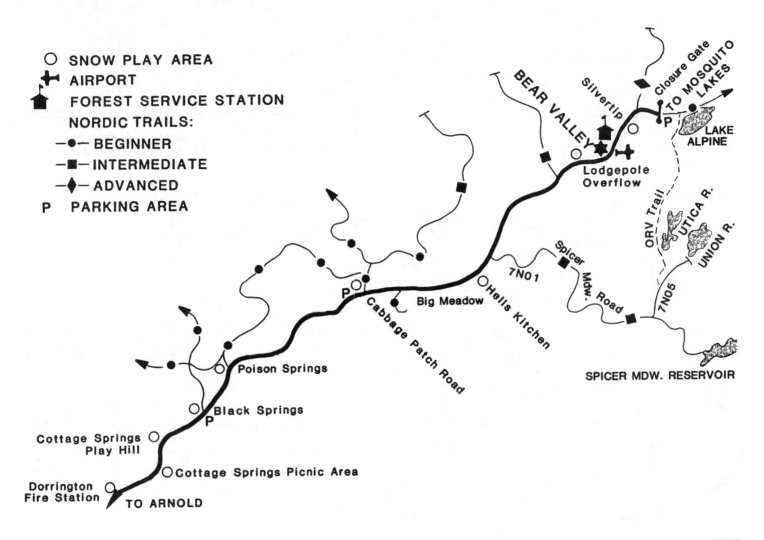

INFORMATION: Calaveras Ranger District, P.O.Box 500, Hathaway Pines 95233, Ph: 209-795-1381

SKIING	RENTALS & LESSONS	RECREATION	ACCOMMODATIONS

Nordic:
  Forest Service
  Roads
  No Groomed Trails
	Nordic Rentals
	  Available at
	  Bear Valley
		Snow Play
		Tobogganing
		Snowmobiling
			Limited Parking
			
			For Lodging
			Information See
			Following Page

TAMARACK PINES LODGE

The Tamarack Pines Lodge and Ski Touring Center is 3 miles west of Bear Valley Village off Highway 4. Located in the beautiful Bear Valley of Stanislaus National Forest at 7,000 feet, this scenic country of open meadows, aspen forest and majestic mountains is a natural ski touring area. The Resort offers 40 kilometers of marked machine-groomed trails that challenge the skills of all levels of skiers from beginner to advanced. Two trails, Bloods and Jacks, provide a 5-1/2 kilometer track to the facilities at Bear Valley. A professional staff of instructors provide both group and private lessons, and the ski shop offers rentals and service. The Lodge offers a hearty meal, cocktails and rooms.

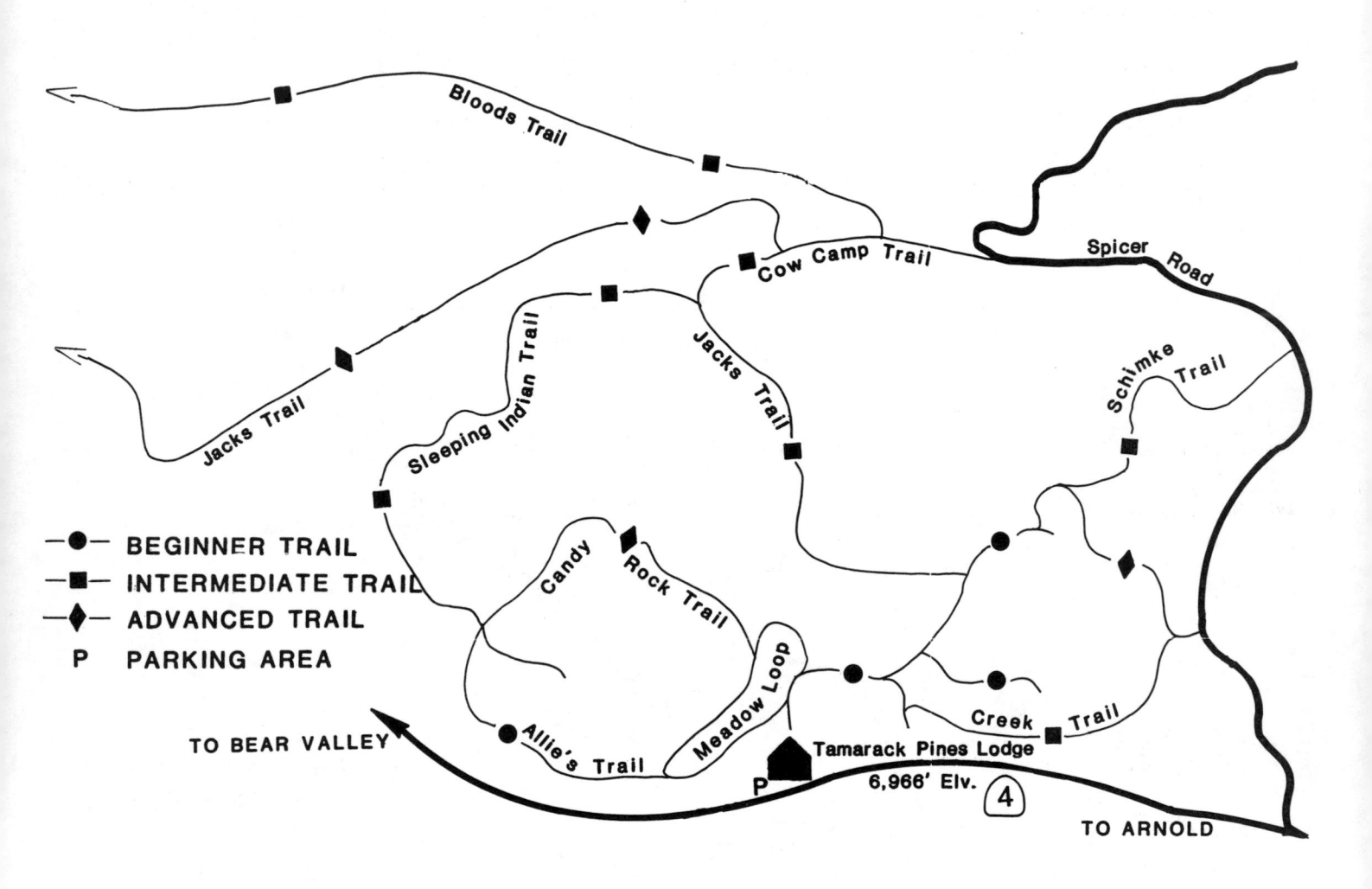

- ● — BEGINNER TRAIL
- ■ — INTERMEDIATE TRAIL
- ◆ — ADVANCED TRAIL
- P — PARKING AREA

| INFORMATION: Tamarack Pines Lodge, P. O. Box 5067, Bear Valley 95223, Ph: 209-753-2080 |

SKIING	RENTALS & LESSONS	RECREATION	ACCOMMODATIONS
Nordic: 40 Kilometers of Machine-Groomed Trails Fee: $7 Children Free with Adult Season: Mid-November Through April	Ski School: Group & Private Lessons Rentals: Combinations	Ski Touring Nearby: Downhill Skiing, Lessons & Rentals Snow Play Areas Snowmobiling Live Entertainment Dancing	Lodge & Restaurant Cocktail Lounge Nordic Ski Shop Lodging/Ski Packages Available Full Facilities at Bear Valley

BEAR VALLEY NORDIC CENTER

The Bear Valley Nordic Center offers one of the largest track systems in the West. Located in the Stanislaus National Forest at an elevation of 7,000 feet, this popular cross-country facility offers 20 trails into this country of scenic beauty and prime snowfall. All trails are marked and groomed and within easy walking distance of the complete facilities at Bear Valley. There is a nice warming hut offering food, drink and a friendly atmosphere. The several picnic sites scattered throughout the trail system offer a relaxing repast. The Nordic Ski School offers a full range of lessons for adults and children. There are special mid-week packages and tours.

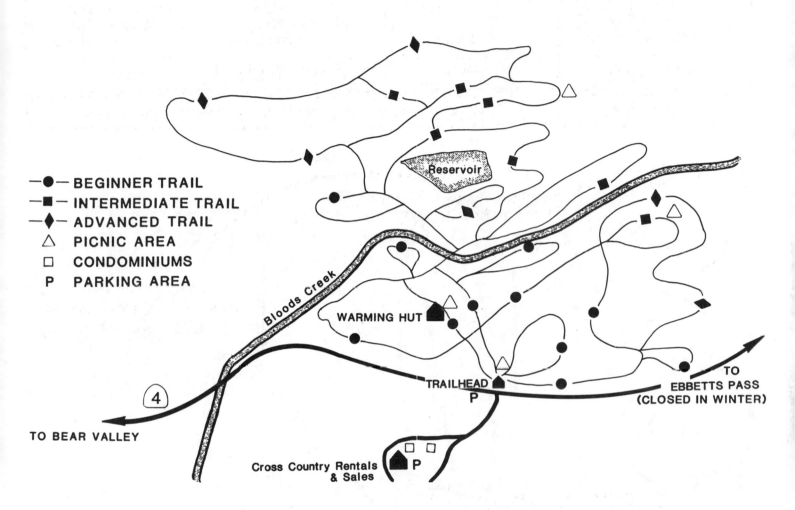

SKIING	RENTALS & LESSONS	RECREATION	ACCOMMODATIONS

Nordic:
   75 Kilometers of
   Groomed Track
Trail Fees:
   Adults – $8
   Children – $4
   Under 7 – Free
 	
Season: Mid-November
   Through April
	Nordic Ski School:
	   Includes Trail Pass
	   Intro. Lesson – $16
	   Lesson & Rental
	      Package – $21
	Private–$25/hr.
	Kinder Ski (4–7) $10
	Telemark–Mt.Reba $28
	Tour du Jour (3–5 Hr)
	   $22 with Lunch
	Rentals & Demos at
	Bear Valley Sports
		Ski Touring
		
		Nearby:
		   Downhill Skiing,
		   Rentals & Lessons
		   Snow Play Areas
		   Snowmobiling
		   Live Entertainment
		   Dancing
			Warming Hut &
			Sundeck
			Snacks, Beer & Drinks
			Picnic Sites with
			Tables
			Bear Trap Basin Hut:
			   2 or 3 Day Tours
			Powderbears Log Cabin
			Mid-Week Specials

INFORMATION: Bear Valley Nordic Center, Box 5005, Bear Valley 95223, Ph: 209-753-2834 or 2844

MT. REBA SKI AREA AT BEAR VALLEY

The Mt. Reba Ski Area at Bear Valley offers alpine skiers a beautiful Central Sierra environment. Surrounded by the Mokelumne Wilderness, this nice family oriented resort offers 21 miles of varied runs with the 1,280 acres of skiable terrain. There are three separate areas for all levels of ability. The annual average snowfall is enhanced by nightly grooming. This complete destination resort offers all the facilities from child care to ski repairs. There is an excellent Ski School and Race Department offering lessons and clinics for all levels of ability. Lodging and other facilities are but 5 minutes away by bus or shuttle. End of the day skiers will find the "Home Run" a pleasant three mile intermediate trail back to Bear Valley.

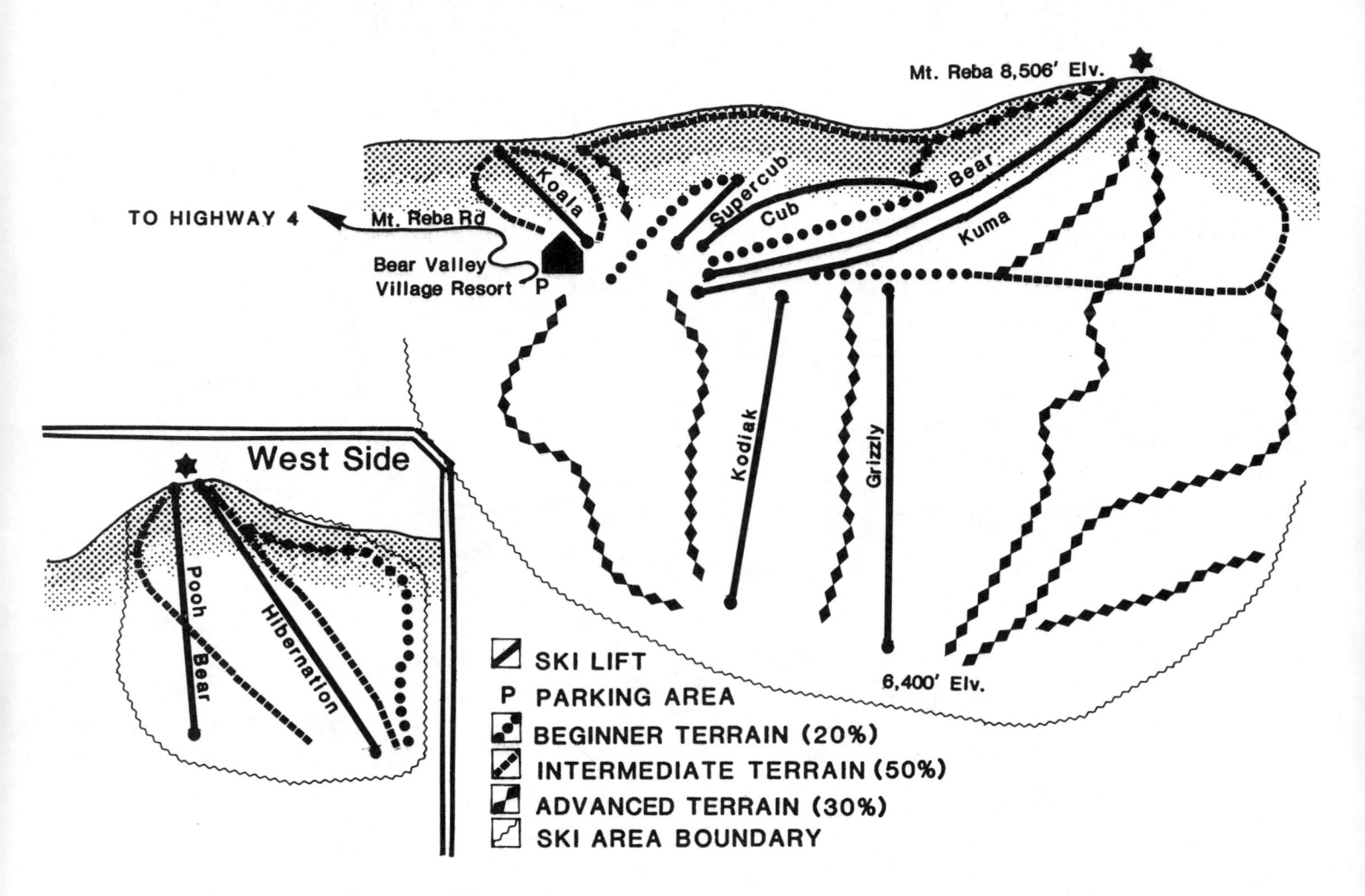

SKI LIFT
P PARKING AREA
BEGINNER TERRAIN (20%)
INTERMEDIATE TERRAIN (50%)
ADVANCED TERRAIN (30%)
SKI AREA BOUNDARY

INFORMATION: Mt. Reba Ski Area, P. O. Box 5038, Bear Valley 95223, Ph: 209-753-2301

SKIING	RENTALS & LESSONS	RECREATION	ACCOMMODATIONS
Alpine: 7 Chairlifts Fees: Half Day/All Day Adults: $18/$24 Seniors & Children: $11/$12 Students $18/$20-$23 NASTAR Racing Season: Mid-November through April	Ski School: Groups Lessons - 2 hrs. - $16 4 hrs. - $25 Private-1 hr.-$32 Skiing Bears (3-7 yrs) Rentals, Lift Ticket & Lunch: $40 Rentals: Combinations - $8-$12	Nordic Skiing, Lessons & Rentals Snow Play Areas Recreation Center Live Entertainment Dancing Nearby: Snowmobiling Ski Touring	Day Lodge & Cafeteria Ski Shop & Repairs Child Care Shuttle Bus Parking for R.V.s Lodging/Ski Packages: Contact - Reservations P.O. Box 5038 Bear Valley 95223 Ph: 209-753-BEAR

LAKE ALPINE SNO-PARK SITE

Located at the end of the plowed section of Highway 4, this Sno-Park Site accommodates 30 vehicles with Permits. Snowmobiles, ORV's and cross-country skiers can travel beyond the Closure Gate all the way to Ebbetts Pass, approximately 16 miles, and beyond. The scenery in this area is spectacular, and intermediate to advanced skiers enjoy the trail to Duck Lake. Be certain to have a Sno-Park Permit if you plan to park at this Site.

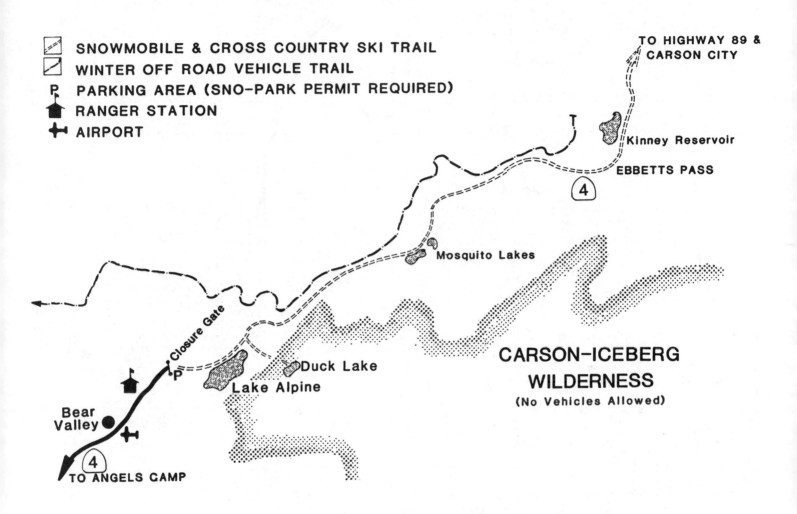

SKIING	RENTALS & LESSONS	RECREATION	ACCOMMODATIONS
Nordic: 　Highway 4 – Open 　to Cross-Country 　Skiing & ORV's 　Only in Winter	Nordic Rentals 　Available at 　Bear Valley	Snow Play Snowmobiles & All Terrain Vehicles SNO-PARK PERMITS ONLY: Contact – California Sno-Park Permit Program P. O. Box 2390 Sacramento 95811 Ph: 916-322-8993	Parking: 30 Vehicles Sno-Park Permit Fees: 　$2 – Day 　$10 – Annual Must Have Permit in Advance

INFORMATION: Calaveras Ranger District, P.O. Box 500, Hathaway Pines 95233, Ph: 209-795-1381

YOSEMITE &
SONORA PASS
AREA

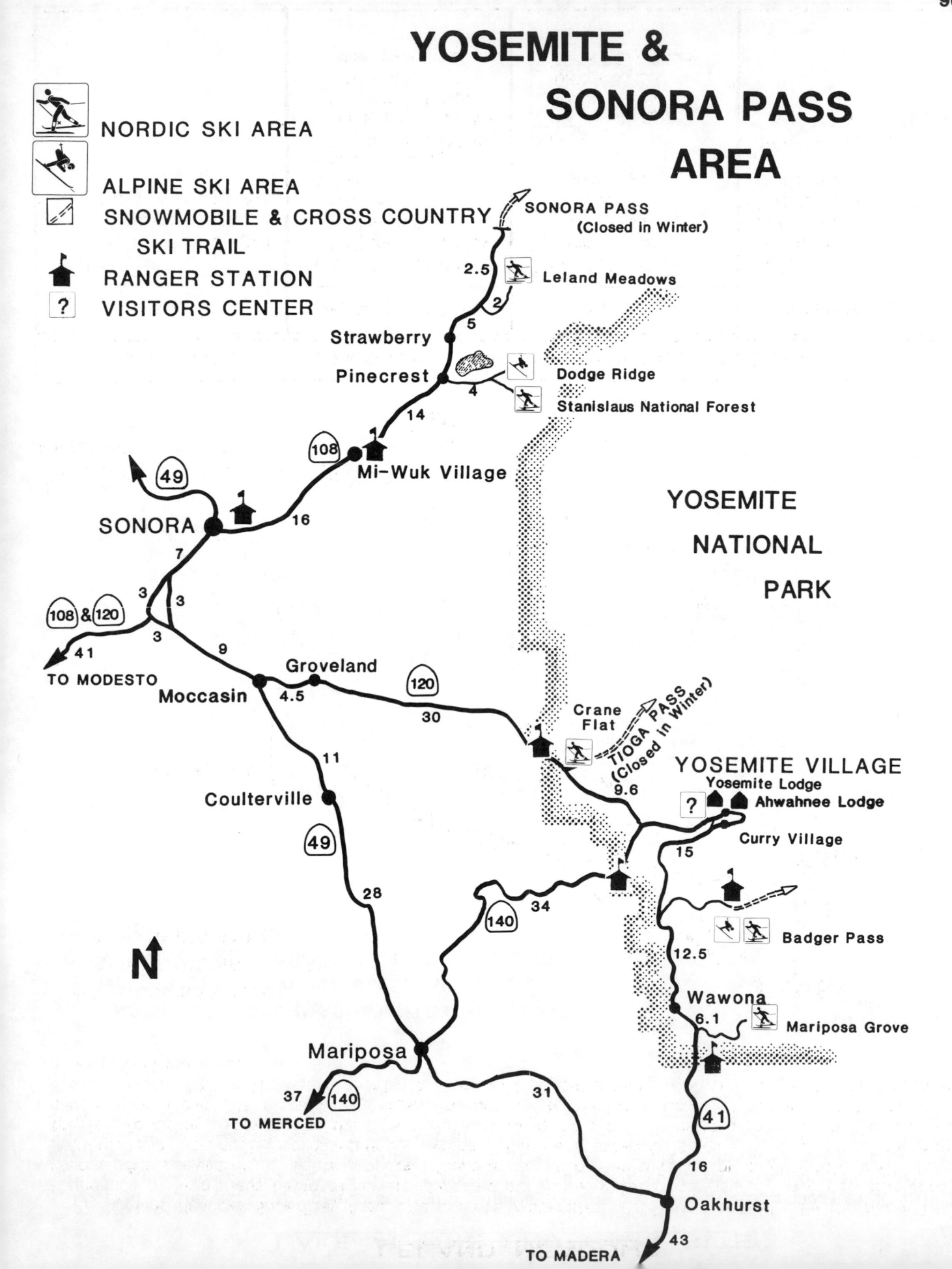

NORDIC SKI AREA

ALPINE SKI AREA

SNOWMOBILE & CROSS COUNTRY
SKI TRAIL

RANGER STATION

? VISITORS CENTER

SONORA PASS
(Closed in Winter)

2.5 Leland Meadows

2

5

Strawberry

Pinecrest

Dodge Ridge

4 Stanislaus National Forest

14

1

108

16

Mi-Wuk Village

49

SONORA

7

3 3

108 & 120

3

41

TO MODESTO

9

Moccasin

4.5

Groveland

120

30

YOSEMITE

NATIONAL

PARK

11

Coulterville

49

28

140 34

140

Crane
Flat

TIOGA PASS
(Closed in Winter)

9.6

YOSEMITE VILLAGE
Yosemite Lodge
? Ahwahnee Lodge

Curry Village

15

Badger Pass

12.5

N

Wawona

6.1 Mariposa Grove

Mariposa

37 140

TO MERCED

31

41

16

Oakhurst

43

TO MADERA

LELAND MEADOWS

The Leland Meadows Snow Play Area is a privately operated facility surrounded by the natural abundance of Stanislaus National Forest. Located off Highway 108 northeast of Pinecrest, this popular resort offers a variety of winter sports. There are over twelve miles of groomed nordic trails for beginner and intermediate cross-country skiers. There are snowmobile tours on U. S. Forest Service trails. To drive a snowmobile, the driver must be 16 years old. There is a toboggan slide, tube and saucer runs along with a stationary rope. In addition to nordic equipment, you can rent all of the above. Overnight facilities are available along with a restaurant, cocktail lounge, dressing room and a large parking area.

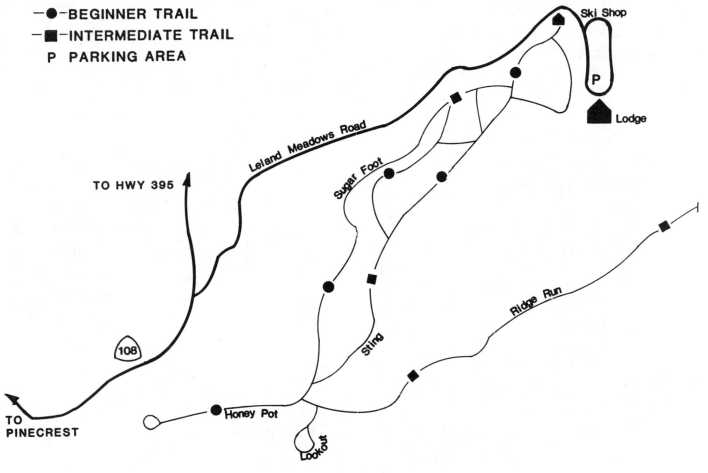

- ●-BEGINNER TRAIL
- ■-INTERMEDIATE TRAIL
- P PARKING AREA

INFORMATION: Leland Meadow Resort, Box 1498, Pinecrest 95364, Ph: 209-965-3745			
SKIING	**RENTALS & LESSONS**	**RECREATION**	**ACCOMMODATIONS**

Nordic:
  12 Miles of Marked
  Groomed Trails
Parking & Trail Fee:
  $3
	Nordic Ski School:
	  By Appointment on
	  Weekends &
	  Holidays
	Rentals:
	  Cross Country –
	  All Day-$9,Half-$7
	  Toboggans – $4-$8
	  Saucers & Tubes –
	  $4 – $6
	  Snow Shoes – $6
		Snowmobile Tours:
		  Single Rider –
		  $25 – $50
		  Double Rider –
		  $25 – $35
		
		Nearby:
		  Ski Touring
		  Alpine Skiing
		  ORV Trails
		  Snow Play Areas
			Lodging
			Restaurant & Bar
			Game Room
			Change Room
			Group Specials
			
			Other Accommodations:
			  See Following Pages

The Dodge Ridge Ski Area has been servicing downhill skiers since 1949. This popular family ski area has recently doubled in size to nearly 800 acres of skiable terrain. The New Prospector Triple Chair has created an additional 6-1/2 miles of intermediate and advanced runs and increased the vertical to 1,600 feet. In addition, there is a new day lodge, The Way Station, at the base of Prospector lift. This is the closest alpine facility to the Monterey and San Francisco Bay Areas offering all the amenities from child care to racing clinics. While primarily a day use resort, there is a complete selection of lodging offering special ski packages.

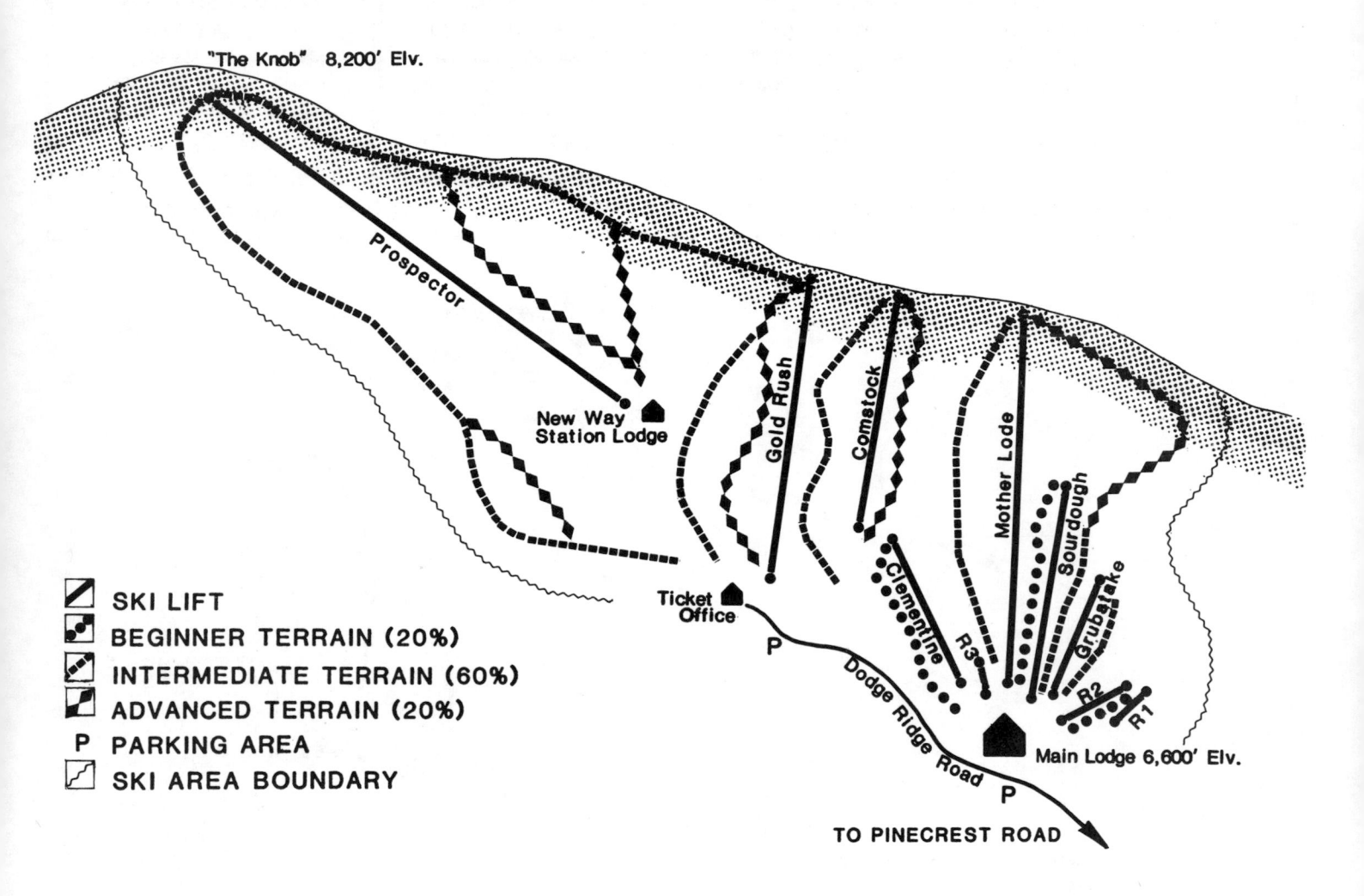

- ◰ **SKI LIFT**
- ◰ **BEGINNER TERRAIN (20%)**
- ◰ **INTERMEDIATE TERRAIN (60%)**
- ◰ **ADVANCED TERRAIN (20%)**
- P **PARKING AREA**
- ◰ **SKI AREA BOUNDARY**

INFORMATION: Dodge Ridge Ski Area, P. O. Box 1188, Pinecrest 95364, Ph: 209-965-3474

SKIING	RENTALS & LESSONS	RECREATION	ACCOMMODATIONS
Alpine: 7 Chairlifts 3 Rope Tows Fees: Adults-$12-$19 Children & Seniors - $6-$10 Race Program & NASTAR Season: Mid November to Mid April Snow Ph:800-233-SNOW	Ski School: Group Lessons: $14 - $21 Private Lessons: $25 per Hour Race Clinic: $15 Skiwee: All Day Lessons, Lifts, Lunch Ages 3-12-$36 Rentals: Adults - $12 Children - $10	Nearby: Cross Country Ski Touring Snowmobiling ORV Trails Snow Play Areas Ice Skating Rink at Long Barn	Restaurant, Beer & Wine Skiers Emporium: Sales, Service & Accessories Child Care: 2-8 yrs. Group Packages & Discounts Special Midweek Ski/ Lodging Packages See Following Pages

STANISLAUS NATIONAL FOREST — SUMMIT RANGER DISTRICT

Highway 108 above Pinecrest is a prime winter sports area. In addition to the downhill skiing at Dodge Ridge, the skier will find an abundance of cross-country opportunities. The Pinecrest area offers 24 miles of marked trails, patroled on most weekends and holidays by the Nordic Ski Patrol. The challenge of these trails vary from beginner to advanced including the open skiing at Telemark Bowl. Snow play is popular at the Pinecrest picnic area and Leland Meadows. Snowmobiling is popular, especially above the winter closure point on the highway at Lilly Creek. There are restricted areas for off-road vehicles. Parking is limited, so it is advisable to check in at the Pinecrest Ranger Station for detailed information.

—●— BEGINNER TRAIL
—■— INTERMEDIATE TRAIL
—◆— ADVANCED TRAIL
P PARKING AREA

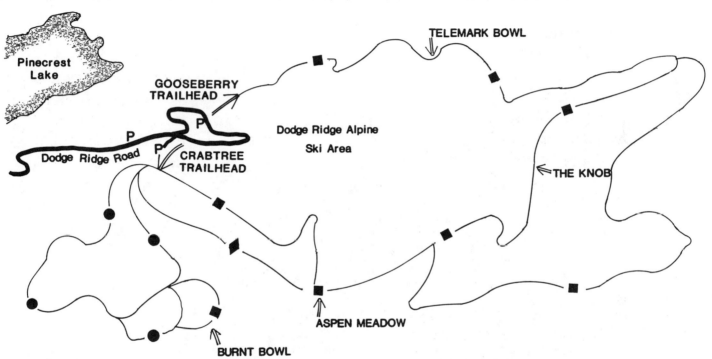

INFORMATION: Summit Ranger District, Star Rt., Box 1295, Sonora 95370, Ph: 209-965-3434

SKIING	RENTALS & LESSONS	RECREATION	ACCOMMODATIONS

Nordic:
    Pinecrest Area:
    24 Miles of
    Marked Trails
    No Fee
Ski Touring
See Leland Meadows
Alpine:
    See Dodge Ridge
	Ski School:
	Nordic-Leland Meadows
	Alpine-Dodge Ridge
	Rentals:
	Leland Meadows Only:
	    Nordic Ski
	    Equipment, Saucers
	    & Tubes, Toboggans
	Dodge Ridge –
	    Downhill Ski Equip.
	Heidi's Ski Shop
	Hwy 108,Cold Springs
		Snow Play Areas
		Snowmobiling Tours
		ORV Trails – See
		    USFS for Details
		Snow Camping
		Ice Skating Rink
		    at Long Barn
			Restaurants
			Stores
			Nordic Ski Rental
			Shop:
			    Morrison's Nordic
			    Experience
			    Hwy. 108 @ Cold
			    Springs
			Lodging Along
			    Highway 108
			    See Page on
			    Area Lodging

BADGER PASS

Badger Pass is a popular family ski resort in beautiful Yosemite National Park. While primarily a beginner (35%) and intermediate (50%) downhill area, skiers of all levels are attracted to this majestic area. There are nine regularly groomed runs within the 100 acres of varied terrain. The vertical drop is 900 feet. The Yosemite Ski School, the oldest in the West, was established in 1928. Its professional staff offers group and private lessons of all levels of ability. Racing clinics and other special classes are offered upon request. NASTAR races are held Wednesday, Saturday and Sunday. In addition to alpine skiing, there are 32 kilometers of set nordic ski track and 90 miles of touring trails, snowcat tours and a Ranger guided snowshoe walk.

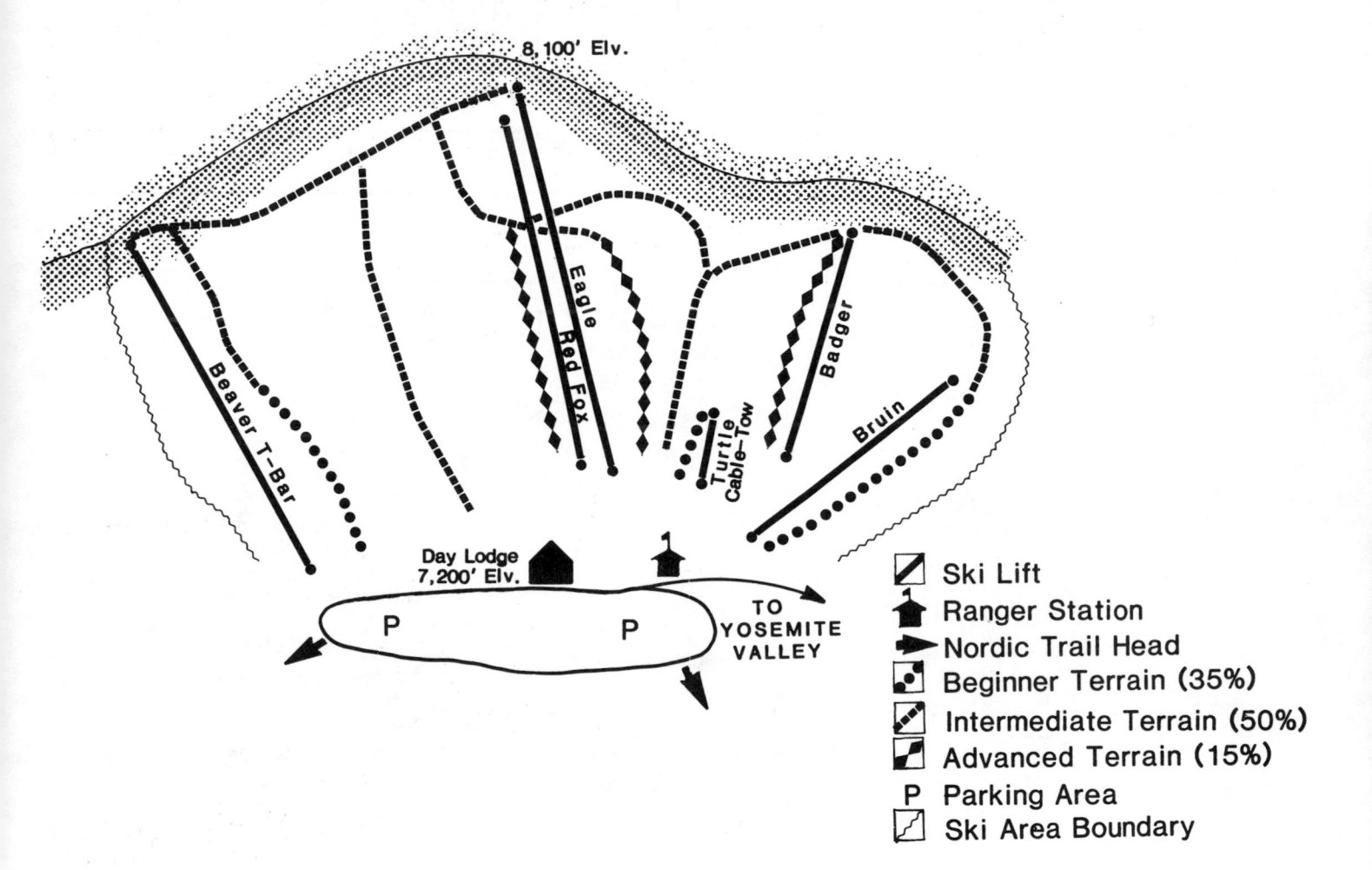

INFORMATION: Badger Pass, Yosemite Park & Curry Co., Yosemite Nat. Park 95389, Ph: 209-372-1330

SKIING	RENTALS & LESSONS	RECREATION	ACCOMMODATIONS

Alpine:
    4 Chairlifts
    1 T Bar/1 Tow
Fees: Seniors - Free
Adults - $10.75-$20.50
Children-$7.50-$10
NASTAR
Season: Thanksgiving
    Through Easter
Snow Ph: 209-372-1338
Reservations:
    Ph: 209-372-2700
	Ski School: Downhill
	    Group (2 hrs.) $16
	    Private (1 hr.) $27
	    Racing Clinics on
	      Request
	Rentals:
	    Adults-$6.75-$14
	    Children - $4.75 -
	    $9.50
	Special Mid-Week &
	Learn to Ski Packages
		Nordic Skiing, Tours,
		Lessons & Rentals
		Ski Touring
		Snowcat Tours
		Ranger Snowshoe Walk
		Live Music - Weekends
		Nearby:
		    Snow Play Areas
		    Ice Skating
		    Naturalist
		      Programs
		    Bus Tours
			Cafeteria & Snack Bar
			Outdoor BBQ-Weekends
			Ski Shop & Repairs
			Child Care-3 Yrs. Up
			Day Lodge
			Free Shuttle Bus from
			    Valley to Badger
			    Pass
			Special Events
			For Lodging See
			Page 97

BADGER PASS NORDIC AREA

Yosemite National Park is one of the most beautiful spots on earth. Enhanced by winter snows, nordic enthusiasts are drawn in increasing numbers to this natural wonderland. Badger Pass is the hub for cross-country skiers where the Yosemite Nordic Ski School offers lessons, tours and ski rentals. There are also 32 kilometers of marked set track from Badger to the scenic overlook at Glacier Point. Virtually the entire Park above 5,500 feet is open to ski touring, snowshoeing and snow camping. Wilderness Permits are required for all overnight backcountry visits and specific rules apply. Most cross-country skiers use the marked trails at Badger Pass (7,200 feet), Crane Flat (6,200 feet), or Mariposa Grove (5,600 feet). These areas offer trails for all levels of ability. Maps and information on winter trails may be obtained at Visitor's Centers and Ranger Stations.

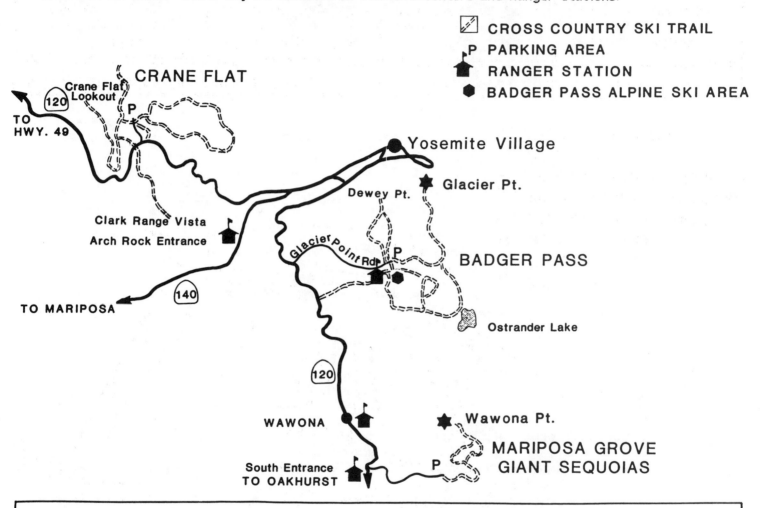

INFORMATION: Nordic Ski School, Yosemite National Park 95389, Ph: 209-372-1244

SKIING	RENTALS & LESSONS	RECREATION	ACCOMMODATIONS

Nordic:
    32 Kilometers of
    Set Track
    90 Plus Miles of
    Marked Trails and
    Over 350 Miles of
    Skiable Roads and
    Trails
 	
Season: Thanksgiving
    Through Mid-April
Snow Ph: 209-372-1338
	Ski School:
	Nordic Intro.,Rentals
	Included:2.5 hrs./$25
	Clinics – 2-1/2 hrs &
	5 1/2 Hrs.–$16.50–$30
	Nordic Downhill –
	4 Hrs. – $32
	2 Hrs. – $16
	Rental Included–$25
	Rentals: Half/Full Day
	Adult – $11.50/$14
	Child – $7.75/$9.50
		Downhill Skiing
		Ski Touring
		Ranger Snowshoe
		    Walks
		Snow Cat Tours
		Snow Camping
		Nearby:
		    Snow Play Areas
		    Ice Skating
		    Naturalist
		        Programs
		    Bus Tours
			Badger Pass:
			    Day Lodge
			    Cafeteria
			    Snack Bar
			    Outdoor Barbecue –
			        Weekends
			    Ski Shop
			    Child Care – 3 Yrs.
			        & Older
			    Shuttle from
			        Yosemite Valley
			    Special Events

ACCOMMODATIONS
Highway 108 — Sonora Pass Area

Winter camping in the Pinecrest area is limited to:

1. Self-contained vehicles in county parking lot.

2. Walk-in tent camping at Pinecrest Campground.

3. Pinecrest Chalet- 12 sites with electrical hookups,
   disposal station, pads to 75 feet, laundromat;
   fee $12.50.

Camping is permitted outside Pinecrest, but access is limited because Forest Service roads are closed during the winter months. An advanced permit is required for groups of 25 or more. For permits and further information contact:

Summit Ranger District
Star Rte. Box 1295
Sonora, CA 95370
Ph: 209-965-3434

For Lodging and other facilities contact:

The Tuolumne County Visitors Bureau
P.O. Box 4020
Sonora, CA 95370
Ph: 209-533-4420

YOSEMITE LODGING

Yosemite West Condominiums
P.O. Box 821
Yosemite, CA 95389
Ph: 209-372-4711
Housekeeping Condos
7 Miles from Badger Pass off Hwy 41
$59-$75/nite

Yosemite Valley
23 Miles from Badger Pass
Bus Service to Ski Area

Hotel/Motel	Double	*SkiPackage
Ahwahnee Hotel	$139.50	$141.20
Yosemite Lodge	$30-62.50	$47.50-86.75
Curry Village	$30-57	$47.50-64.75

*Ski Package (2 nite minimum)
Includes: Lodging, 2 Downhill Lessons
and All Day Lift Ticket, or 1 All Day
Nordic Lesson or Touring Class per
Person per Day.

Yosemite and Curry County Reservations:
      510 East Home
      Fresno 93727
      Ph: 209-252-4848

Campgrounds Open in Winter
Information: 209-372-4461

Hogden Meadow (Near Big Oak Flat off Hwy 120)	107 Tent/RV sites	$6/nite
Lower Pines (Yosemite Valley)	173 Tent/RV sites	$7/nite
Sunnyside Walk-In (Yosemite Valley)	38 Tent sites	$2/nite
Wawona (Hwy 41 @ Wawona)	100 Tent/RV sites	$6/nite

There are no RV hookups in Yosemite Campgrounds.

HIGHWAY 395 AREA

TO BRIDGEPORT
25

MONO LAKE

LEE VINING

120

5

158

Grant Lake

6

9

Silver Lake

June Lake

2.5

3.6

June Lake

1.5

June Mountain

Obsidian Dome

P

395

10

Legend:

- NORDIC SKI AREA
- ALPINE SKI AREA
- P   SNO PARK PERMIT SITE
- SNOWMOBILE & CROSS COUNTRY SKI TRAIL
- YEAR-ROUND CAMPGROUND
- RANGER STATION
- AIRPORT

Shady Rest

Mammoth Mtn.

Minaret R.

5

1

203

MAMMOTH LAKES

L. Mary Rd.

2,5

?

2.3

Info. Center

Sierra Meadows

LAKE CROWLEY

Twin Lakes

Tamarack Lodge

Horseshoe Lake

Lake Mary

12

3

Tom's Place

89

6

395

22

Rock Creek

P

Rock Creek Winter Lodge

Rock Creek Lake

3

BISHOP

JOHN

MUIR

WILDERNESS

168

9

9

Lake Sabrina

P

BISHOP CREEK LODGE

Bishop Creek

16

TO BIG PINE

South Lake

N

BISHOP CREEK AREA

Although the Bishop Creek area is no longer a part of the Sno-Park program, it offers many opportunities for cross-country skiing. The U.S. Forest Service maintains 3 kilometers of easy trails. Experienced ski mountaineers can continue into North Lake, Lake Sabrina and on to South Lake. There is parking at Bishop Park campground for those venturing into the Sabrina Basin. Wilderness Permits are required for those venturing into the John Muir Wilderness. Alpine Expiditions offers a guide service, tours, instructional workshops and survival courses.

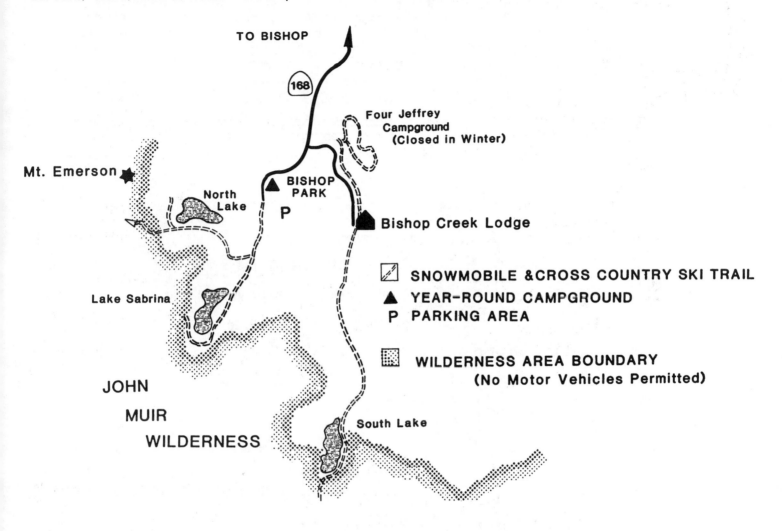

TO BISHOP

168

Four Jeffrey
Campground
(Closed in Winter)

Mt. Emerson

North
Lake

BISHOP
PARK

P

Bishop Creek Lodge

SNOWMOBILE & CROSS COUNTRY SKI TRAIL

YEAR-ROUND CAMPGROUND

P PARKING AREA

Lake Sabrina

WILDERNESS AREA BOUNDARY
(No Motor Vehicles Permitted)

JOHN

MUIR

WILDERNESS

South Lake

INFORMATION: White Mountain Ranger District, 798 N. Main St., Bishop 93514 Ph: 619-873-4207			
SKIING	**RENTALS & LESSONS**	**RECREATION**	**ACCOMMODATIONS**

Nordic:
USFS: Beginners
3 Km. Groomed Trails
Bishop Creek Lodge:
26 Km. Groomed Trails
Fee for Use
	Ski School at Bishop
	Creek Lodge
		Alpine Expeditions
		224 Sneden, P.O. 1571
		Bishop 93514
		Ph: 619-873-5617
		Ski Touring, Telemark,
		& Ski Mountaineering
		Guide Service
		Snowmobiling in
		    Designated Areas
		Snow Play Areas
		Snow Camping
			Bishop Creek Lodge
			P.O. Box 1628
			Bishop 93514
			Ph: 619-873-4484
			    Housekeeping Units
			    2 to 6 People

ROCK CREEK SNO-PARK SITE

This Site is located about 6 miles from Highway 395 at the end of the plowed section of Rock Creek Road. Sno-Park Permits are required. Snow play and cross-country skiing are the primary activities. For a remote backcountry experience, cross-country skiers can ride a snow cat or ski two miles into Rock Creek Winter Lodge at an elevation of 9,300 feet. Most guests take part in the ski packages which include lodging, meals and ski touring. There are 14 rustic cabins. Permits are available for those wishing to venture into the John Muir Wilderness Area. Also available are three backcountry ski huts which can be rented by individuals or groups. In this high country, avalanches are common so extreme caution is advised.

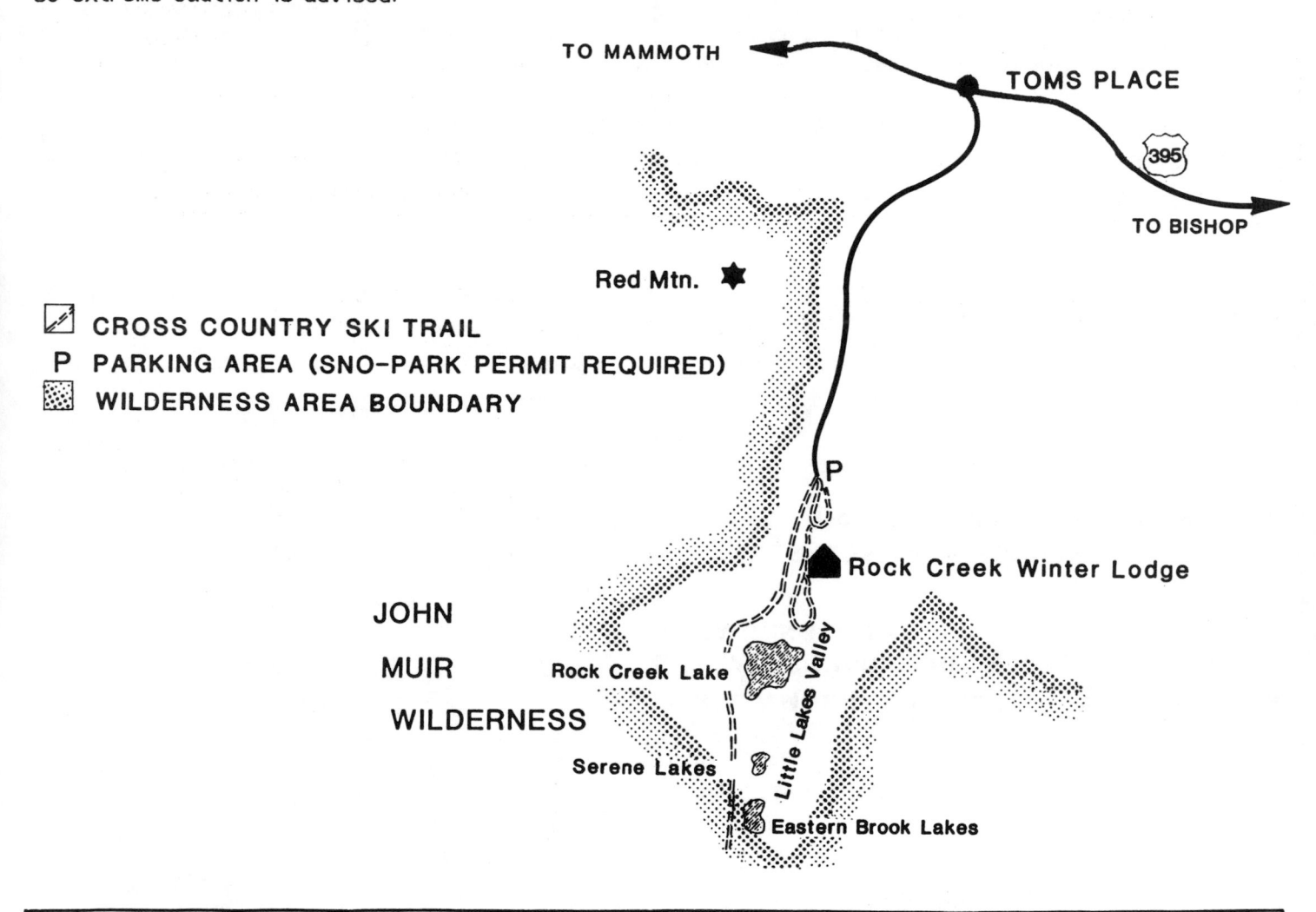

INFORMATION: Rock Creek Winter Lodge, Rt. 1, Box 5, Mammoth Lakes 93546, Ph: 619-935-4464

SKIING	RENTALS & LESSONS	RECREATION	ACCOMMODATIONS

Nordic:
  Beginner,
  Intermediate &
  Advanced
30 Km. Marked
Trails
25 Km. Set Track
	At Lodge:
	  Ski School - $20
	  Rentals - $10
	  Guided Tours
		Snow Play
		SNO-PARK PERMITS
		ONLY:
		Contact -
		California Sno-Park
		Permit Program
		P. O. Box 2390
		Sacramento 95811
		Ph: 916-322-8993
			Parking at Sno-Park
			Site - 30 Vehicles
			Sno-Park Permit Fees:
			  $2 - Day
			  $10 - Annual
			Must Have Permit in
			  Advance
			Lodge: Ski Packages
			  Backcountry Hut
			  System
			  Restaurant
			  Warming Hut

SHADY REST AREA — INYO NATIONAL FOREST

Located just before the Town of Mammoth Lakes, Shady Rest-Mammoth Knolls Trail System is an excellent area for cross-country skiers, particularly when heavy storms make the higher elevations inaccessible. The "Blue Diamonds Trails" wind through forests and into the Inyo Volcanic Craters. The scenery is beautiful along the way. Shady Rest Campground is open to tent campers in winter. R. V. Sites are available at the Mammoth Mountain R.V. Park across Highway 203. Mammoth Lakes is one of the most extensive winter recreation areas in California, offering snow activities of every kind. The Forest Service Visitor Center is open all winter, and maps and books are available.

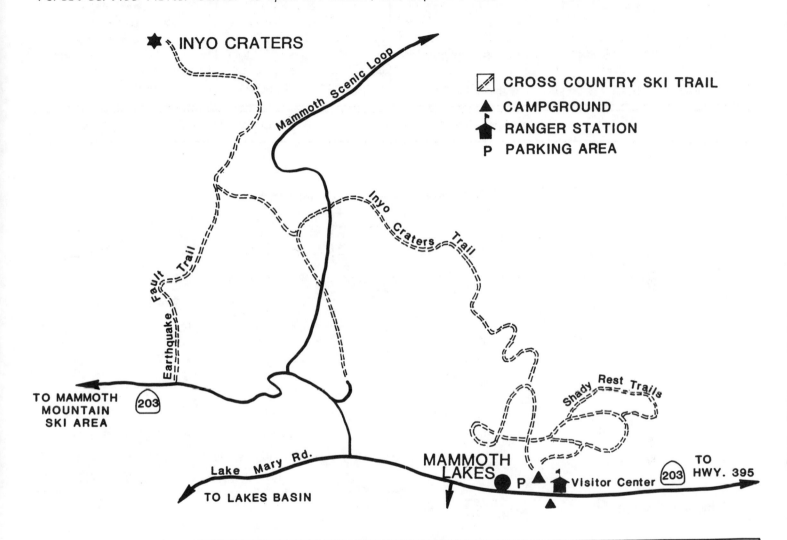

| INFORMATION: Mammoth Ranger District, P.O. Box 148, Mammoth Lakes 93546. Ph: 619-934-6611 |

SKIING	RENTALS & LESSONS	RECREATION	ACCOMMODATIONS

Nordic:
  Beginner,
  Intermediate &
  Advanced –
  16 Kilometers
  Marked Trails
	Not Available at Site	Nearby:
		  Downhill Skiing
		  Snow Play Areas
		  Snowmobiling
			Winter Tent Camping
			  at Shady Rest
			  Campground
			R. V. Sites at Mammoth
			  R.V. Park
			Visitor Center:
			  Open Monday –
			  Saturday
			  8:00 a.m. –
			  4:30 p.m.
			Full Facilities in
			  Mammoth Lakes

SIERRA MEADOWS SKI TOURING CENTER

This facility offers over 20 kilometers of cross-country trails for all levels of ability. Mammoth Meadows has one of the most consistently ideal snow conditions in the area, and the trails are well groomed by machine. Moonlight skiing is popular as well as the Sleigh Ride Dinners from the Touring Center. Hot spiced wine or cider can be enjoyed during the horse-drawn sleigh ride followed by a complete home cooked meal and entertainment. The warming hut has a cafe and a small accessory shop. This is a good spot to introduce the family to the fun of cross-country skiing in beautiful surroundings.

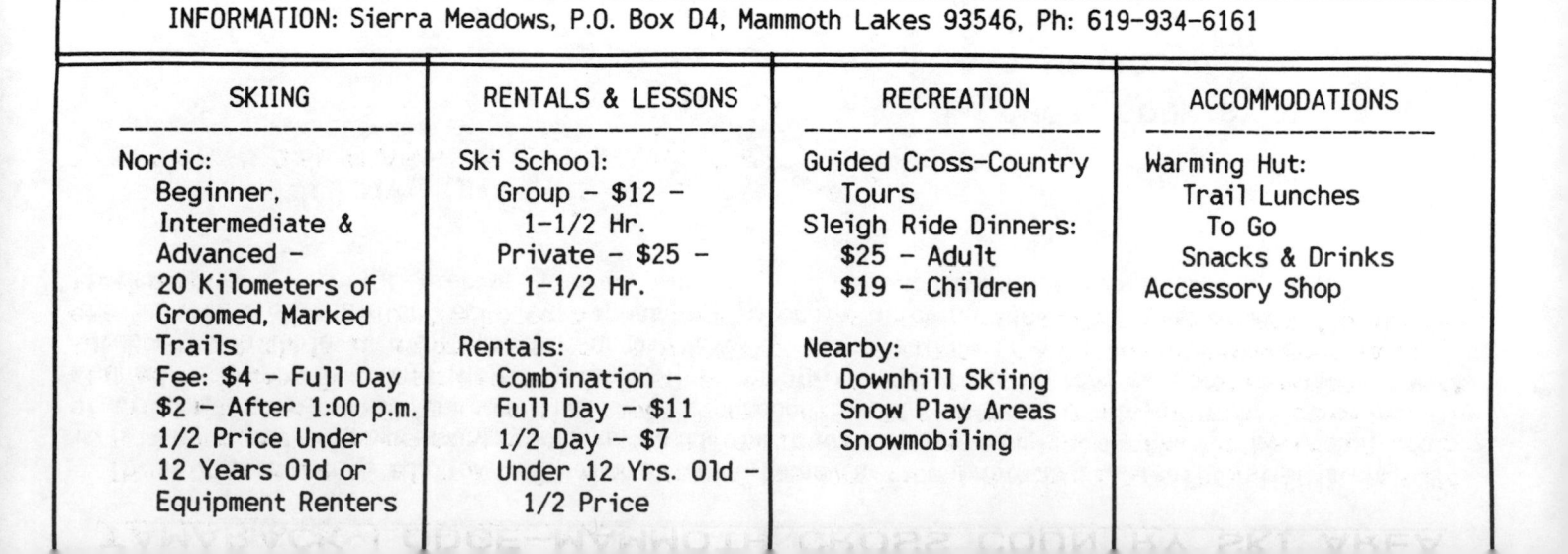

INFORMATION: Sierra Meadows, P.O. Box D4, Mammoth Lakes 93546, Ph: 619-934-6161

SKIING	RENTALS & LESSONS	RECREATION	ACCOMMODATIONS

Nordic:
  Beginner,
  Intermediate &
  Advanced –
  20 Kilometers of
  Groomed, Marked
  Trails
Fee: $4 – Full Day
$2 – After 1:00 p.m.
1/2 Price Under
12 Years Old or
Equipment Renters
	Ski School:
	  Group – $12 –
	  1-1/2 Hr.
	  Private – $25 –
	  1-1/2 Hr.
	
	Rentals:
	  Combination –
	  Full Day – $11
	  1/2 Day – $7
	  Under 12 Yrs. Old –
	  1/2 Price
		Guided Cross-Country
		  Tours
		Sleigh Ride Dinners:
		  $25 – Adult
		  $19 – Children
		
		Nearby:
		  Downhill Skiing
		  Snow Play Areas
		  Snowmobiling
			Warming Hut:
			  Trail Lunches
			  To Go
			  Snacks & Drinks
			Accessory Shop

This Lodge is centered in a 2,500 acre area of the magnificent Mammoth Lakes Basin. Built in 1924, it is a complete cross-country resort with well marked trails and set tracks into the beautiful lakes of this high country. Skiers can also depart from here on snow camping trips. The Ski School is staffed with certified instructors and offers a variety of lessons and clinics. Accommodations are at the Lodge, which includes breakfast, or in the surrounding cabins. The Lakefront Restaurant serves evening meals. Guests of the Lodge are treated to an "apres ski" cocktail hour and a complimentary trail pass.

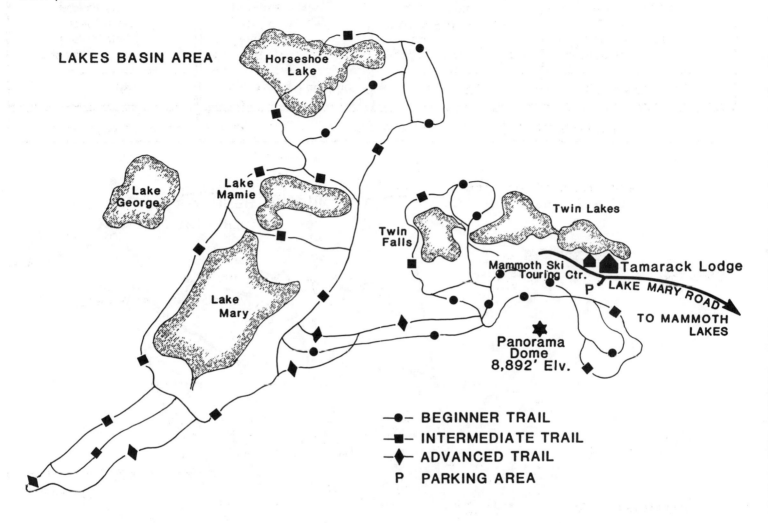

INFORMATION: Tamarack Lodge, P.O. Box 69, Mammoth Lakes 93546, Ph: 619-945-2442

SKIING	RENTALS & LESSONS	RECREATION	ACCOMMODATIONS

Nordic:
  Beginner,
  Intermediate,
  Advanced
  30 Km. of Marked
  Trails
  75 Km of Set Track
Fees:
  Adults: $3–$6
  Children: $2–$4
  Seniors: Free
	Ski School:
	  Beg./Intermed: $18
	  Adv./Telemark: $20
	  Includes Trail Fee
	  Lesson/Tour/Lunch:
	    $35
	Rentals – Combos:
	  Adults: $17
	  Children: $6–$12
	  Demos: $20
		Guided Day and
		  Moonlight Tours
		Snow Camping
		Nearby:
		  Downhill Skiing
		  Snowmobiling
			Lodge:
			Bed & Breakfast –
			  From $30 for 2
			Cabins –
			  From $40 for 2
			Restaurant
			Ski Shop

MAMMOTH MOUNTAIN

Mammoth Mountain is one of the largest ski areas in America. Spectacular Eastern Sierra scenery, abundant snow, and a complete modern facility compliment this ever popular Alpine resort. This vast mountain has 152 trails down a vertical of 3,100 feet.   The runs are enhanced by extensive grooming. The ski school and race department offer a complete line of lessons, programs and special events. There is a Children's Ski School and a Day Care Center. The three day lodges, one at mid-mountain, have food and service facilities, and Mammoth Mountain Inn has a variety of overnight accommodations along with a nice restaurant and cocktail lounge. Mammoth's skiing season is the longest in the Sierras stretching from November through June.

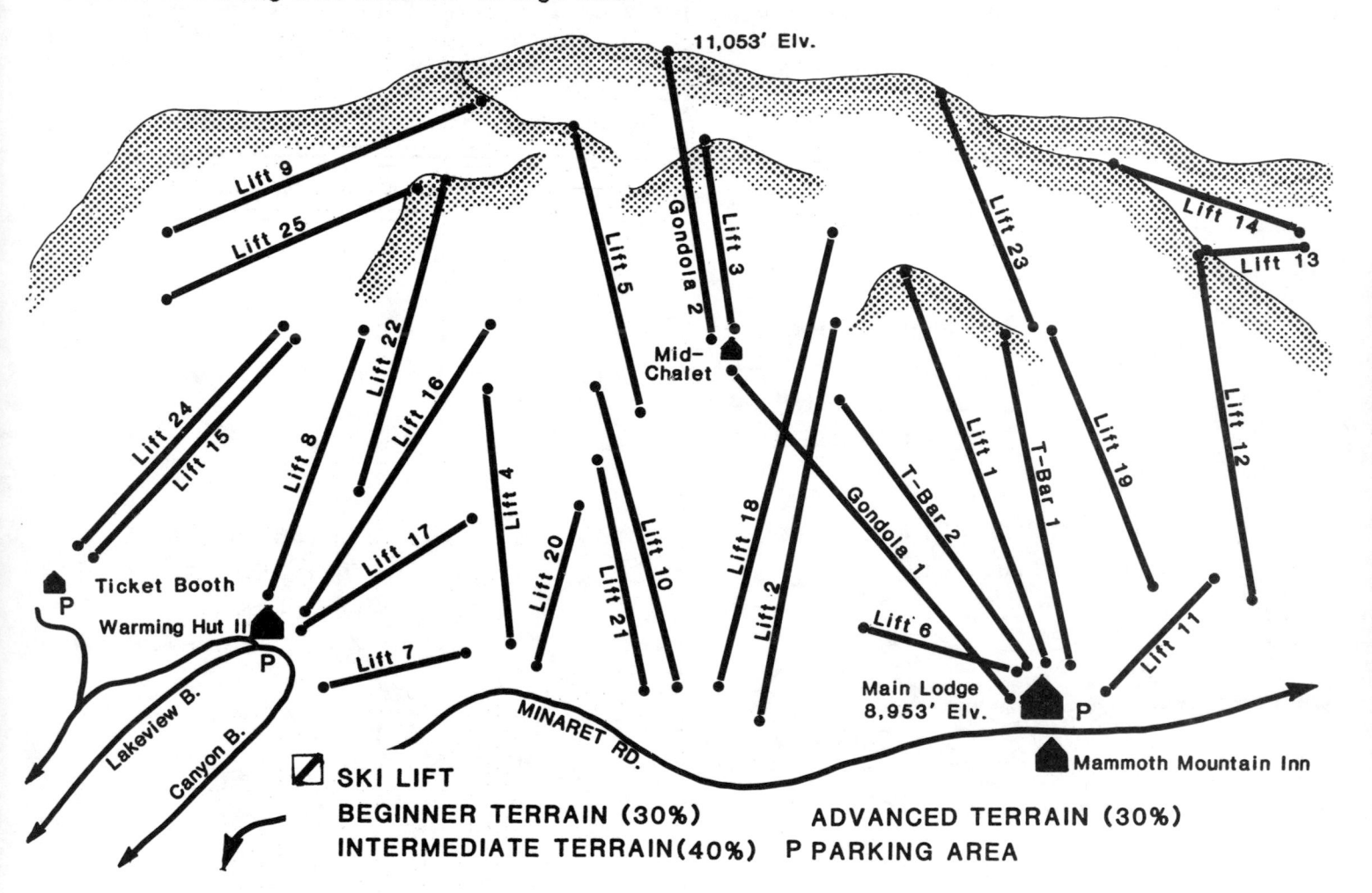

SKI LIFT
BEGINNER TERRAIN (30%)
INTERMEDIATE TERRAIN (40%)
ADVANCED TERRAIN (30%)
P PARKING AREA

INFORMATION: Mammoth Mountain Ski Area, P.O. Box 24, Mammoth Lakes, Ca. 93546 Ph: 619 934-2571

SKIING	RENTALS & LESSONS	RECREATION	ACCOMMODATIONS

Alpine:
  2 Gondolas
  25 Chairlifts
  2 Pomas
  2 T Bars
Fees:PM only/Full Day
  Adult:$17/$24
  Child:$9/$12
  After May 1st
  Adult:$17, Child:$9
Snow Ph: 619-934-6166
	Ski School
	  Group:
	  All Levels $22
	  Private $37/hr.
	  Pre-Ski School $14
	  Ages 4-6, Half Day
	  Race Clinic, Entry
	  Included $16
	Rentals:
	  Standard: $12
	  Cross-Country: $9
	  Demos Available
		Race Department
		  Auto. Pay Courses
		  NASTAR
		  Scheduled Races
		Nearby:
		  Cross-Country
		  Helicopter Skiing
		  Snow Camping
		  Snow Play
		  Snowmobiling
		  Sleigh Rides
		  Live Entertainment
			3 Day Lodges/Cafe.
			Restaurant & Bar
			Ski Shop & Repairs
			Day Care Center
			Mammoth Mt. Inn
			Hotel, Motel, Condos
			  $45-$165
			P.O. Box 353
			Mammoth Lakes, Ca.
			       93546
			Ph: 800-228-4947
			L.A.800-934-2581

JUNE LAKE CROSS COUNTRY AREA

Located just off Highway 395 are excellent cross-country trails. Maintained by the U.S. Forest Service, the June Lake Junction Trail is for intermediate skiers, with a small loop for beginners. The Obsidian Dome Area offers 12 kilometers of trails for all levels of ability. At 8,000 feet elevation there are spectacular views of recent volcanos and Jeffrey Pine forests. Weather permitting, the U.S. Forest Service grooms these trails periodically. Snowmobiles are prohibited.

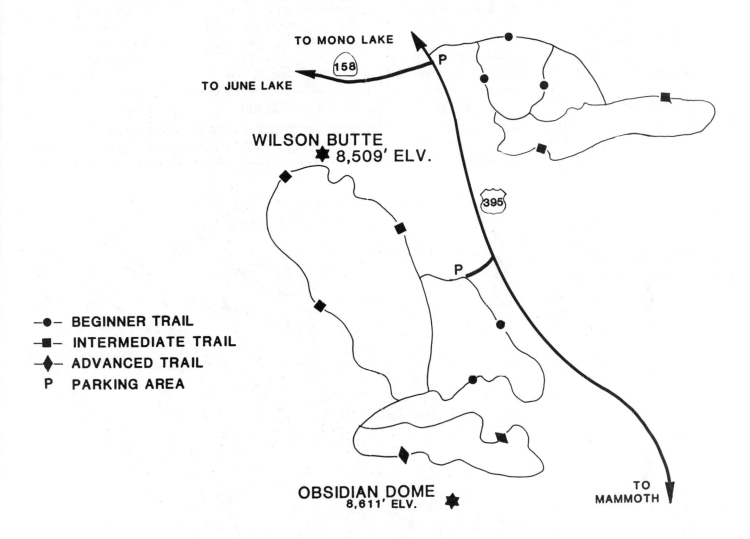

TO MONO LAKE

158

TO JUNE LAKE

P

WILSON BUTTE
8,509' ELV.

395

P

—●— BEGINNER TRAIL
—■— INTERMEDIATE TRAIL
—◆— ADVANCED TRAIL
P   PARKING AREA

OBSIDIAN DOME
8,611' ELV.

TO
MAMMOTH

INFORMATION: U.S. Forest Service, P.O. Box 10, Lee Vining 93541 Ph: 619-647-6525

SKIING	RENTALS & LESSONS	RECREATION	ACCOMMODATIONS

Nordic:
  Beginner, Intermed.
  & Advanced
  22 Kilometers of
  Marked Trails
	Not Available at Site	Nearby:
		  Downhill Skiing
		  Snow Play Areas
		  Snow Camping
			Numerous Facilities in Area (see following pages)

June Mountain, just down the road from Mammoth, offers uncrowded slopes, excellent intermediate runs in a relaxed atmosphere. Located in a beautiful alpine setting off the eastern slopes of the Southern Sierras, this downhill area has 23 miles of well groomed terrain. There are 25 runs down a 2,562 foot vertical. Snowmaking covers 40 acres. There are runs for every level of ability, from beginner to expert. In addition to group and private lessons, the Ski School offers a special multi-day learning package. The Children's Ski Center provides specialized instruction. The main lodge, Grand Chalet Schweizerhof, is at mid-mountain and Alpenhaus is located at the base.

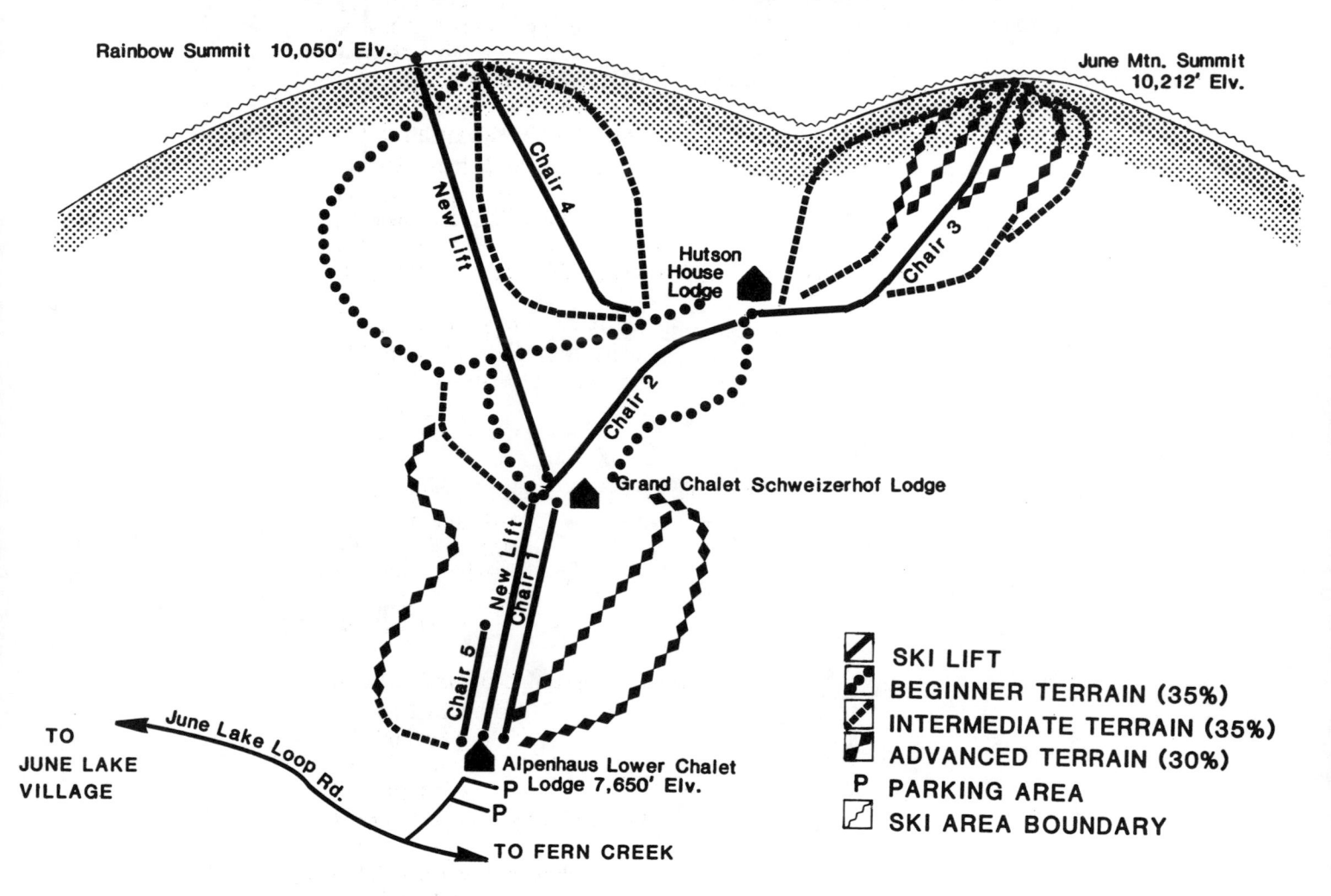

INFORMATION: June Mountain, P. O. Box 146, June Lake 93529, Ph: 619-648-7733

SKIING	RENTALS & LESSONS	RECREATION	ACCOMMODATIONS

Alpine:
    8 Chairlifts
    Fee
Season:
Thanksgiving
    through Easter
 	
Snow Ph: 619-648-7545
or 213-935-8866
	Ski School:
	Group – All Day
	    or Half Day
	Private Lessons
	Children's Ski Center
	    Ages 4 to 12 yrs.
	Snow Playground –
	    4 to 6 yrs.
	Rentals:
	Combination
		Nearby:
		    Cross Country
		    Skiing, Rentals
		    Snow Touring
		    Snow Play Areas
		    Snowmobiling
		    Helicopter Skiing
			Grand Schweizerhof:
			    Cafeteria & Bar
			    Ski Rentals
			    Ski Shop
			Alpenhaus:
			    Ticket Office
			    Apres Ski Bar
			Motels & Condos:
			Rainbow Ridge
			Reservation Service
			Ph: 619-648-7811

MAMMOTH LAKES ACCOMMODATIONS

Mammoth Lakes Resort Association
P.O. Box 123
Mammoth Lakes 93546
Ph: 800-367-6572
    619-934-2712
Vacation Information, Reservation Referrals,
Hotel, Lodge or Condominium.

Condo Connection
P.O. Box 789
Mammoth Lakes 93546
Ph: 800-468-6386
    619-934-3187
Condominium Reservations

Eastern Sierra Reservations
P.O. 1058
Mammoth Lakes 93546
Ph: 800-421-8240
    619-934-3000
Summit Condominiums (near lifts)

Resort Reservations
P.O. Box 8527
Mammoth Lakes 93546
Ph: 800-MAM-MOTH
    619-934-4541
Lodge and Condominium Reservations

Mammoth Properties
P.O. Box 408
Mammoth Lakes 93546
Ph: 800-227-SNOW
    619-934-4242

High Country Management and Reservations
P.O. Box 7338
Mammoth Lakes 93546
Ph: 800-321-3261
    619-934-7260
Condominium Reservations

Mammoth Realty and Reservation Bureau
P.O. Box 8
Mammoth Lakes 93546
Ph: 800-462-5571
    619-934-2528
Condominium Reservations and Sublet

MAMMOTH LAKES, continued...

Mammoth Sierra Reservations
P.O. Box 7054
Mammoth Lakes 93546
Ph: 800-325-8415
    619-934-8472
Condominium Reservations

Ski Time Reservations Inc.
P.O. Box 911
Mammoth Lakes 93546
Ph: 800-462-5584
    213-754-8463
    619-934-8144

JUNE LAKE AREA RESERVATIONS:

June Lake - June Mountain Reservation Service
P.O. Box 216
June Lake 93529
Ph: 800-648-2211
    619-648-7794
Vacation Planning, Accommodations

Rainbow Ridge Realty and Reservations
P.O. Drawer C
June Lake 93529
Ph: 800-462-5589
    619-648-7811

June Lake Chamber of Commerce
P.O. Box 2
June Lake 93529
Ph: 619-648-7584

RV PARKS and CAMPING:

MAMMOTH:

Mammoth Mountain RV Park
P.O. Box 288
Mammoth Lakes 93546
Ph: 619-934-3822
130 RV sites, Electricity & Water Hookups,
Hot Showers, Disposal Station, Cable TV, Spa

MAMMOTH LAKES, continued...

United States Forest Service
Crowley Lake and Shady Rest Campgrounds
Mammoth Lakes Visitors Center
P.O. Box 148
Mammoth Lakes 92546
Ph: 619-934-2505
Open to Snow Camping

Golden Pines Trailer Park
P.O. Box 253
June Lake 93529
Ph: 619-648-7743
8 Sites, Full Hookups, Heated Restrooms & Showers

SNOWMOBILE RENTALS:

Mammoth Lakes Snowmobile Rentals
P.O. Box 34
Mammoth Lakes 93546
Ph: 619-935-4263
Rentals and Wilderness Tours

DJ's Snowmobile Rentals
Rte. #1 Box 76
Mammoth Lakes 93546
Ph: 619-935-4480
Rentals, Guided and Special Tours (by reservation)

HIGHWAY 168 – SIERRA NATIONAL FOREST

KAISER WILDERNESS

LAKESHORE

P Eastwood

P Rancheria

.5

Road Closed – Winter Sports Only!

HUNTINGTON LAKE

2

Huntington
Lake Resort
(Open in Winter –
By Reservations Only)
Ph. 209-893-3226

Sierra Summit Ski Area

168

7

NORDIC SKI AREA

ALPINE SKI AREA

P   SNOW PARK PERMIT SITE

SNOWMOBILE & CROSS COUNTRY
SKI TRAIL

BIG CREEK

7

Tamarack Lodge
Sierra National Forest

TO FRESNO
50

6

168

SHAVER
LAKE

N

EASTWOOD SNO-PARK SITE

This parking area is an excellent starting point for both cross-country skiers and snowmobilers. Adjacent to the Kaiser Wilderness area (no motor vehicles permitted in Wilderness), advanced skiers and snowmobilers can enjoy the 5-mile climb rising 2,000 feet in elevation to Kaiser Pass where the views are spectacular. There is also an unplowed forest road with trails leading to the summit of Bear Butte.

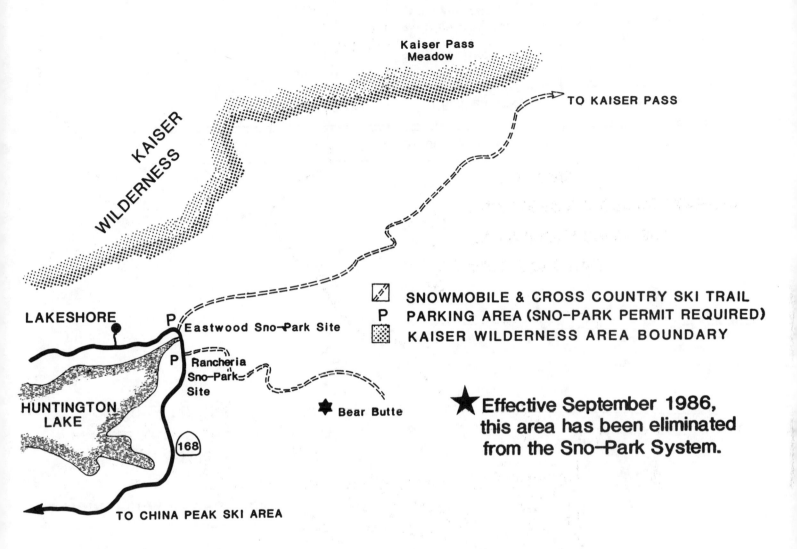

SNOWMOBILE & CROSS COUNTRY SKI TRAIL
P PARKING AREA (SNO-PARK PERMIT REQUIRED)
KAISER WILDERNESS AREA BOUNDARY

★ Effective September 1986, this area has been eliminated from the Sno-Park System.

INFORMATION: Pineridge Ranger District, P.O. Box 300, Shaver Lake 93664, Ph: 209-841-3311			
SKIING	**RENTALS & LESSONS**	**RECREATION**	**ACCOMMODATIONS**
Nordic: Intermediate & Advanced Trails	Not Available at Site	Snowmobiling SNO-PARK PERMITS ONLY: Contact – California Sno-Park Permit Program P. O. Box 2390 Sacramento 95811 Ph: 916-322-8993	Parking: 30 Vehicles Sno-Park Permit Fees: $2 – Day $10 – Annual Must Have Permit in Advance

RANCHERIA SNO—PARK SITE

At the entrance to Rancheria Campground off Highway 168, this small site can accommodate 10 vehicles with Sno-Park Permits. Snow camping is permitted, and there are looped trails for cross-country skiers which offer pretty views of Huntington Lake. Snowmobiles and all terrain vehicles are prohibited within the campground. Further trails go on to Black Butte. Be certain to have a Sno-Park Permit if you intend to use this parking site.

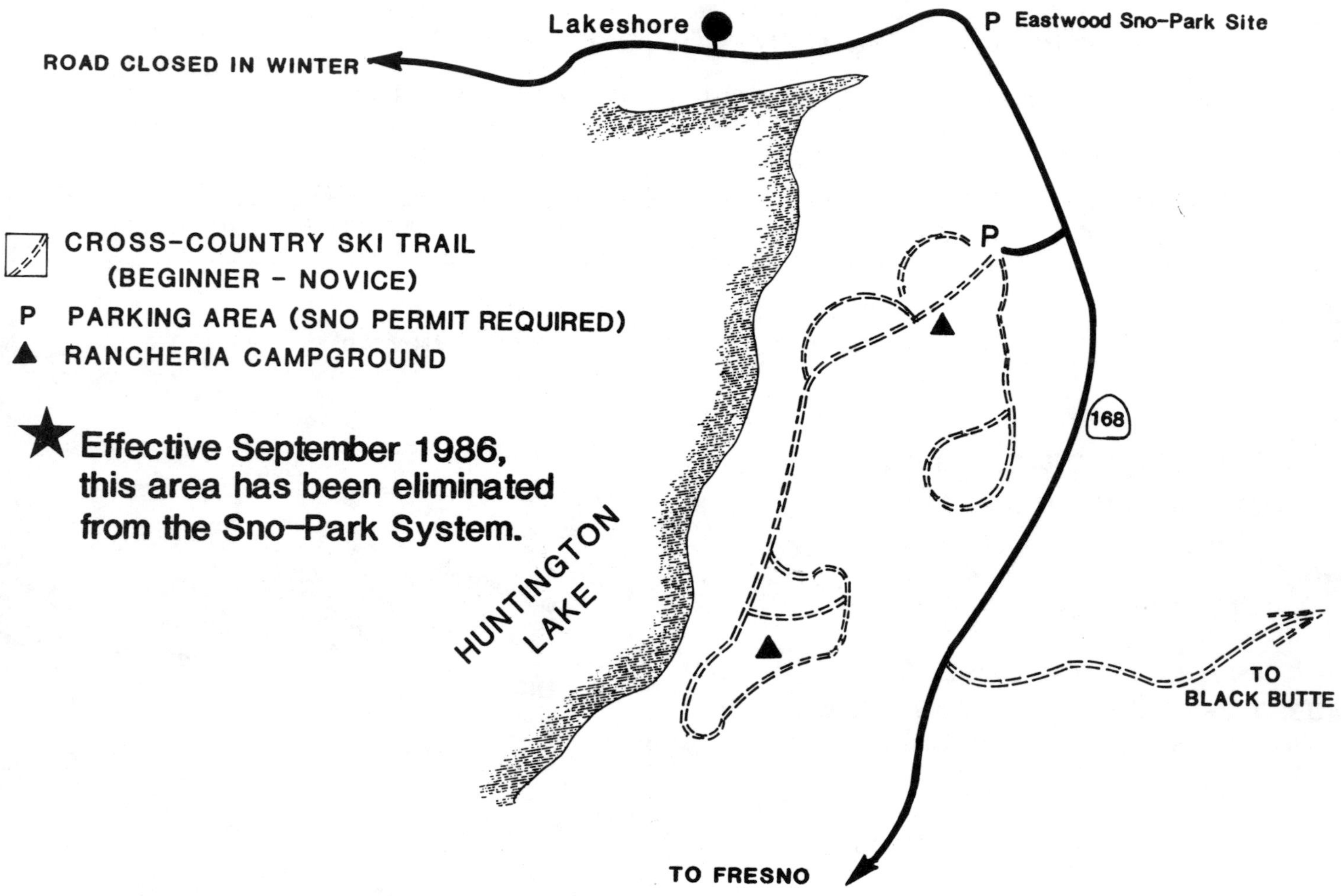

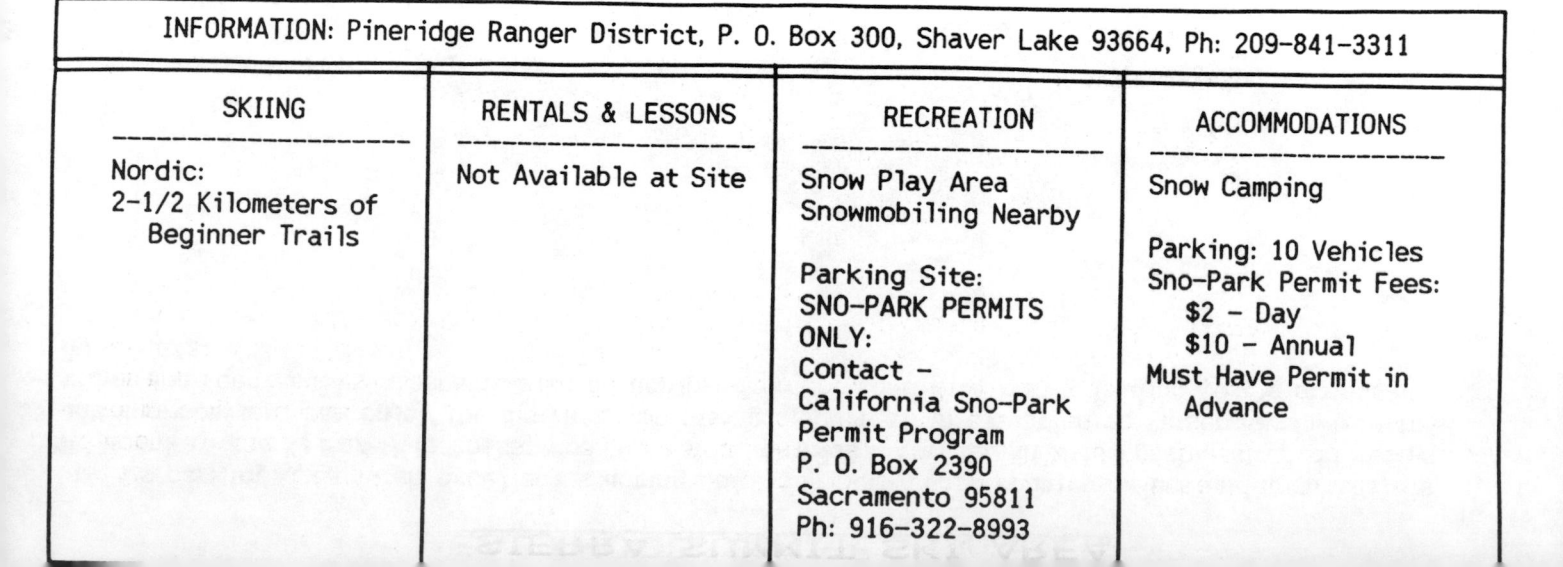

Lakeshore

ROAD CLOSED IN WINTER

P Eastwood Sno-Park Site

▨ **CROSS-COUNTRY SKI TRAIL**
   (BEGINNER - NOVICE)
P **PARKING AREA (SNO PERMIT REQUIRED)**
▲ **RANCHERIA CAMPGROUND**

★ **Effective September 1986, this area has been eliminated from the Sno-Park System.**

HUNTINGTON LAKE

P

(168)

TO BLACK BUTTE

TO FRESNO

INFORMATION: Pineridge Ranger District, P. O. Box 300, Shaver Lake 93664, Ph: 209-841-3311			
SKIING	**RENTALS & LESSONS**	**RECREATION**	**ACCOMMODATIONS**
Nordic: 2-1/2 Kilometers of Beginner Trails	Not Available at Site	Snow Play Area Snowmobiling Nearby Parking Site: SNO-PARK PERMITS ONLY: Contact – California Sno-Park Permit Program P. O. Box 2390 Sacramento 95811 Ph: 916-322-8993	Snow Camping Parking: 10 Vehicles Sno-Park Permit Fees: $2 – Day $10 – Annual Must Have Permit in Advance

SIERRA SUMMIT SKI AREA

Sierra Summit Ski Area is 67 miles north-east of Fresno in the Huntington Lake area of the Sierra National Forest. Formerly called the China Peak Ski Area, this facility is continually being upgraded. Snowmaking equipment will be added for this season. There are 230 acres of varied skiable terrain. These well-groomed slopes accommodate all levels of ability. The vertical off the mountain is 1,600 feet. The Nordic Center offers rentals (tour and telemark equipment), lessons and tours. There is a mile and a half set track, and the surrounding countryside offers nordic opportunities. This is a complete destination resort offering a full range of services and accommodations.

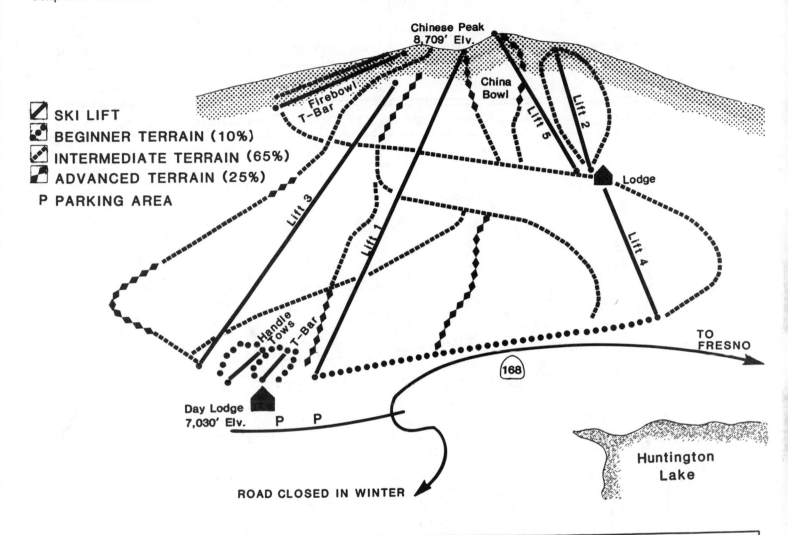

SKIING	RENTALS & LESSONS	RECREATION	ACCOMMODATIONS

Alpine:
  5 Chairlifts
  2 T Bars
  1 Handle Tow
Fees: Adults–$15–$21
Children – $9 – $14
Season: Thanksgiving
  to Mid–April
Nordic: 1-1/2 Mile
  Set Track
Snow Ph: 209-893-3311
or 209-233-3330
	Ski School:
	  Ph: 209-893-6680
	Alpine: Group/Pvt.
	  $15-$25/$30/hr.
	Nordic:
	  Group – $15
	  Afternoon Tour-$10
	Rentals: Alpine –
	  Adult – $12.50
	  Child – $9
	  Nordic – Tour-$10
	  Telemark – $15
		Nearby:
		  Nordic Trails
		  Ski Touring
		  Snow Play Areas
		  Snowmobiling
		  Snow Camping
		R. V. Camping with
		  Electric & T.V.
		  Hookups:
		Reservations –
		  Ph: 209-893-3305
			2 Bars & Restaurants
			Snack Bar & 2 BBQ's
			Sundecks
			Sport Shop
			Race Clinics
			Child Care (6 & Under)
			Special Packages
			Lodging:
			  Ph: 209-893-3305
			Reserve Lifts by
			Ticketron or Teletron:
			Ph: 800-447-7477

INFORMATION: Sierra Summit Ski Area, P. O. Box 236, Lakeshore 93634, Ph: 209-893-3316

Several marked nordic trails can be found in the Pineridge Ranger District of the Sierra National Forest ranging from 7,000 to 7,500 feet in elevation. In addition, any snow-covered forest service road can be used by cross-country skiers. Snowmobiles are restricted in some areas, but there are some excellent marked routes which are posted. The Pineridge Ranger District has a Nordic Ski Patrol which can provide information and guidelines for all types of snow activities.

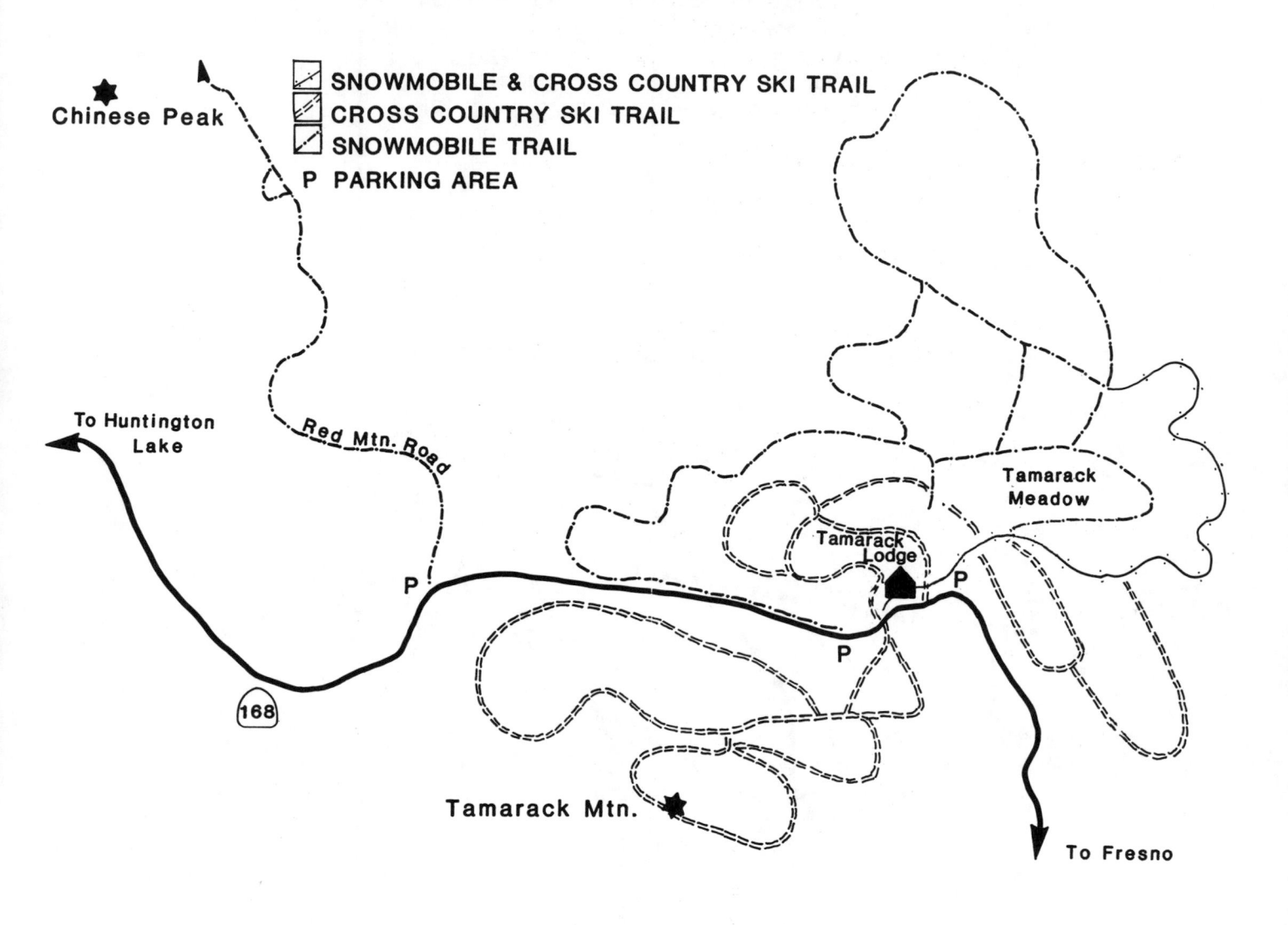

★ Chinese Peak

☑ SNOWMOBILE & CROSS COUNTRY SKI TRAIL
☑ CROSS COUNTRY SKI TRAIL
☑ SNOWMOBILE TRAIL
P PARKING AREA

To Huntington Lake

Red Mtn. Road

168

Tamarack Mtn. ★

Tamarack Meadow

Tamarack Lodge

To Fresno

INFORMATION: Pineridge Ranger Dist., P. O. Box 300, Shaver Lake 93664, Ph: 209-841-3311

SKIING	RENTALS & LESSONS	RECREATION	ACCOMMODATIONS

Nordic:
  Beginner Trails up
  to 5-1/2 miles long
	Not Available at Site	Snow Play
		Snowmobiling
			Tamarack Lodge
			P. O. Box 175
			Lakeshore 93634
			Ph: 209-893-3244
			  1 Bedroom Studio
			  Units

SEQUOIA, KINGS CANYON & HWY. 190 AREA

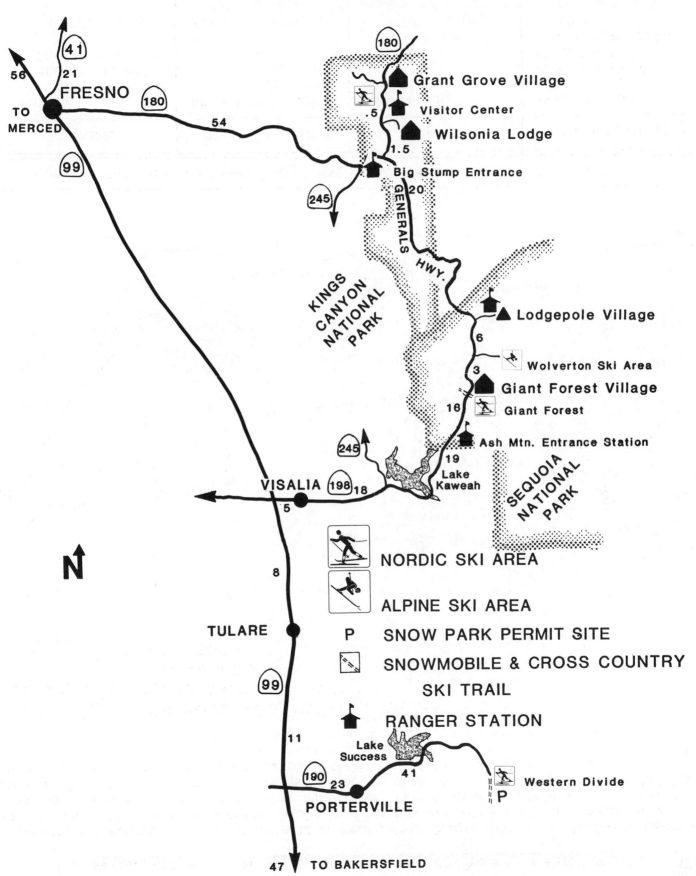

NORDIC SKI AREA

ALPINE SKI AREA

P SNOW PARK PERMIT SITE

SNOWMOBILE & CROSS COUNTRY
SKI TRAIL

RANGER STATION

Grant Grove of the Kings Canyon National Park provides another opportunity to ski among the giant sequoia trees. There are five well-marked trails within the Park ranging in difficulty from easy to moderately advanced. There are two ski touring centers in the Village. Sequoia Ski Touring has ski rentals, nordic lessons and guided tours throughout this area. Wilsonia Ski Touring provides lessons and guided tours within the Park and surrounding backcountry. Wilsonia features guided overnight hut tours along a 4-mile novice trail to the hut at Big Meadows. A new hut has just been opened, Park Ridge. This will be the first in a series of huts connecting Grant Grove to Big Meadows. Ski and snowshoe rentals are offered at the Wilsonia Lodge and Sequoia Ski Touring.

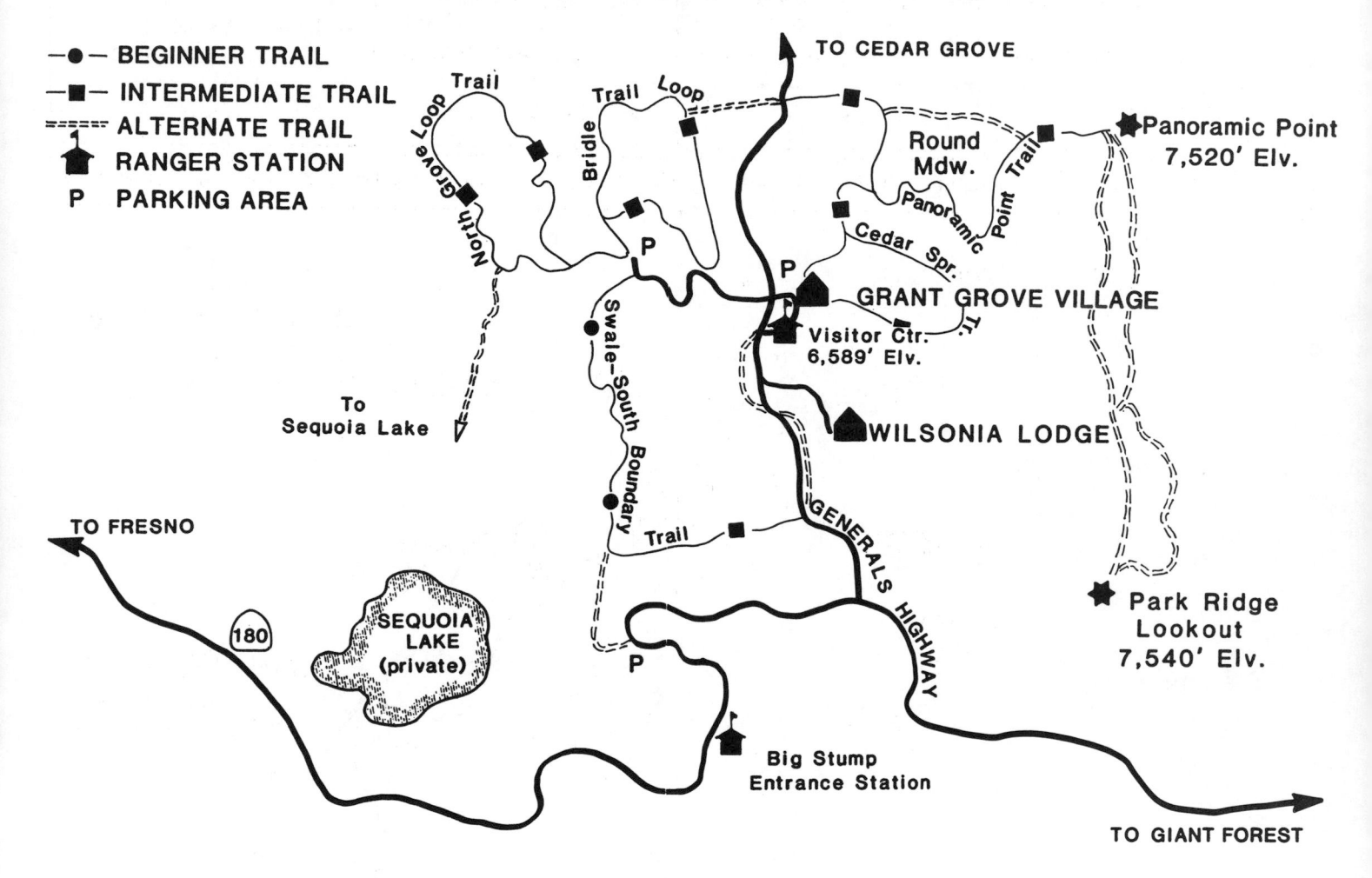

SKIING	RENTALS & LESSONS	RECREATION	ACCOMMODATIONS

Nordic:
   32 Miles of Marked
   Trails
   Ski Touring
 	
Season: November to
May
	Wilsonia Ski Touring:
	  Ph: 209-335-2404
	Lessons & Day Tours –
	  $8 – $16
	Guided Hut Tours –
	Meals Furnished –
	  $75 – $110
	Wilsonia Lodge: Ski &
	  Snowshoe Rentals
	Sequoia Ski Touring
	and Montecito-Sequoia
	Lodge
		Snow Shoe Walks
		Snow Play
		
		Nearby:
		  Snowmobiling
		  Downhill Skiing
			Wilsonia Lodge for
			Reservations:
			Ph: 209-335-2310
			Kings Cyn. Nat'l Park
			Grant Grove Lodge
			P. O. Box 789
			Three Rivers 93271
			Ph: 209-561-3314
			Market & Coffee Shop
			Service Station
			Closed Tues & Weds
			Ski Touring Center

INFORMATION: Grant Grove, Kings Canyon National Park 93633, Ph: 209-335-2315

SEQUOIA NATIONAL FOREST — BIG MEADOWS AREA

The Big Meadows Area along the Generals Highway, Highway 180, between Grant Grove and Giant Forest is in the Sequoia National Forest. The Forest Service maintains marked nordic trails at Quail Flat and Big Meadows, and the Buck Rock Snowmobile Trail offers a 15 mile loop and a 26 mile loop. Snow play is popular at Quail Flat. Sequoia Ski Tours, Wilsonia Ski Touring and Montecito-Sequoia Lodge provide guided cross-country tours into this scenic backcountry area. The Montecito-Sequoia Lodge is a complete nordic resort offering home-cooked meals with lodging, ski lessons, rentals, tours and an ice skating lake. Parking can be a problem, but there are cleared areas along Generals Highway at Quail Flat, Big Meadows Road and Woodward Creek.

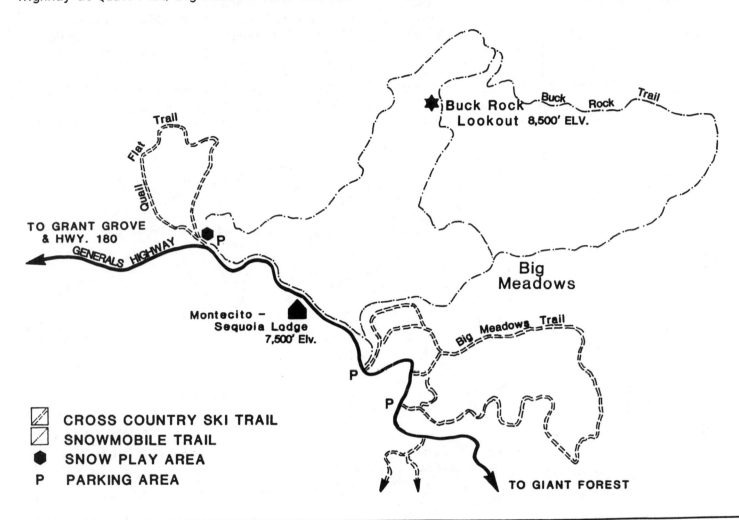

CROSS COUNTRY SKI TRAIL
SNOWMOBILE TRAIL
SNOW PLAY AREA
P   PARKING AREA

INFORMATION: Hume Lake Ranger Dist., 35860 E. Kings Canyon Rd., Dunlap 93621, Ph: 209-338-2251

SKIING	RENTALS & LESSONS	RECREATION	ACCOMMODATIONS

Nordic:
  50 Miles of Marked
  Trails
  Ski Touring
 	
Snow Ph: 209-336-2881
	Montecito-Sequoia
	Lodge:
	  Lessons: $8 – $14
	  Rental: Nordic
	  Combination for
	  2 Days – $15
	  Snowshoes & Poles
	    $5
	  Ice Skates/Fee-$5
	
	See Page for Wilsonia
	& Sequoia Ski Touring
		Snow Shoeing
		Snow Play
		Snowmobile & ATV
		  Trails
		Ice Skating
		Ski Football
		
		Nearby:
		  Alpine Skiing
		  Snow Camping
			Montecito-Sequoia
			Lodge
			1485 Redwood Dr.
			Los Altos 94002
			Ph: 209-565-3388
			  Lodging & Meals
			  Cocktail Lounge
			  Recreation Rooms
			  Special Packages
			Other Facilities at
			Giant Forest Village
			or Grants Grove

GIANT FOREST — LODGEPOLE

The Giant Forest and Lodgepole/Wolverton sections of the Sequoia National Park are prime ski touring areas. Although these areas are popular with cross-country skiers and snowshoers, the winter majesty of the Giant Sequoias seems to create an aura of solitude. There are 35 miles of marked trails for every level of ability. The Pear Lake Ski Hut is available for overnight use — reservations are required. Wilderness Permits are needed for all overnight tours, and there is no snow camping within Giant Forest. Sequoia Ski Touring offers rentals, lessons and tours. The Wolverton Ski Area is a small downhill facility for alpine skiers and those nordic skiers who wish to develop their telemark technique. There are lodging and facilities in Giant Forest Village, and the Lodgepole campground is open.

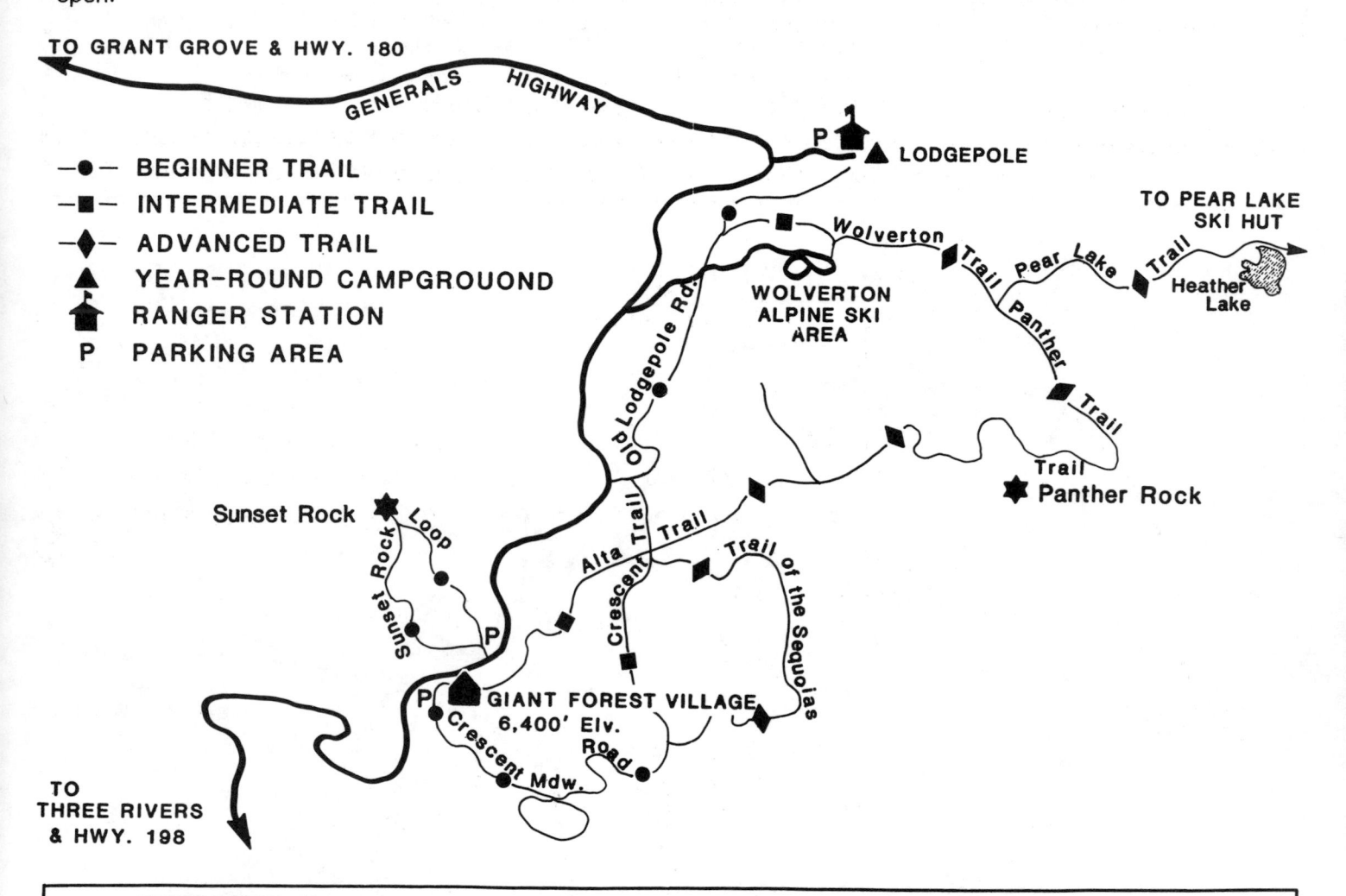

SKIING	RENTALS & LESSONS	RECREATION	ACCOMMODATIONS

Nordic:
    35 Miles of Marked
    Trails
 	
Season: Late November
to April
	Sequoia Ski Touring:
	Nordic School –
	Groups:
	2 Hr. Lesson – $12
	Sequoia Tours–$9–$18
	Private: $22 Hr.
	    Rentals:
	Nordic Combinations –
	    Adult – $11
	    Children – $8
		Downhill, Lessons &
		    Rentals
		Ranger Led Snowshoe
		    Walks
		Ski Touring
		Snow Camping (Outside
		    Giant Forest)
		Moonlight Tours
		Pear Lake Ski Hut:
		    Chief Ranger
		    Sequoia Nat. Park
		    Three Rivers 93271
			Giant Forest Village:
			    Cafeteria
			    Cocktail Lounge
			    Gift Shop & Market
			    Post Office &
			Lodgepole Campground
			    No Fee
			Motel, Cabins:
			    $34 – $65
			P. O. Box 789
			Three Rivers 93271
			Ph: 209–561–3314

INFORMATION: Sequoia Ski Touring, Sequoia National Park 93262, Ph: 209-565-3461

WOLVERTON SKI AREA

Wolverton Ski Area is in the scenic Sequoia National Park of the southwestern Sierras. This small downhill resort offers two rope tows and a platter lift. There are six groomed runs off a vertical of 480 feet. Beginner and intermediate skiers have all the terrain as there are no advanced runs. Cross country skiers have made this a popular area for developing their downhill (telemark) techniques. This is a family oriented facility providing a snack bar, accessories, repairs, a ski school and rentals. There are complete accommodations nearby. An abundance of nordic trails and snow play opportunities are found in this beautiful area.

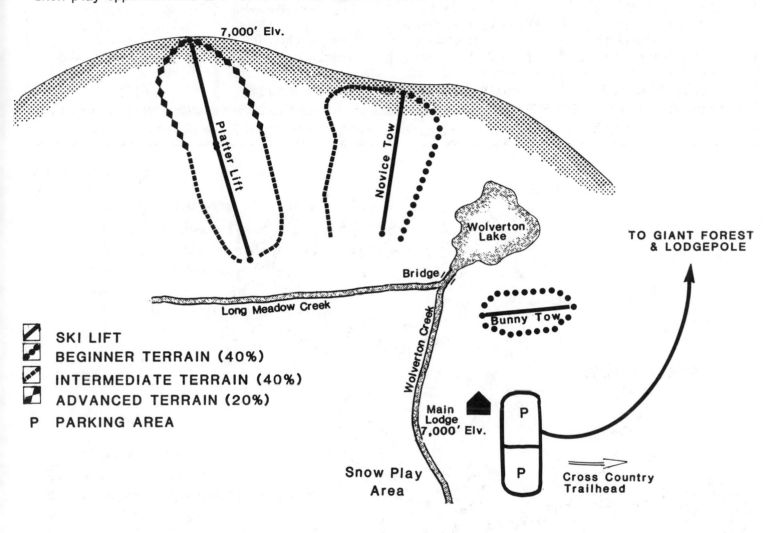

- SKI LIFT
- BEGINNER TERRAIN (40%)
- INTERMEDIATE TERRAIN (40%)
- ADVANCED TERRAIN (20%)
- P PARKING AREA

INFORMATION: Wolverton Ski Area, Sequoia National Park 93262, Ph: 209-561-3314

SKIING	RENTALS & LESSONS	RECREATION	ACCOMMODATIONS

Alpine:
    2 Rope Tows
    1 Platter
Fee: Adults–$10–$14
Children–$6–$9
 	
Season: Late November to Early April
Open Saturday & Sunday & Holiday Periods
	Ski School:
	    Group – $9/2hrs.
	    Private – $22/hr.
	
	Rental Package:
	    Adults–$13.50
	    Children–$9.75
		Cross Country Skiing
		Ski Touring
		Snow Play
		Snow Camping
			Snack Bar
			Ski Shop & Repairs
			Sun Deck
			Campgrounds: No Hookups, No Fee in Winter
			
			Full Facilities Nearby
			
			For Cabin Reservations:
			Call Above Number

Located 41 miles east of Porterville, these two locations for Snow Play are part of the California Sno-Park Permit System. 15 vehicles are allowed at each site for day use parking only. The Quaking Aspen Campground, which is closed in winter, is adjacent to a meadow ideal for easy cross-country skiing and snow play. There is also a small hill for tobogganing. Areas are exclusively designated for snowmobiles and cross-country skiing. Facilities are limited and the road is closed beyond this area in winter. Allow extra time for traveling this section of Highway 190, and be certain to have a Sno-Park Permit.

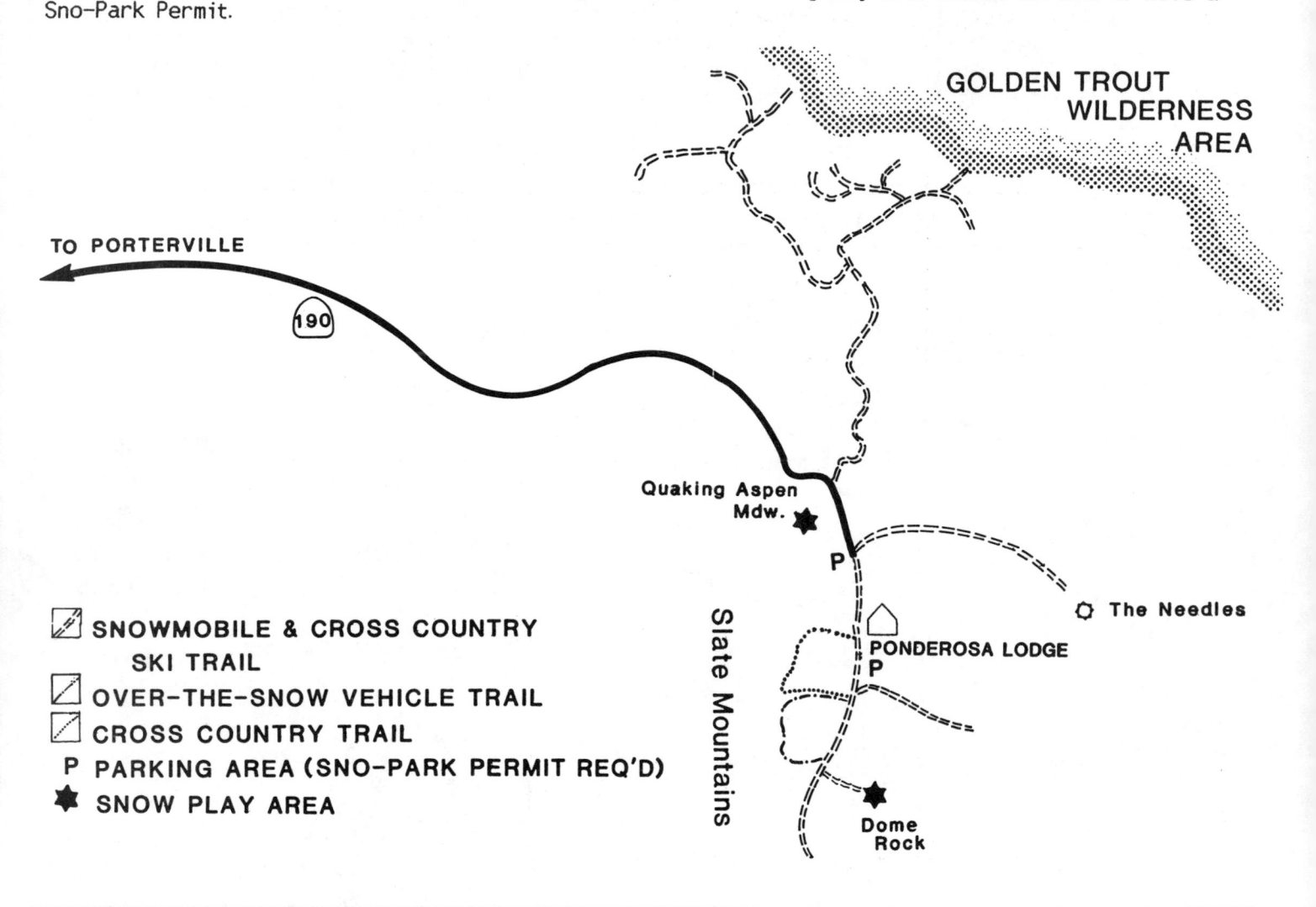

GOLDEN TROUT WILDERNESS AREA

TO PORTERVILLE

190

Quaking Aspen Mdw.

P

The Needles

Slate Mountains

PONDEROSA LODGE
P

Dome Rock

SNOWMOBILE & CROSS COUNTRY SKI TRAIL

OVER-THE-SNOW VEHICLE TRAIL

CROSS COUNTRY TRAIL

P PARKING AREA (SNO-PARK PERMIT REQ'D)

SNOW PLAY AREA

INFORMATION: Tule River R. D., USFS, 32588 Highway 190, Porterville 93257, Ph: 209-539-2607

SKIING	RENTALS & LESSONS	RECREATION	ACCOMMODATIONS

Nordic:
  Beginner and
  Intermediate
  Trails & Meadows
	Nordic Ski Rentals &
	  Instructions:
	Ponderosa Lodge,
	Star Route 2
	Springville 93265
	Ph: 209-542-2579
	
	Snowmobile Rentals &
	  Guided Tours:
	High Sierra
	Snowmobiles
	Ph: 209-542-2893
		Snow Play Areas
		Snowmobiles:
		  Designated Areas
		Tobogganing
		SNO-PARK PERMITS
		ONLY:
		Contact –
		California Sno-Park
		Permit Program
		P. O. Box 2390
		Sacramento 95811
		Ph: 916-322-8593
			Ponderosa Lodge:
			Overnight
			Accommodations –
			  Ph: 209-542-2579
			
			Parking: 15 Vehicles
			
			Sno-Park Permit Fees:
			  $2 – Day
			  $10 – Annual
			Must Have Permit in
			Advance

The Greenhorn Mountain Area, at 7,000 feet in the Sequoia National Forest, offers a variety of snow sports. Located 60 miles northeast of Bakersfield, Shirley Meadows Ski Resort has a small alpine area with beginner (10%), intermediate (70%) and advanced (20%) runs. There is one lift and two rope tows. The vertical is 400 feet. There is a Ski School, rentals and a warming hut. Although there are no designated snow play areas, there are opportunities outside the ski area wherever it is safe to park. Nordic trails are located at Windy Gap and the Shirley Loop. The unplowed roads north of Greenhorn Summit are popular with snowmobile and ATV enthusiasts. Facilities are limited in this area and parking is a problem as there are no plowed parking areas outside the Ski Resort.

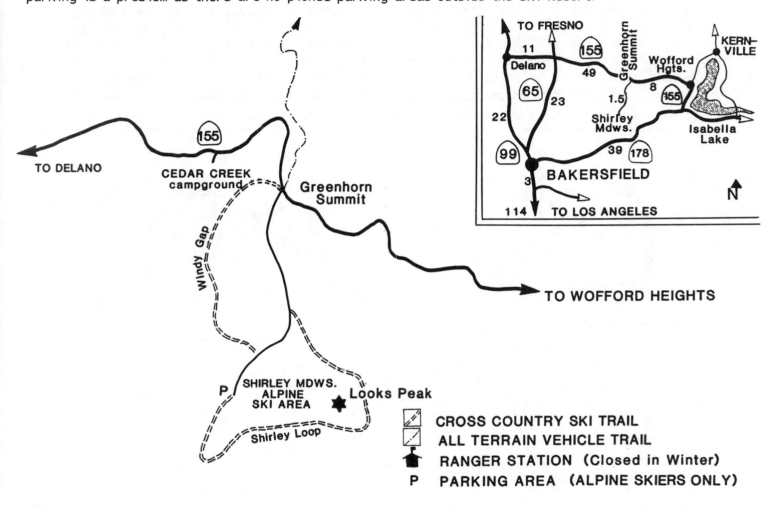

CROSS COUNTRY SKI TRAIL
ALL TERRAIN VEHICLE TRAIL
RANGER STATION (Closed in Winter)
P   PARKING AREA (ALPINE SKIERS ONLY)

INFORMATION: Greenhorn Ranger Dist., 800 Truxtun Ave., Bakersfield 93301, Ph: 805-861-4212

SKIING	RENTALS & LESSONS	RECREATION	ACCOMMODATIONS
Alpine – Shirley Meadows: – 1 Chairlift 2 Rope Tows Fee: Adult – $15 Child – $10 Weekends & Holidays Only – Fri. & Sat. Night Skiing Season: Dec.–April 24 Hr. Recording: 805-861-4214	Shirley Meadows Alpine Ski School: Group – $15 Private – $18 Hr. Rentals: Combinations – $12 Nordic Trails: Windy Gap – 3 Mi. Shirley Loop –5 Mi.	ATV & Snowmobile Trails Snow Play (Outside Downhill Area) Ski Touring Snow Camping No Snow Patrol	Shirley Meadows Ski Resort P. O. Box Q Wofford Heights 92340 Ph: 805-861-4212 Snack Bar Warming Hut Food & Gas at Glennville & Wofford Heights, Isabella and Kernville

MOUNT PINOS

The Mount Pinos area of the Los Padres National Forest is popular with Southern California's ever-growing group of nordic ski enthusiasts. Located 20 miles west of the Gorman Exit of I-5 between Los Angeles and Bakersfield, this winter sports area provides 14 miles of set track and 21 miles of marked wilderness trails. These trails range from easy to advanced. For those venturing overnight into the backcountry, it is necessary to check in with the Ranger Station. The marked trails are patrolled on weekends. Facilities are limited at the ski area, but Frazier Ski and Pack offers rentals, lessons and tours. This is a day use area under the jurisdiction of the Forest Service.

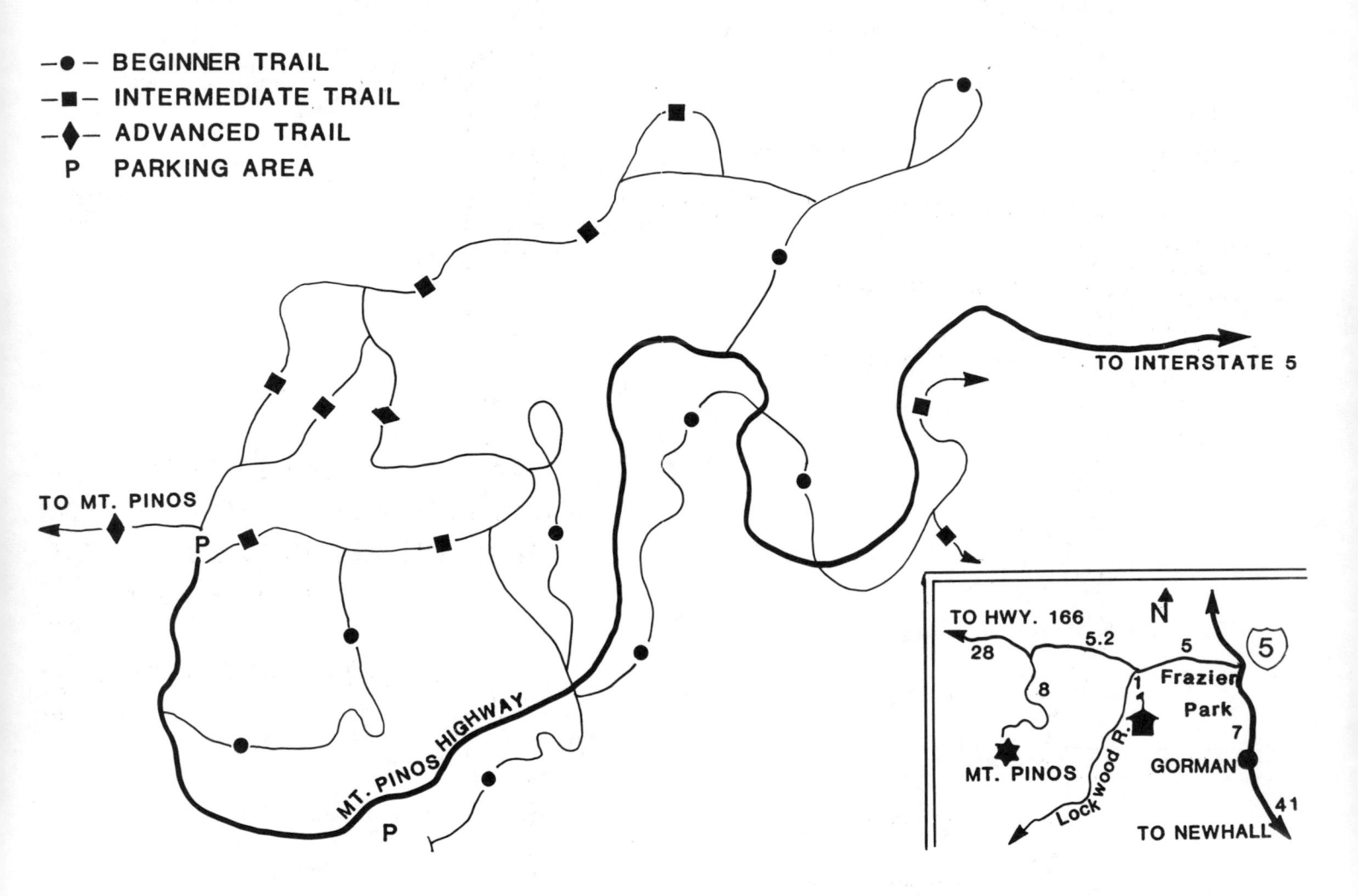

—●— BEGINNER TRAIL
—■— INTERMEDIATE TRAIL
—♦— ADVANCED TRAIL
P   PARKING AREA

INFORMATION: Mt. Pinos Ranger District, Star Rte. 400, Frazier Park 93225, Ph: 805-245-3731

SKIING	RENTALS & LESSONS	RECREATION	ACCOMMODATIONS
Cross-Country 14 Miles of Groomed Set Track 21 Miles of Marked Trails Season: December Through March Snow Ph: 805-245-3050	Frazier Ski & Pack Frazier Park Ph: 805-245-3438 Cross Country, Lessons, Tours, Ski & Snowshoe Rentals Mt. Pinos Winter Spts. Lake of the Woods Ph: 805-245-3760 Toboggans, Scooters, Sleds, Saucers, Snowshoe Rentals	Snow Play Ski Touring Snowshoeing Snow Camping	Mel Potrero Park: Westside Recreation and Park District P. O. Box 1406 Taft 93268 Ph: 805-763-4246 Camping: Fee - $8 Lodge: Fee - $2.50 Closed Wed. & Thurs. Other Facilities in Gorman & Frazier Park

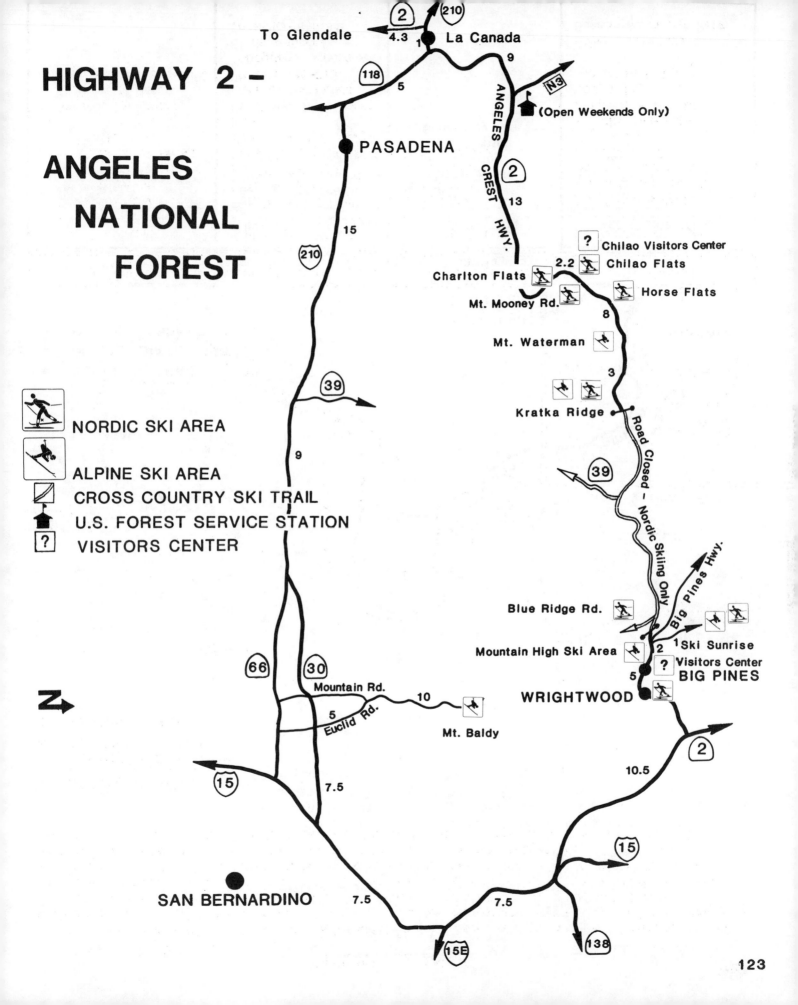

HIGHWAY 2 —

ANGELES

NATIONAL

FOREST

To Glendale

La Canada

(2) (210)

4.3 1

9

(118)

5

N3

(Open Weekends Only)

PASADENA

ANGELES CREST HWY.

(2)

13

15

(210)

? Chilao Visitors Center

2.2 Chilao Flats

Charlton Flats

Horse Flats

Mt. Mooney Rd.

8

Mt. Waterman

3

(39)

Kratka Ridge

NORDIC SKI AREA

ALPINE SKI AREA

CROSS COUNTRY SKI TRAIL

U.S. FOREST SERVICE STATION

? VISITORS CENTER

9

Road Closed — Nordic Skiing Only

(39)

Big Pines Hwy.

Blue Ridge Rd.

2

1 Ski Sunrise

Mountain High Ski Area

2 ? Visitors Center

5 BIG PINES

N

(66) (30)

Mountain Rd.

10

Euclid Rd.

5

WRIGHTWOOD

Mt. Baldy

(2)

7.5

10.5

(15)

(15)

7.5

SAN BERNARDINO

7.5

7.5

(15E)

(138)

ARROYO SECO RANGER DISTRICT — ANGELES NATIONAL FOREST

The Angeles Crest Highway, State Highway 2, 23 miles from La Canada offers a variety of winter sports opportunities. This area is under the jurisdiction of the Arroyo Seco Ranger District of the Angeles National Forest. In addition to Kratka Ridge and Mr. Waterman downhill ski areas, the Forest Service recommends five untracked nordic ski trails off and along the Highway. These are primarily for beginner and intermediate cross-country skiers. They vary from the marked 2.5 mile loop at Charlton Flats to the 10.5 mile beginner/intermediate tour along the unplowed Highway 2 from Islip Saddle to Vincent Gap. Parking along the Highway can be a problem, although there is cleared parking at each trailhead. This is a day use area with limited facilities. All vehicles must stay on plowed, paved roads, including 4 wheel drive vehicles, ATC's, ATV's and ski bikes.

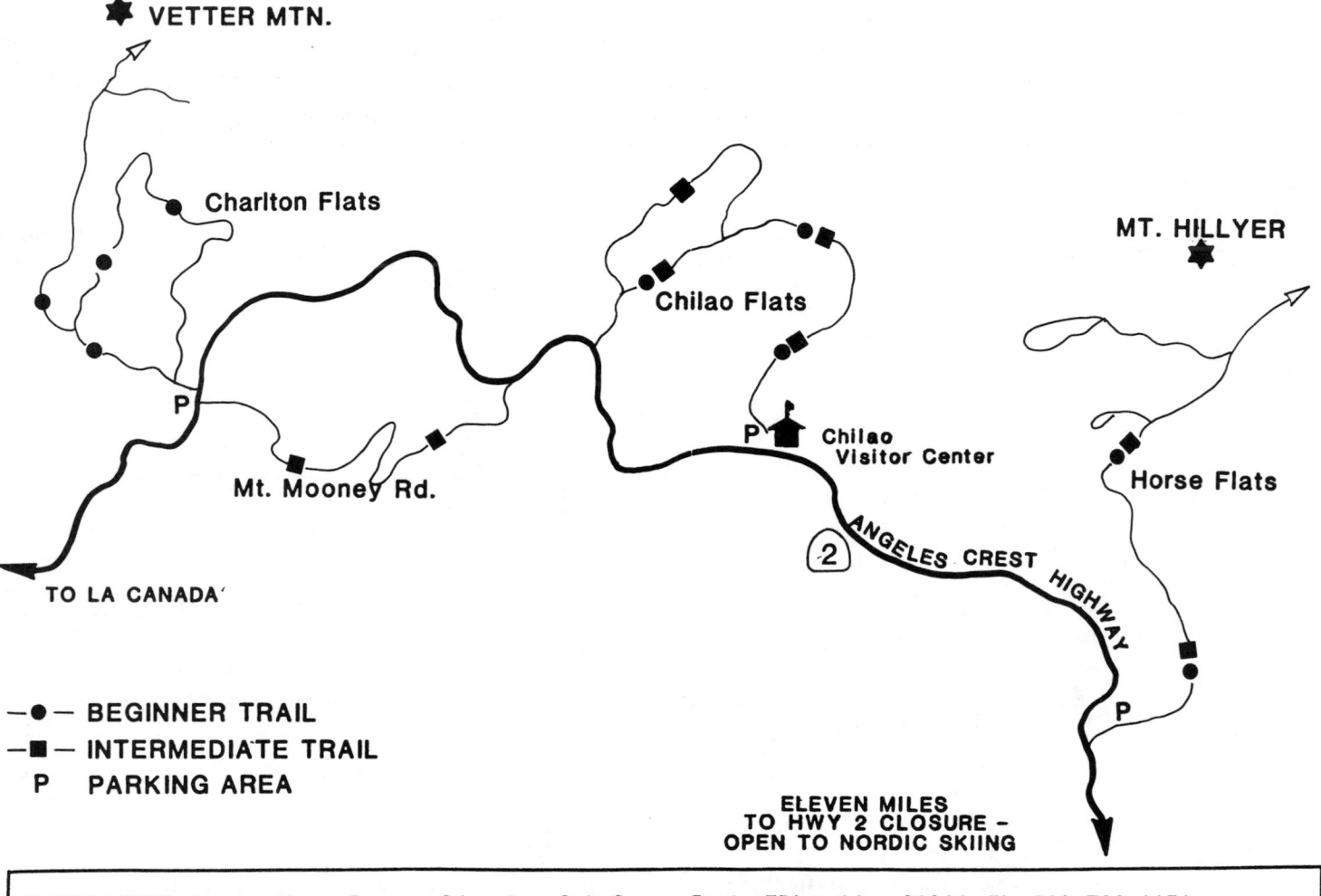

✱ VETTER MTN.

Charlton Flats

Chilao Flats

MT. HILLYER
✱

Mt. Mooney Rd.

P Chilao
Visitor Center

Horse Flats

② ANGELES CREST HIGHWAY

P

TO LA CANADA'

—●— BEGINNER TRAIL
—■— INTERMEDIATE TRAIL
  P PARKING AREA

**ELEVEN MILES
TO HWY 2 CLOSURE -
OPEN TO NORDIC SKIING**

INFORMATION: Arroyo-Seco Ranger District, Oak Grove Park, Flintridge 91011, Ph: 818-790-1151

SKIING	RENTALS & LESSONS	RECREATION	ACCOMMODATIONS

Nordic:
  17.5 Miles of
  Trails
	See Page on Kratka
	Ridge Ski Area and
	Mt. Waterman Ski Area
		Nearby:
		  Alpine Skiing
		  Ski Touring
		  Snow Camping
		  Snow Play Areas
			See Pages on Kratka
			Ridge Ski Area and
			Mt. Waterman Ski Area

MT. WATERMAN

Mt. Waterman is a small day use alpine resort in the Angeles National Forest just 33 miles from La Canada. Located in an area of Southern California's most consistent snowfall, this family owned facility has been serving skiers since 1939. It has 25 runs off a vertical of 1,600 feet. The slopes are groomed on a daily basis. Both group and private lessons are offered at the Ski School, and the Race Department offers a variety of races, clinics and group programs supported by state of the art equipment. This family oriented facility allows up to two children under 12 years of age to ski free with a paying adult.

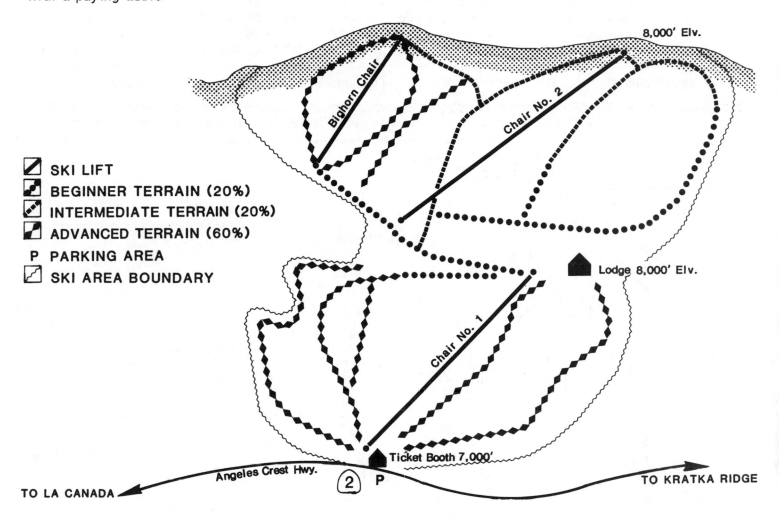

- SKI LIFT
- BEGINNER TERRAIN (20%)
- INTERMEDIATE TERRAIN (20%)
- ADVANCED TERRAIN (60%)
- P PARKING AREA
- SKI AREA BOUNDARY

8,000' Elv.

Bighorn Chair

Chair No. 2

Lodge 8,000' Elv.

Chair No. 1

Ticket Booth 7,000'

Angeles Crest Hwy.

② P

TO LA CANADA

TO KRATKA RIDGE

INFORMATION: Mt. Waterman Ski Lifts, 817 Lynnhaven Lane, La Canada 91011, Ph: 818-796-4368

SKIING	RENTALS & LESSONS	RECREATION	ACCOMMODATIONS

Alpine:
  3 Chairlifts
Fees: Adults–$14–$22
Seniors & Children
  Under 12 – Free
 	
Season: Mid–November
  Through April
 	
Snow Ph: 818–790–2002
	Ski School:
	  Group – $12
	  Private – $22 Hr.
	  Race Clinics
	
	Rentals:
	  Combination:
	  Full Day – $12
	  Half Day – $8
		Nearby:
		  Ski Touring
		  Snow Camping
		  Snow Play Areas
			Warming Hut
			Snack Bar
			Bar
			Reserved Lift Tickets
			Through Ticketron
			
			Nearby:
			  Newcomb's Ranch
			  Restaurant, Bar &
			  Live Entertainment
			  Saturday Night

Kratka Ridge Ski Area is a small day use facility in the Angeles National Forest. Just a short drive from downtown Los Angeles on the Pacific Crest Highway above La Canada, this resort offers both alpine and nordic skiing. The downhill area provides 35 acres of skiable terrain for all levels of ability. The vertical drop is 750 feet and the largest run is one-half of a mile. There is a complete line of support facilities including a ski school, rentals and cafeteria. The Nordic Center in conjunction with Sports Chalet offers a variety of cross-country programs such as ski touring, telemarking and winter camping. Snow coverage is sometimes a problem so it is advisable to call for current conditions.

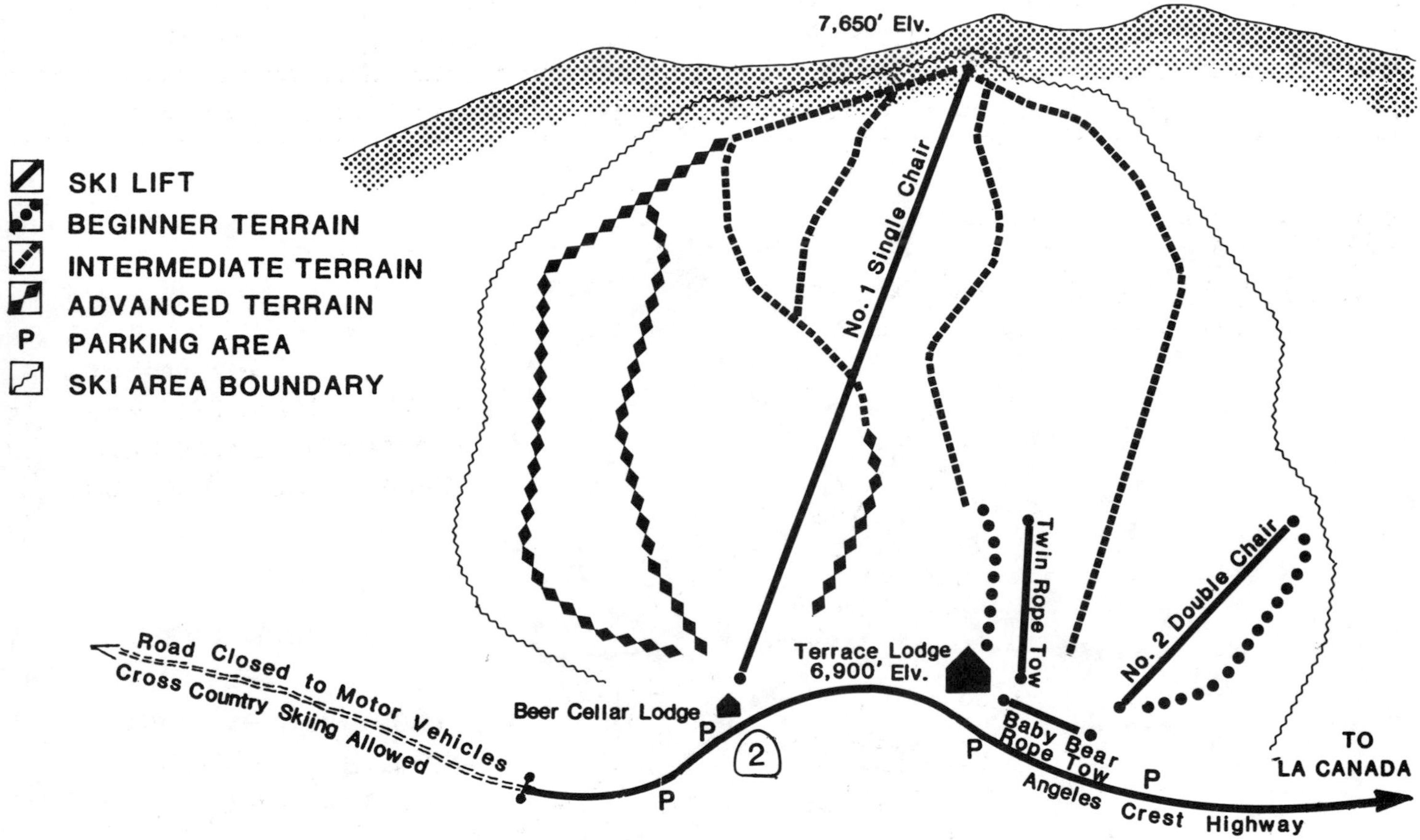

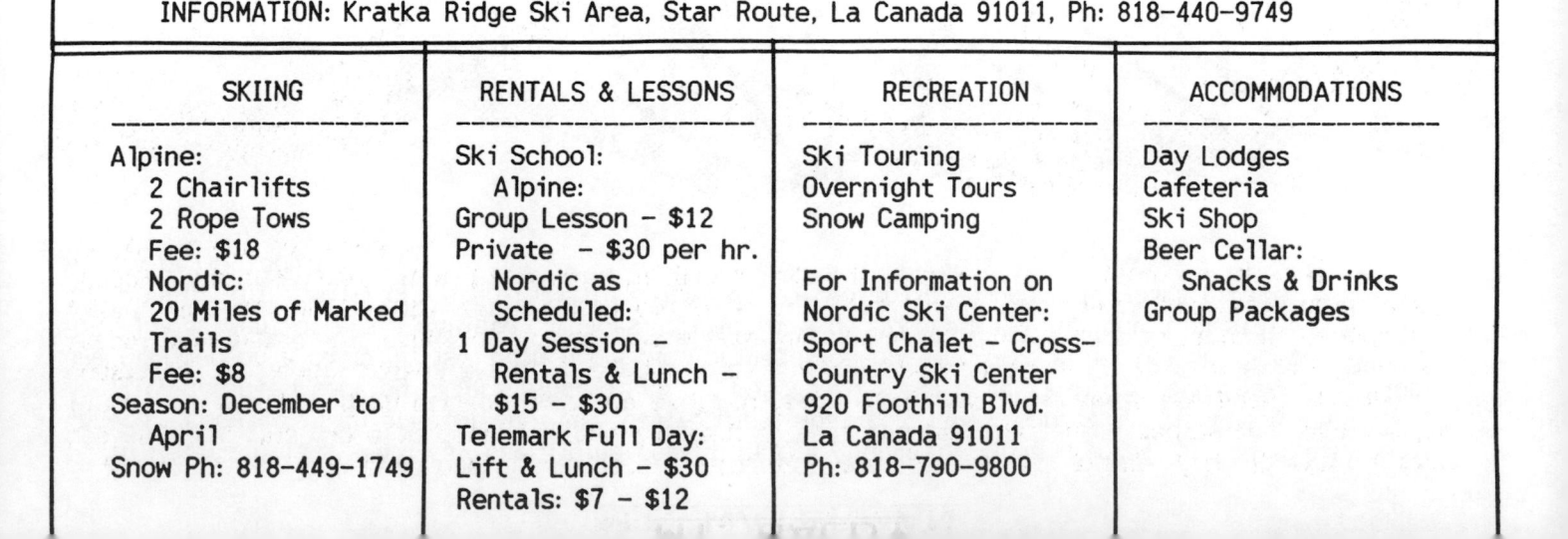

Legend:
- SKI LIFT
- BEGINNER TERRAIN
- INTERMEDIATE TERRAIN
- ADVANCED TERRAIN
- P PARKING AREA
- SKI AREA BOUNDARY

7,650' Elv.

No. 1 Single Chair

Twin Rope Tow

No. 2 Double Chair

Terrace Lodge 6,900' Elv.

Beer Cellar Lodge

Baby Bear Rope Tow

Road Closed to Motor Vehicles
Cross Country Skiing Allowed

Angeles Crest Highway

TO LA CANADA

INFORMATION: Kratka Ridge Ski Area, Star Route, La Canada 91011, Ph: 818-440-9749

SKIING	RENTALS & LESSONS	RECREATION	ACCOMMODATIONS
Alpine: 　2 Chairlifts 　2 Rope Tows 　Fee: $18 Nordic: 20 Miles of Marked Trails 　Fee: $8 Season: December to April Snow Ph: 818-449-1749	Ski School: 　Alpine: Group Lesson – $12 Private – $30 per hr. 　Nordic as 　Scheduled: 1 Day Session – 　Rentals & Lunch – 　$15 – $30 Telemark Full Day: Lift & Lunch – $30 Rentals: $7 – $12	Ski Touring Overnight Tours Snow Camping For Information on Nordic Ski Center: Sport Chalet – Cross- Country Ski Center 920 Foothill Blvd. La Canada 91011 Ph: 818-790-9800	Day Lodges Cafeteria Ski Shop Beer Cellar: 　Snacks & Drinks Group Packages

Mt. Baldy has long been one of Southern California's most popular ski areas. Just 45 minutes from Los Angeles, this close-in downhill resort offers 24 well groomed runs supported by four chair lifts. There is a vertical drop off the mountain of 2,140 feet. Extensive snowmaking equipment provides consistent and early season skiing. Beginning and intermediate runs are groomed nightly. The ski school provides a full range of lessons for adults and children, and the race department offers an extensive program for both recreational and serious skiers. There are seven team races held each Sunday. The new Lodge at mid mountain, Mt. Baldy Notch, offers a pleasant interlude with its cafeteria, bar and sundeck.

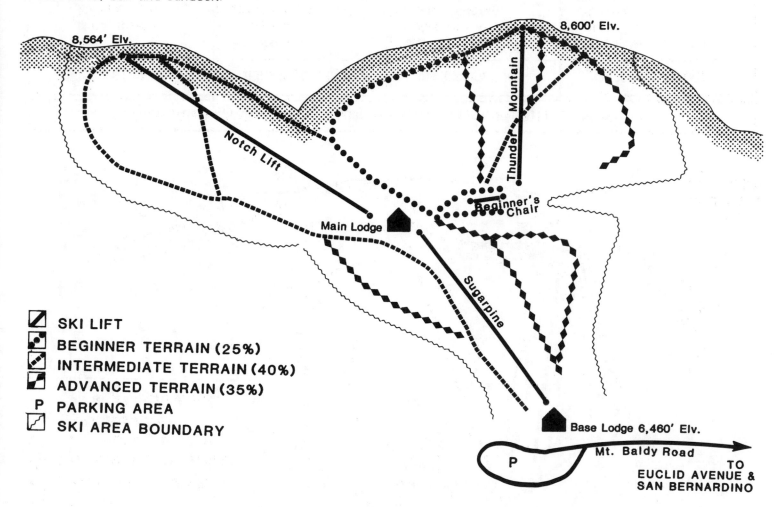

SKI LIFT

BEGINNER TERRAIN (25%)

INTERMEDIATE TERRAIN (40%)

ADVANCED TERRAIN (35%)

P PARKING AREA

SKI AREA BOUNDARY

INFORMATION: Mt. Baldy Ski Area, P. O. Box 459, Mt. Baldy 91759, Ph: 714-946-9653

SKIING	RENTALS & LESSONS	RECREATION	ACCOMMODATIONS
Alpine: 　4 Chairlifts Fees: Adults–$16–$24 Seniors – Half Price Children – $10–$15 Students – $12–$18 Sunday Team Races Season: Late November 　to April Snow Ph: 714-981-3344	Ski School: 　Group Lessons–$10 　Private Lessons – 　By Appointment–$25 Sandy's Ski Rentals: 　Combinations – $12 　Half Day & Child 　Rates Available	Nearby: 　Cross Country 　Skiing 　Snow Play: Glacier Picnic Area– Parking – 20 Vehicles Manker Campground– Parking – 100 Vehicles	Day Lodge & Cafeteria Snack Bar, Barbecue & Sundeck Ski Shop Advance Tickets:Ticketron or Ticketmaster Lodging Information: 　Chamber of 　Commerce 　Ph: 714-946-9643

Mountain High Ski Area is a relatively easy drive from the major population centers of Southern California. This resort is actually two separate ski areas less than a mile apart. Mountain High East was formerly Holiday Hill. There are over 200 acres of varied terrain enhanced by extensive snowmaking and daily grooming. The 39 runs offer a variety of challenges to all levels of ability from novice to expert. The vertical is 1,600 feet and the longest run is a mile and a half. There are excellent support facilities including a large ski school and extensive rental equipment. Children under 10 may ski free when accompanied by an adult. There is night skiing seven nights a week.

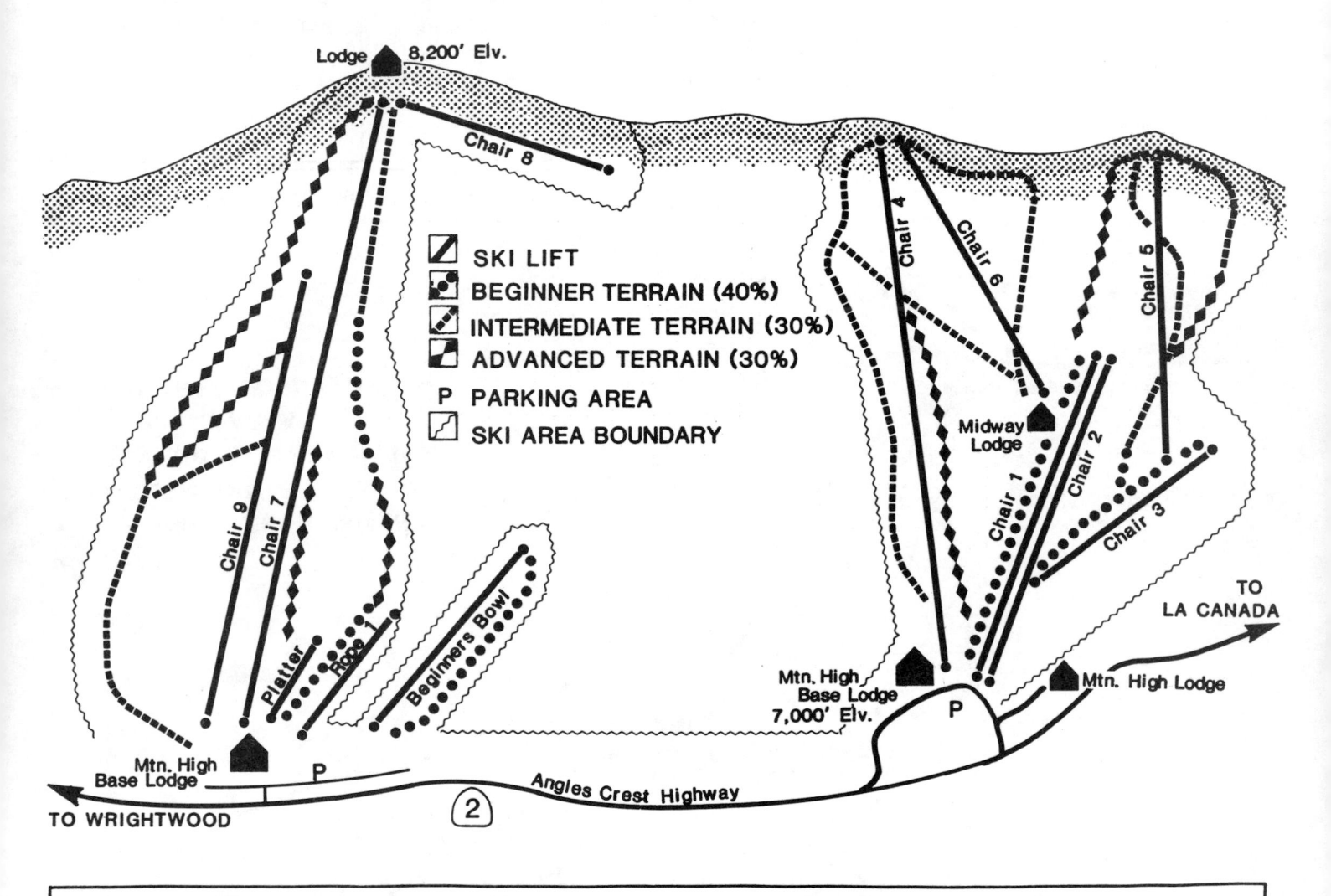

INFORMATION: Mtn. High Ski Area, Box 993, Wrightwood 92397, Ph: 213-460-6911

SKIING	RENTALS & LESSONS	RECREATION	ACCOMMODATIONS
Alpine: 　10 Chairlifts 　1 Poma 　1 Rope Tow Night Skiing 3-10pm Fees: 　Day/Half Day/Nite Adult:$22/$16/$16 Child:$13/$11/$11 Season: Mid- November to Mid- April	Ski School: 　Group: $12 　Private: $32 Hr. 　Children's Buckaroo 　Program: 9 am to 　3 pm – Lift, 　Lesson & Lunch – 　3 to 7 Yrs. Old 　$28 Rentals: 　Combination – $12	Nearby: 　Nordic Skiing 　Ski Touring 　Snow Play Areas 　Snowmobiling 　Live Entertainment 　Dancing	5 Food Service Areas 4 Bars 2 Ski Shops Shuttle Bus Service Group Discounts Ticket Reservations 　Through Ticketron Mountain High Lodge: 　Cabins, Restaurant, 　Bull Wheel Saloon 　Ph: 619-249-5474

Ski Sunrise is an easy ninety minute drive from Los Angeles, just up the road from Mountain High Resort. This popular downhill area has some of the steepest advanced runs in Southern California. There are over 100 acres of well-groomed open runs down a vertical of 800 feet. There is a separate beginner's area and a variety of intermediate and advanced runs. Snowmaking covers 15% of the terrain. Lift tickets are limited. The Ski School features The America Teaching Methods, and uses Scorpion Skis for easy learning, offering first time and advanced beginner packages. There are attractive group discounts. The parking lot and facilities are located near the top of the mountain, so you ski down to the lifts.

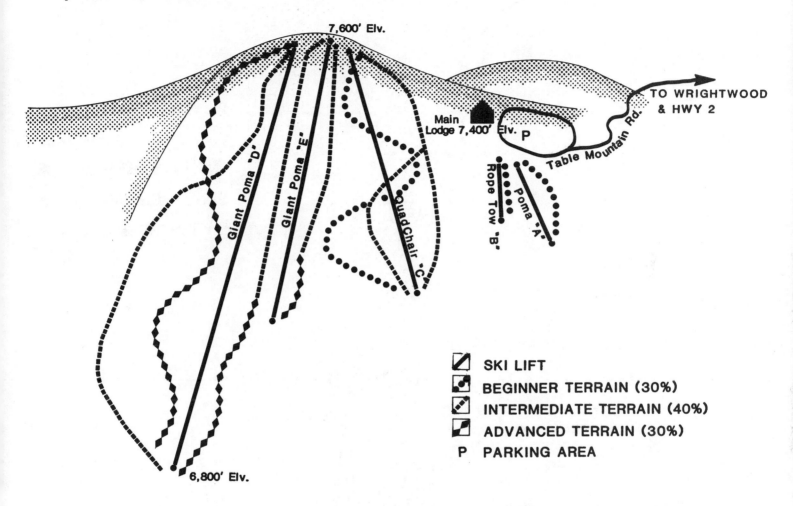

SKIING	RENTALS & LESSONS	RECREATION	ACCOMMODATIONS

Alpine:
  1 Chairlift
  3 Pomas
  1 Rope Tow
Fees: Adults–$20
Children – $8 – $10
Seniors & Under
5 Yrs. – Free
 	
Season: Late November
to Mid-April
	Ski School:
	  Group – $12
	  Private – $25 Hr.
	  Children's Ski/Play
	  Program
	
	Rentals:
	  Combinations – $12
		Nearby:
		  Cross Country
		    Skiing
		  Snow Play Areas
		  Snow Camping
			Day Lodge
			Cafeteria
			Sun Deck
			Mountain Shop
			R. V. Parking
			Campground
			Limited Lift Tickets:
			Reserve Through
			Ticketron &
			Ticketmaster
			Special Package &
			Group Discounts

INFORMATION: Ski Sunrise, P.O. Box 645, Wrightwood 92397, Ph: 619-249-6150

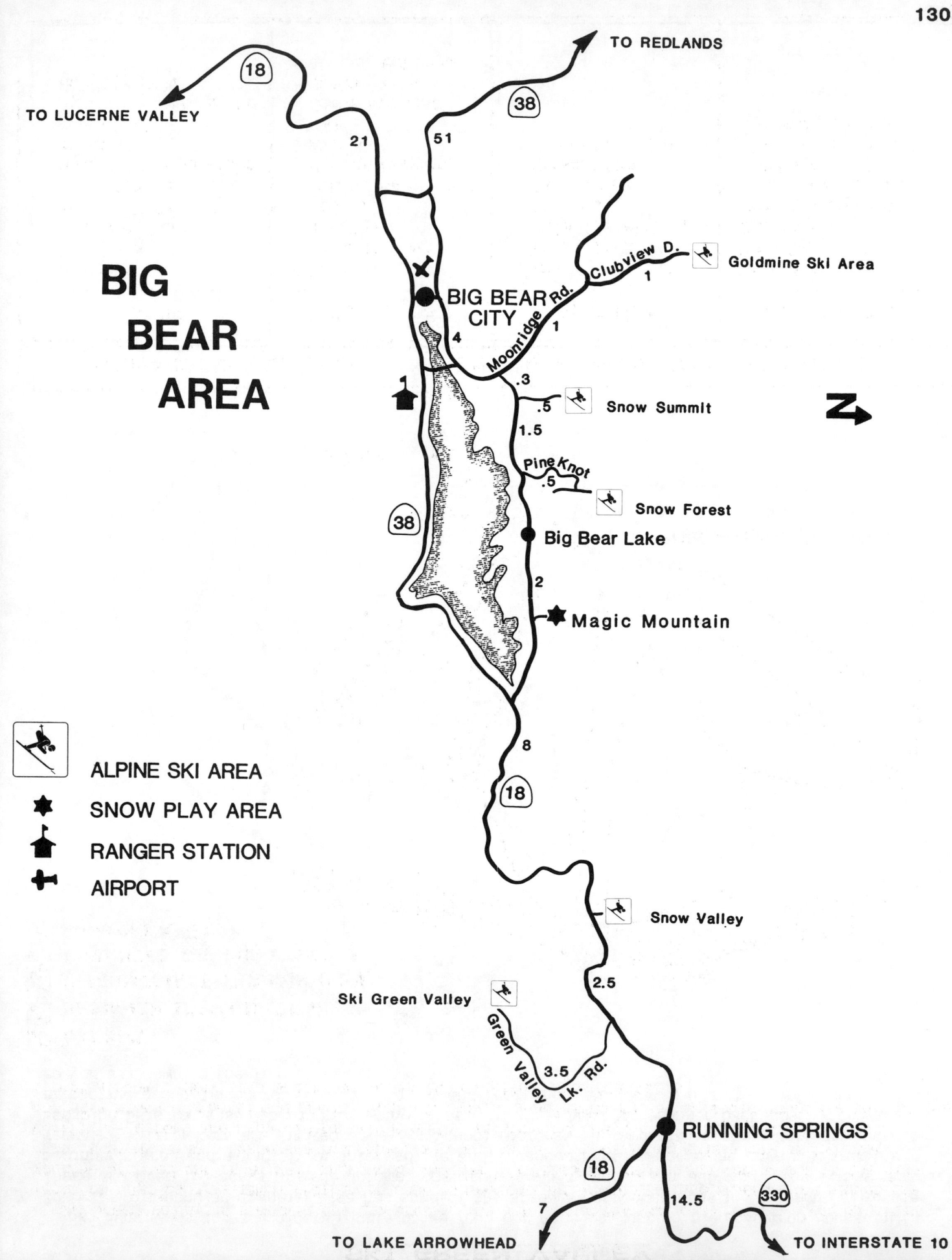

BIG BEAR AREA

TO LUCERNE VALLEY

18

TO REDLANDS

38

21   51

Clubview D.   Goldmine Ski Area

Moonridge Rd.   1

BIG BEAR CITY

1

4

.3

.5   Snow Summit

1.5

Pine Knot

.5

Snow Forest

38

Big Bear Lake

2

Magic Mountain

8

18

Snow Valley

2.5

Ski Green Valley

Green Valley Lk. Rd.

3.5

RUNNING SPRINGS

18

330

7   14.5

TO LAKE ARROWHEAD   TO INTERSTATE 10

ALPINE SKI AREA

SNOW PLAY AREA

RANGER STATION

AIRPORT

SKI GREEN VALLEY

Ski Green Valley is a modest day use area in the San Bernardino National Forest. Just 85 miles from Los Angeles, this small facility is open to weekend and holiday alpine skiers. The slopes are machine groomed and relatively uncrowded, and the lift rates are nominal in comparison to the other resorts in the area. There are two rope tows and 2 poma lifts carrying skiers up the 350 foot vertical. Lessons are provided for all levels of ability from beginner to advanced. There is a complete stock of rental equipment. Goggles, gloves, sunglasses and other accessories are sold at the ticket window. There is a snack bar in the warming hut featuring pizza.

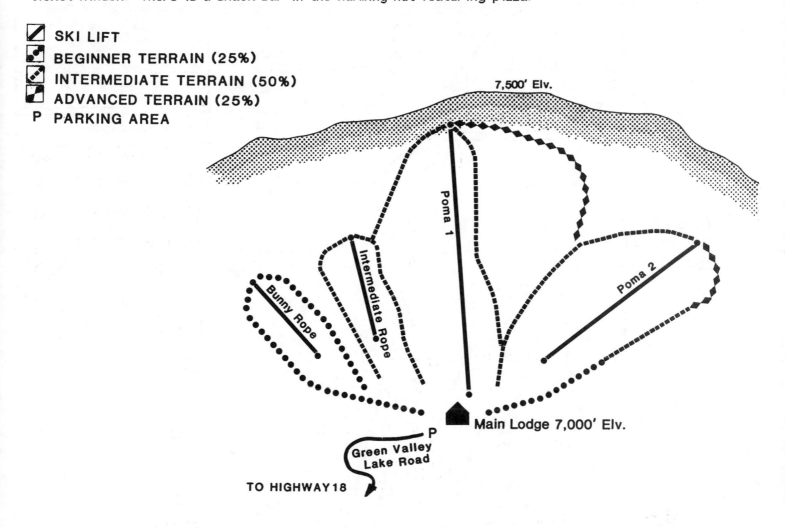

SKI LIFT
BEGINNER TERRAIN (25%)
INTERMEDIATE TERRAIN (50%)
ADVANCED TERRAIN (25%)
P PARKING AREA

7,500' Elv.

Poma 1

Poma 2

Intermediate Rope

Bunny Rope

P

Main Lodge 7,000' Elv.

Green Valley Lake Road

TO HIGHWAY 18

INFORMATION: Ski Green Valley, P. O. Box 202, Green Valley Lake 92341, Ph: 714-867-2338

SKIING	RENTALS & LESSONS	RECREATION	ACCOMMODATIONS

Alpine:
    2 Pomas
    2 Rope Tows
Fees: Full Day – $14
        Half Day – $12
Season: Late November
to April
Hours: 9:00 a.m. to
4:30 p.m. Weekends and
Holidays Only
	Ski School:
	    Group Lessons –
	    1-1/2 Hrs:
	    Beginner &
	    Intermediate – $10
	    Private Lessons
	    Available
	Rentals:
	    Combinations: $7
	    Junior Rates for
	    10 yrs. and under
		Nearby:
		    Cross Country
		    Skiing, Rentals &
		    Lessons
		    Ski Touring
		    Snowmobiling
		    Snow Play Areas
			Day Lodge
			Snack Bar
			Accessories
			Rooms & Housekeeping
			    Accommodations in
			    Village
			Other Facilities in
			    Running Springs

Snow Valley is one of Southern California's major ski areas. It offers 9-1/2 hours of skiing daily. A "Late-Day/Nite" ticket provides evening skiing from 1 p.m. to 9 p.m. five nights a week. The facilities close at 5 p.m. on Mondays and Tuesdays. Located on the western slope of the San Bernardino Mountains, this area's 230 acres of skiable terrain is complemented by extensive snowmaking and immaculate groomed trails. There are 35 runs down a 1,100 vertical off the mountain accommodating skiers of all levels of skill. Advanced skiers have their own separate side of the mountain with 2 chairlifts. This modern day-use facility has all the amenities. Lift tickets are limited so reservations are advised. Reserved ticket holders are offered preferred parking.

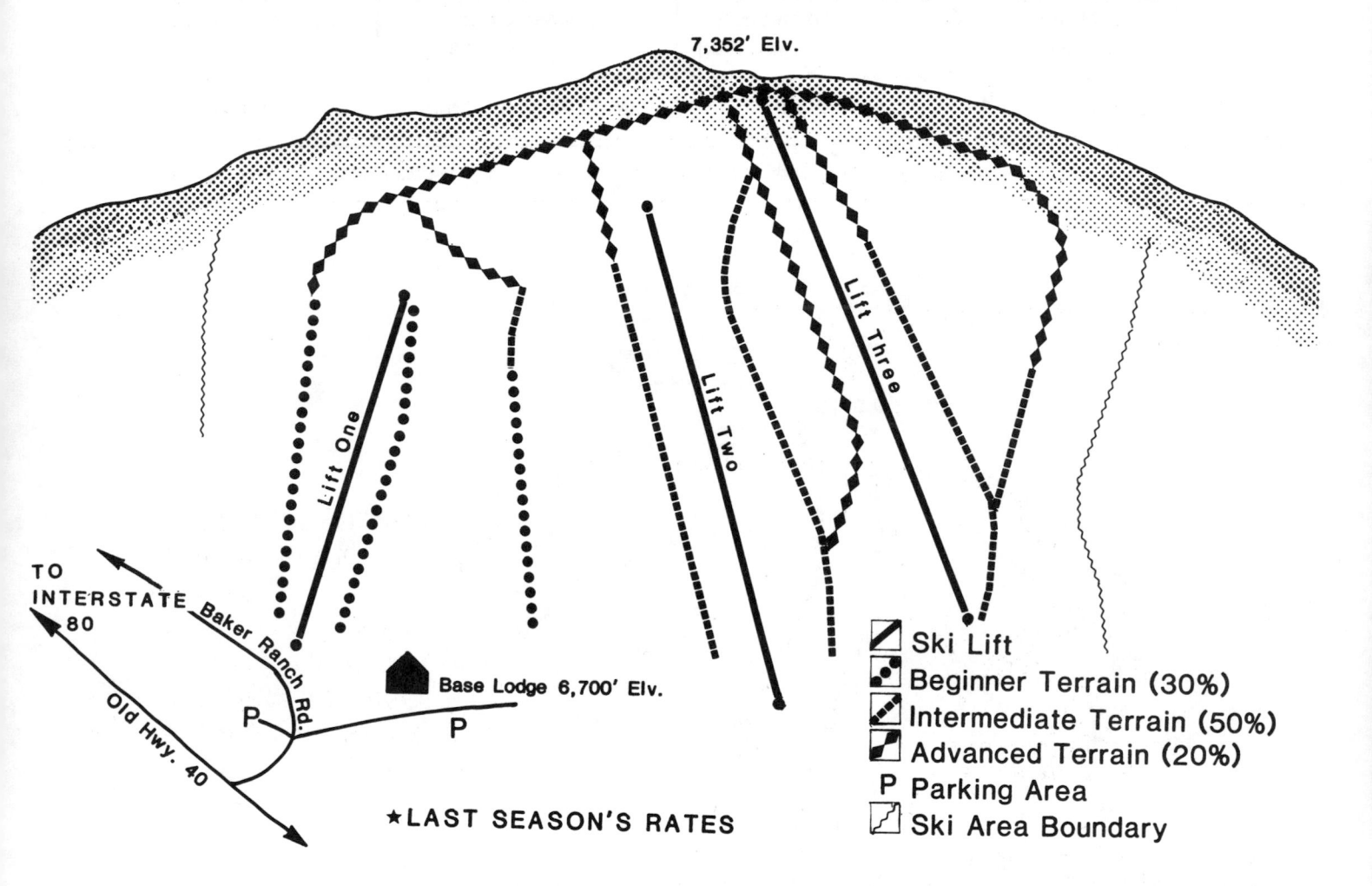

7,352' Elv.

Lift One

Lift Two

Lift Three

TO INTERSTATE 80

Baker Ranch Rd.

Old Hwy. 40

P

P

Base Lodge 6,700' Elv.

Ski Lift
Beginner Terrain (30%)
Intermediate Terrain (50%)
Advanced Terrain (20%)
P Parking Area
Ski Area Boundary

★LAST SEASON'S RATES

INFORMATION: Snow Valley, Box 8, Running Springs 92382, Ph: 714-867-2751

SKIING	RENTALS & LESSONS	RECREATION	ACCOMMODATIONS

Alpine:
   13 Chairlifts
Fees: $15 - $25
Hours: 7:30 a.m. to
   5:00 p.m. Daily
Night Skiing: 1:00 p.m.
   to 9:00 p.m. Except
   Mondays and
   Tuesdays
Snow Phones:
   714-867-5151 or
   714-625-6511
	Ski School:*
	   Group Lessons –
	   Half Day – $14
	   All Day – $20
	   Private – $35/hr.
	Rentals:*
	   Combinations –
	   Seniors & Children
	   $9
	   Adults – $12
		Nearby:
		   Cross Country
		   Ski Touring
		   Snowmobile Rentals
		   Snow Play Areas
		   Live Entertainment
			Restaurant & Bar
			Snack Bars
			Ski Shop
			Paved Parking for
			   3,000 Cars
			Lift Ticket
			Reservations:
			Ticketron or Phone
			   714-567-5111 or
			   714-625-6611
			For Lodging See
			Following Pages

SNOW FOREST

Snow Forest is a small expanding ski area on the slopes above the south shore of Big Bear Lake. There are 160 acres of skiable terrain down a vertical of 1,200 feet. There are groomed runs for all levels of ability and a separate area on Siberia Mountain for beginner and low-intermediate skiers. Lynn Mountain is serviced by a 3,000 foot triple chairlift. Lift tickets are limited, so reservations are advised. There is a ski school offering both group and private lessons. The rental shop offers a complete line of equipment including Scorpion skis and snow boards. The two lodges at the base of each mountain offers hot food, beer and wine.

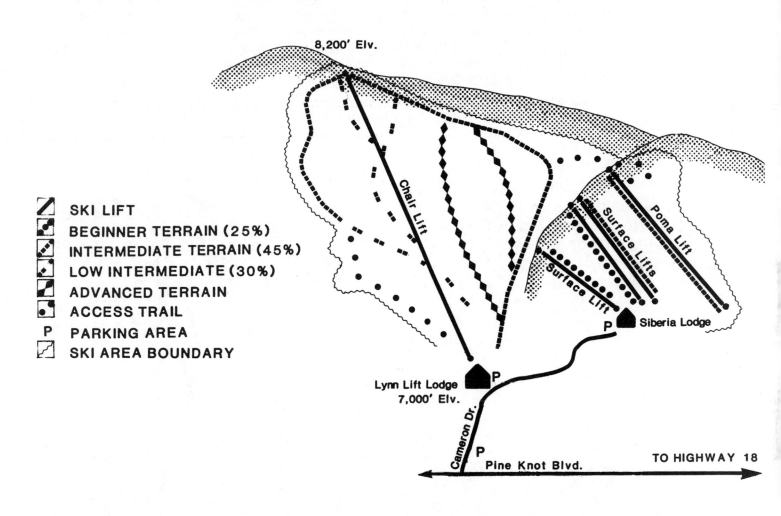

SKI LIFT
BEGINNER TERRAIN (25%)
INTERMEDIATE TERRAIN (45%)
LOW INTERMEDIATE (30%)
ADVANCED TERRAIN
ACCESS TRAIL
P PARKING AREA
SKI AREA BOUNDARY

8,200' Elv.

Chair Lift

Poma Lift

Surface Lifts

Surface Lift

Siberia Lodge
P

Lynn Lift Lodge
7,000' Elv.
P

Cameron Dr.

P
Pine Knot Blvd.

TO HIGHWAY 18

INFORMATION: Snow Forest Ski Area, P. O. Box 1711, Big Bear 92314, Ph: 714-866-8891

SKIING	RENTALS & LESSONS	RECREATION	ACCOMMODATIONS

Alpine:
  1 Chairlift
  1 Poma Lift
  3 Rope Tows
Fees: Adults—$10—$17
Seniors — $10
Children — $8 – $13
Group & Mid-Week
Rates
Season: Late December
to Early April
Snow Ph: 714-866-5503
	Ski School:
	  Group Lessons:
	   $10/1.5 hrs.
	  Private: $25/hr.
	Rentals:
	Combinations – $7–$9
	Snow Boards – $8–$12
	Breakage Insurance–$1
		Nearby:
		Cross Country Skiing,
		Lessons, Rentals &
		  Tours
		Snow Play & Slide
		Snowmobile & ATV
		Grand Prix Track,
		Rentals & Tours:
		Adventure Expeditions
		  P.O. Box 3084
		  Big Bear 92315
		  Ph: 714-866-7216
			2 Day Lodges
			2 Restaurants
			2 Beer & Wine Bars
			Shuttle Bus from
			  Parking Lot
			Lift Ticket Reserv:
			Ticketron or Ticket
			  Master
			For Lodging See
			Following Page

SNOW SUMMIT

Snow Summit is one of the most popular ski areas in the San Bernardino Mountains. Weekend lift tickets are often sold out, so advanced reservations are a must. There are 210 acres of well-groomed terrain with a vertical drop of 1,200 feet. Extensive snowmaking covers 94% of the skiable runs. Night skiing is a featured attraction, weather permitting. It is wise to check the snow report for current conditions. In addition to the regular Ski School agenda, there are special mid-week beginners packages and a Kiddy Ski School. A complimentary beginners orientation is offered each morning. The Race Department offers a variety of recreational racing programs. NASTAR racing is held every Thursday, Saturday and Sunday. League racing is held on Tuesday, Wednesday and Friday nights.

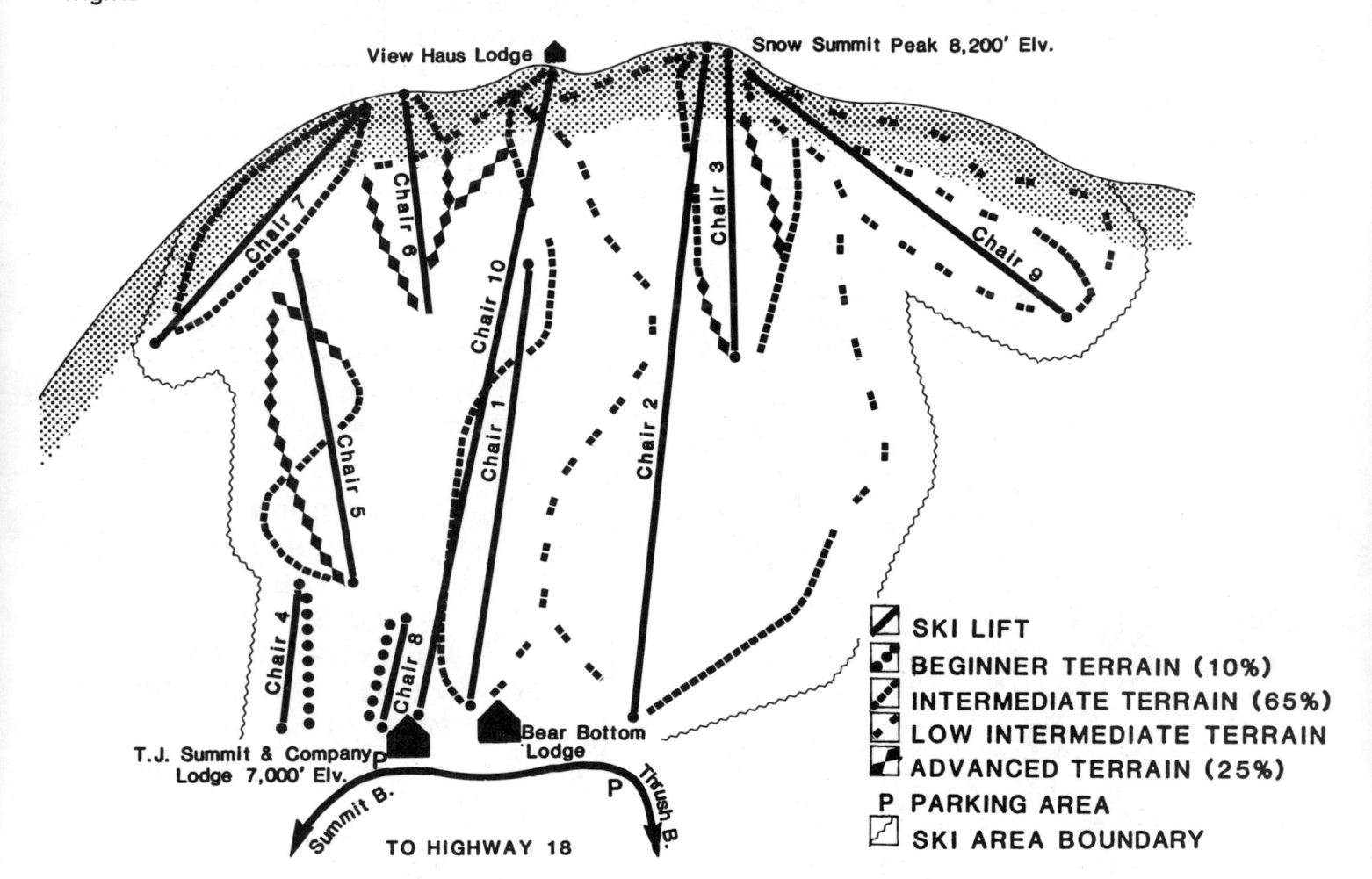

INFORMATION: Snow Summit, Big Bear Lake 92315, Ph: 714-866-5766

SKIING	RENTALS & LESSONS	RECREATION	ACCOMMODATIONS

Alpine:
  10 Chairlifts
Fees: $10.50 to $23.50
Night Skiing
NASTAR - Coin
Operated Race Course
Season: Mid November
to Mid April
Snow Phone:
  714-866-4621
	Ski School:
	  Group Lessons -
	  $15 - $20
	  Race Clinic - $15
	  Private - $30 Hour
	Children-9 to 12 yrs
	  $13 - $18
	Kiddy Ski School -
	  4 to 8 yrs - 1/2
	  Day-$15, All-$25
	Rentals: $11 for
	  Combinations
		Special Events
		
		Nearby:
		  Cross Country
		  Skiing, Lessons &
		  Rentals
		  Ski Touring
		  Snow Play Areas
		  Snowmobile Rentals
		  Live Entertainment
			TJ Summit: Cafeteria
			Bear Bottom Lodge:
			  Snack Bar, BBQ
			View Haus: Restaurant
			Ski Shop
			Lift Ticket
			Reservations:
			  Ticketron or Phone:
			  714-866-5841
			Lodging Reservations:
			  Ph: 714-866-5878

GOLDMINE SKI AREA

The Goldmine Ski Area is one of Southern California's prime alpine resorts. There are 250 acres of varied terrain enhanced by extensive snowmaking equipment which can cover 100% of the area. The vertical is 1,800 feet. The well-groomed runs challenge all levels of ability. The Ski School features specifically tailored instructions from beginner to advanced techniques. Minor's Camp, a Skiwee program, offers a full day of supervised instruction for children. The Race Department offers various programs and clinics including NASTAR. There are 2 fully equipped race hills. In addition to the complete day use facilities, Goldmine offers a Tuesday Premium Day (gifts), a Wednesday Lady's Day (free lessons & cocktails) and a Thursday Race Day (free clinic & NASTAR).

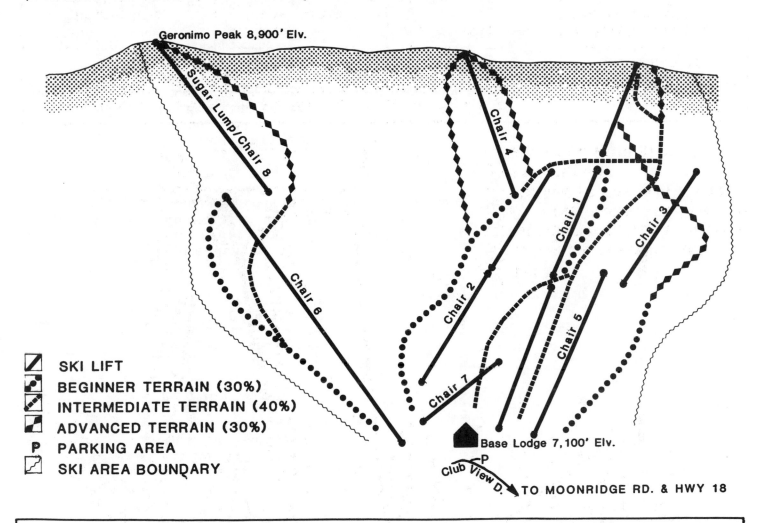

SKI LIFT
BEGINNER TERRAIN (30%)
INTERMEDIATE TERRAIN (40%)
ADVANCED TERRAIN (30%)
P   PARKING AREA
SKI AREA BOUNDARY

Geronimo Peak 8,900' Elv.
Sugar Lump/Chair 8
Chair 4
Chair 1
Chair 3
Chair 6
Chair 2
Chair 5
Chair 7
Base Lodge 7,100' Elv.
Club View D.
TO MOONRIDGE RD. & HWY 18

INFORMATION: Goldmine Ski Resort, P. O. Box 6812, Big Bear Lake 92315, Ph: 714-585-2519

SKIING	RENTALS & LESSONS	RECREATION	ACCOMMODATIONS

Alpine:
  8 Chairlifts
Fees: Adults-$13-$23
Children-$6-$10
NASTAR Racing:
  2 Race Hills
Season: Thanksgiving
  to Easter
Snow Ph: 714-585-2517
	Ski School:
	  Groups – $13-$19
	  Private – $26 hr.
	Miner's Camp: 4-12 yr.
	  Skiwee Program-
	  Supervised
	  Instruction, Lunch
	  & Snacks-8:30-3:30
	  Fee: $27
	Rentals:
	  Combination – $10
	  Miner`s Camp – $5
		Nearby:
		  Cross Country
		  Skiing, Lessons &
		  Rentals
		  Ski Touring
		  Snowmobile Rentals
		  ORV Trails
		  Snow Play Areas
			Cafeteria, Deli, Pizza
			Patio – Barbecue
			Cocktail Lounge
			Ski Shop
			
			Lodging: See
			Following Page
			
			Teletron Reservations
			  Ph: 213-410-1062
			Ticketmaster –
			  Ph: 213-480-3232

BIG BEAR LAKE AREA

Big Bear Lake Tourists and Visitors Bureau
P.O. Box 3050
Big Bear Lake, CA. 92315
24 Hour/7 Day Recreation Service for a Variety of Lodging
Ph:714-866-5878

Big Bear Chamber of Commerce
P.O. Box 2860
41647 Big Bear Blvd.
Big Bear Lake, CA. 92315
General Information
Ph: 714-866-5652

Big Bear Ranger District
P.O. Box 290
Fawnskin, CA. 92333
Ski Touring and Snowmobiling Trails, Snow-Camping Information

Alpine Slide at Magic Mountain
P.O. Box 6141
Big Bear Lake, CA. 92315
Tubing Hill, Chairlift, Alpine Slide, New Water Slide, Snack Bar
Ph: 714-866-4626

Adventure Expeditions of the Wilderness, Inc.
P.O. Box 3084
Big Bear Lake, CA. 92315
Snowmobile Wilderness Tours, ATV Grand Prix Track, Summer Day
and Extended Tours, ATV Riding Academy
Ph: 714-866-7216
   714-585-5453

One of the most unique winter sports areas is located in the Mount San Jacinto State Park and Wilderness Area. Palm Springs Aerial Tramway carries passengers from a desert environment at 2,643 feet elevation to the snow-covered mountains of the San Jacinto Wilderness Area at 8,516 feet, all in 15 minutes. The Nordic Center at the top of the Tramway rents cross-country ski equipment or snowshoes. There are two loops of marked trails to follow. 30,000 acres of remote areas offer the experienced winter backcountry traveler opportunities for snow camping. Permits are required. Check at the Ranger Station for details.

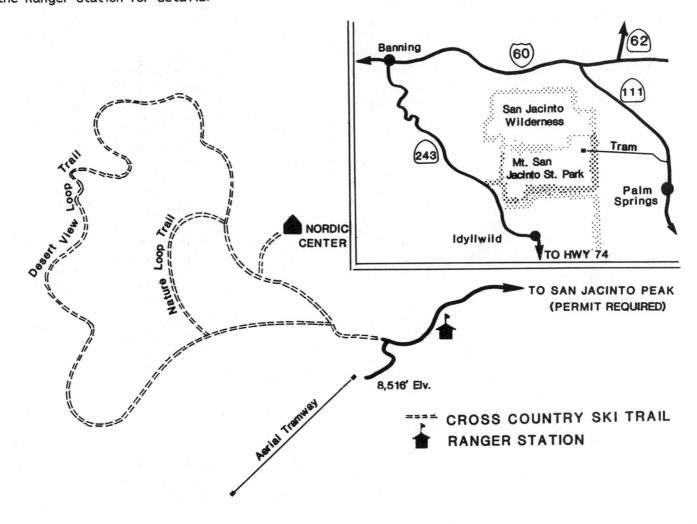

INFORMATION: Palm Springs Nordic, P.O. Box FF, Palm Springs 92263, Ph: 619-327-6002			
SKIING	**RENTALS & LESSONS**	**RECREATION**	**ACCOMMODATIONS**

Nordic:
  Beginner,
  Intermediate &
  Advanced – 2 Miles
  of Marked Trails:
  Mt. San Jacinto
  State Park
  P.O. Box 308
  Idyllwild 92349
  Long Valley
  Ranger Station:
  Ph: 619-327-0222
	Ski School:
	  Basic Lesson-1-1/2
	  Hr. – $10 a Person
	  Advanced – 2 Hr. –
	  $18 a Person
	Rentals:
	  Combination –
	  Adult-$6 hr/$15 Day
	  Child-$4 hr/$8 Day
	  Snowshoes – $8/Day
	  Sleds – $4/hr.
	  Snowboots – $1.50/hr.
		Snow Play Areas
		Snow Camping
		Championship Dog Sled
		  Races – January
		  X-C 5-10K Race,
		  March
		Aerial Tramway:
		  $11.95 Round trip
		Group Packages:
		  Ph: 619-325-1449
		Snow & Ski Conditions
		  Ph: 619-325-4227
			Cafeteria & Day Lodge
			Snack Bar
			Warming Hut
			
			Hours:
			  Weekdays– 10:00 am
			  to Dusk
			  Weekends-8:00 am
			  to Dusk
			
			Full Facilities in
			Palm Springs

LEE CANYON

Lee Canyon is just 47 miles northwest of the exciting desert environment of Las Vegas. Located in a beautiful alpine setting beneath the slopes of Mount Charleston in the Toiyabe National Forest, this popular area offers a variety of winter recreation opportunities. The downhill ski area has 40 acres of varied terrain. There are 14 groomed trails off a vertical of 990 feet. These runs vary in difficulty from the beginning area at Rabbit Peak to the advanced challenge at Slot Alley and Flying Home. The Lee Canyon Ski Area is operated by permit from the Forest Service, and offers complete day use facilities. There is a special skiers bus service to and from Las Vegas. Below the Ski Area on Highway 156, there is a snowplay area, gentle nordic slopes and restricted snowmobiling.

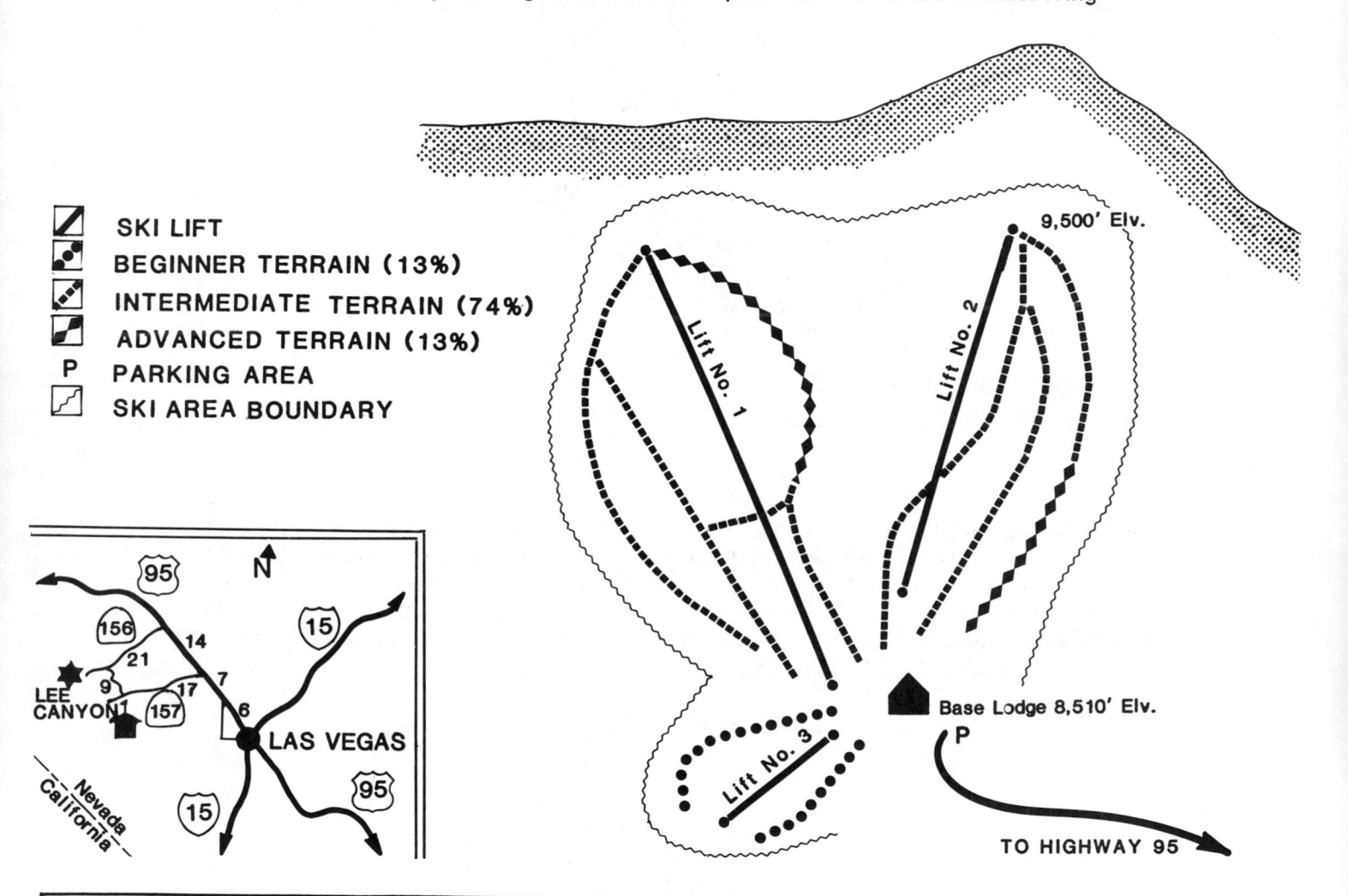

SKI LIFT
BEGINNER TERRAIN (13%)
INTERMEDIATE TERRAIN (74%)
ADVANCED TERRAIN (13%)
P   PARKING AREA
SKI AREA BOUNDARY

Lift No. 1
Lift No. 2
Lift No. 3
9,500' Elv.
Base Lodge 8,510' Elv.
TO HIGHWAY 95

LAS VEGAS
LEE CANYON
Nevada
California
N

INFORMATION: Ski Lee, 1552 Winwood St., Las Vegas NV 89108, Ph: 702-872-5462

SKIING	RENTALS & LESSONS	RECREATION	ACCOMMODATIONS
Alpine: 3 Chairlifts Fee: $15 Season: Thanksgiving to Easter Snow Ph: 702-646-5462	Ski School: Group Lessons Private Lessons Special Racing Clinics by Arrangement Rentals: At Resort or – Ski Lee Rentals 2395 N. Rancho Rd. Las Vegas	Nearby: Nordic Skiing Ski Touring Snow Play Areas Snowmobiling For Information on Lee Canyon: Las Vegas Ranger District 550 E. Charleston Las Vegas NV 89104 Ph: 702-388-6255	2 Day Lodges Coffee Shop Cocktail Lounge Ski Shop Sun Deck Las Vegas Shuttle Bus Lift & Rental Reservations & Group Tours – Programs: Ph: 702-646-0008

SNO-PARK PERMIT SYSTEM

The new California Sno-Park System has been developed for those who enjoy an informal and easy access to uncrowded snow play areas, cross-country skiing and snowmobiling. There are presently 16 established sites in the Sierras, from the Yuba Pass site to the Western Divide site in Sequoia National Forest. New sites are expected to be added in the future.

These Sno-Park sites offer safe, cleared parking by permit only. Those who park in these areas without a permit are subject to a $75 fine. The fee for an annual permit is $10, while a daily permit is $2. Permits may be purchased at many sporting goods stores, the California State Automobile Association (members only) , or by sending a check or money order to:

> Sno-Park Permits
> P.O. Box 2390
> Sacramento, CA. 95811
> 916-322-8593

SNOWPLAY

Snowplay can be enjoyed by the entire family. This popular recreation requires a little caution, a day change of clothes, and imagination. Toboggans and tubes are great fun, but difficult to maneuver.   Sleds are easier to steer, yet require a harder surface pack. Always check the hill you have chosen for possible obstructions and hazards. Observe all local safety rules and regulations. Park in a safe area off the road and enjoy the snow. Perhaps, make a snow man.

WINTER DRIVING

Since winter recreation sites are usually in mountainous areas of inclement weather, snow, ice, mudslides and low visibility can create driving problems. Here are a few tips that will reduce stress and increase the safety of winter driving:

1. Always check road conditions and weather with your local Department of Transportation's 24 hour phone report.

2. Before you leave home, be sure that your vehicle is in good mechanical condition. Brakes, lights, turn signals and emergency flashers should all be operating properly. The battery should be fully charged and the exhaust system free of any dangerous leaks. Proper anti-freeze should be in the engine's cooling sytem. Replace worn tires and wiper blades, and be sure to carry an extra supply of anti-freeze type window washing solution. Always have plenty of gas when entering snow country.

3. Always carry chains, even if you have snow tires, and use caution when putting them on. Carry extra chain tensors, tarp, flashlight, flares, shovel, ice scraper and other equipment that may be needed in an emergency situation.

4. Slow down when driving on slippery roads. Allow extra space between the car in front of you and yourself, use low gears as you go downhill and around curves. Avoid abrupt changes in speed or direction. Never slam on the brakes, but tap them gently, yet rapidly. Start slowly for better traction, and always drive defensively.

5. When in a skid remain calm and turn into the direction the rear of your car is heading; leave your car in gear and when it has straightened out, straighten your steering wheel.

6. Be prepared for cold weather by having ample layers of warm clothing and a pair of gloves within easy reach. Highly visible, brightly colored clothing is helpful in an emergency. A thermos of hot drink and snacks are often welcome. A couple of blankets and first aid kit are invaluable in an emergency.

ROAD CONDITIONS

The California Department of Transportation 24 hour phone
reports on highway and weather conditions at the following numbers:

Angels Camp.....209-736-4564
Auburn..........916-885-3786
Bakersfield.....805-393-7350
Bishop..........619-873-6366
Chico...........916-895-8111
Eureka..........707-444-3077
Fresno..........209-247-2871
Grass Valley....916-272-2171
Jackson.........209-223-4455
Marysville......916-743-4681
Merced..........209-383-4291
Modesto.........209-521-2240
Oakland.........415-654-9890
Oroville........916-535-7900
Placerville.....916-622-7355

Quincy..........916-283-1045
Redding.........916-244-1500
Sacramento......916-445-7623
Salinas.........408-757-2006
San Francisco...415-557-3755
San Jose........408-289-1161
Santa Rosa......707-585-0326
Sonora..........209-532-0227
So. Lake Tahoe..916-577-3550
Stockton........209-931-4848
Ukiah...........707-462-0155
Vallejo.........707-643-8421
Walnut Creek....415-938-1180
Yreka...........916-842-1217

In Nevada Call:

Reno............702-793-1313
Las Vegas.......702-385-6500

HELI-SKIING

Heli-skiing is said to be the ultimate skiing experience. After a breathtaking helicopter ride to your preselected slope, you are left with your group and expert guide in the backcountry wilderness. Below, a vast panorama of open bowls, timbered runs and gentle slopes covered with virgin powder await your tracks down an unspoiled vertical of thousands of feet. These runs vary in length and difficulty in terrain.

This type of skiing is not for everyone. Downhill skiers must have advanced intermediate skills or better. Since each group's run is geared for their level of ability, always provide an accurate assessment of your skills to the operator. Nordic skiers should have a basic understanding of cross-country skills, but again, tours are selected by the group's level of ability. Good physical condition is a factor; however there are handicapped tours available. Heli-skiing is expensive to operate and enjoy, but the thrill and challenge to dedicated wilderness skiers makes it well worth the cost.

Helicopter Services
(Reservations Advised)

Mammoth Heli-Ski
P.O. Box 600
Mammoth Lakes, CA. 93456
619-934-4494

Introductory Package
(2 runs): $75
Full Day: $225
Group Rates (7 or more):
$195
Scenic Flights (4 or
more): $25 per person

Sierra Helicopter Ski
P.O. Box 8038
Truckee, CA. 95737
916-587-4573

Base Operation:
2000 Loop Road
Squaw Valley, CA.

North Lake Tahoe
Alpine:
One Run: $50
Half Day: $150
All Day: $250
Nordic Tours: $50
Scenic Tours: $50
Mono Lake Two Day
Package: $650

Tahoe Heli-Ski
P.O. Box 6240
Stateline, NV. 98949
702-588-2228

Half Day and Full Day
Tours Available

WILDERNESS TRAVEL

Those venturing into snow country should be prepared for the hazards of winter travelling. The harsh realities of extreme cold, snow, and whiteout are always a possibility. It is wise to check current weather conditions; study the area you are entering and the route you have chosen. Advanced planning, common sense and good physical condition helps to ensure an enjoyable outing.

Always leave word with a responsible person before leaving. This person should have a description of the area and the route you have chosen. Your departure time and estimated time of arrival and return are essential. Be sure to check back with them when you return. When overdue, this person should contact the local sheriff in the area you are touring so that any necessary action can be taken immediately.

It is never wise to enter the wilderness alone. Always travel with partner or a group. Companions are invaluable in the event of an emergency.

Dressing properly for protection from the elements is essential. Gloves, a wool watch cap, and waterproof outer garments are necessary. Since winter time temperatures can vary up to 80 degrees, light weight layers of clothing can be added or removed with changing weather conditions. Wool and other heat retaining materials, such as polypropylene, are your best protection in wet, cold environments. Always carry a complete change of clothing.

Advanced meal planning is of prime importance. High energy foods are necessary to maintain body temperature and stamina in cold environments. Drink plenty of water when travelling and carry water or a container for melting and the necessary chemicals to treat melted snow. Never eat snow; it offers limited water and burns calories by using your body heat to melt the snow.

A map of the area and a compass are often needed in backcountry travel. It is essential that you know how to use these directional aids prior to your planned expedition. Trail maps of the area are usually available at recreation sites and ranger stations.

Always carry a survival kit. This kit can be tailored to individual needs, but a basic kit includes the following items:

Water Proof Matches	Whistle
Candles	Flashlight
Firestarter (lighter)	Tool Kit
50' Nylon Rope	Wide Tape for Repairs
Tarp	High Energy Food
Space Blanket	Water Container
General Purpose Knife	First Aid Kit
Folding Saw	Sunscreen
Signal Mirror	Sunglasses
Flares	Survival Manual

SNOWMOBILING

This growing winter sport combines the thrill of motorcycle riding with the adventure of ski touring. Although a relatively new winter sport in the west, snowmobiling is rapidly gaining popularity. Most major winter sports areas have commercial outfitters offering tours, rentals and sales.

Those who have their own snowmobiles will find a variety of areas where they may enjoy this activity. These areas are generally located near snow play and cross-country ski areas. They are marked by orange diamonds. All wilderness areas and many parts of our forests are closed to snowmobiles; always check with the nearest ranger station before venturing out in an area that isn't marked.

A good source of information on snowmobiling is the California/Nevada Snowmobile Association which has 27 active clubs. For further information, and the snowmobile club nearest you, contact:

Mr. Bud Hooker
California/Nevada Snowmobile Assn.
685 Placerville Dr. , Suite 415
Placerville, CA 95667
Ph: 916-638-SNOW

Wilderness Ethics

Those travelling by skis, snowshoes and snowmobile often share the same wilderness area. Good judgment and common courtesy often make for a more enjoyable journey. The following are a few generally accepted guidelines which should be followed no matter the type of recreation you choose.

1. Always park your vehicle off the road.
2. Snowmobilers should always check to be sure that snowmobiling is permitted in the area they have chosen.
3. Respect both private and public property and the privacy of others.
4. Snowmobilers should operate at a minimum speed when approaching or passing skiers or snowshoers.
5. Skiers and snowshoers should yield the track to oncoming snowmobilers.
6. Snowmobiles are not permitted in developed ski areas.
7. Use gates when travelling through fenced lands.
8. What you carry in, carry out. Keep our parklands clean !!
9. Always stop when encountering animals and give them the right of way.
10. Respect the natural environment by avoiding small trees, bushes and other vegetation
11. Avoid leaving human waste on the trail or near any water source.
12. Never travel alone into the backcountry.
13. All come to the aid of those in distress.

WINTER SAFETY

Winter recreation can be a safe and enjoyable experience, but it is not risk free. There are some basic risks related to the winter environment.

Frostbite: This condition occurs when an unprotected part of the skin, especially the extremities and nose, ears and cheeks, is exposed to freezing temperatures. Snowmobilers are especially susceptible with the additional drop in ambient temperature due to the wind chill factor. The symptoms are a loss of feeling and a chalky white appearance of the skin. The affected area should be warmed immediately, but never rubbed. Immersion in warm water is the best method. Frostbite is a serious condition, equal to that of a bad burn. Those afflicted should see a doctor immediately.

Hypothermia: Like frostbite, hypothermia is a serious condition. It occurs when the body loses heat more quickly than it is able to produce heat. This lowering of basal body temperature leads to mental and physical collapse and, if left untreated, eventually to death.

Hypothermia is caused by exposure to cold, aggravated by wetness, wind and exhaustion. To prevent this condition stay dry and warm by wearing materials that retain heat even when wet. Good examples of such materials are wool and polypropylene. For added protection against the elements, wear waterproof outer garments and eat high energy foods.

When a member of your party shows uncontrollable shivering, slurred speech, memory lapses, disorientation, drowsiness and a lack of concern for their physical well being, these are the symptoms of hypothermia. Immediately move the victim to a sheltered area, remove all their wet clothes and attempt to restore proper body temperature. Skin to skin contact in a sleeping bag with a warm individual is the best method. When the victim is thoroughly warmed, they should be taken to safety.

Avalanche: Avalanches may occur at any time during the winter months. While avalanche prediction is not an exact science, it is wise to obey all warning signs and check with the National Weather Service before entering the wilderness. Avoid mountainous terrain during or immediately after heavy snowfall or prolonged periods of high wind. Developed recreation areas and trails usually post avalanche warning signs. When travelling in snow country avoid crossing steep side hills and entering steep narrow canyons. The safest routes are along ridgetops on the windward side away from edges. If ridgetop travel is impossible, use the valleys away from the bottoms of the slopes.

Altitude Sickness and Hyperventilation: Altitude sickness is a common complaint at higher elevations. The lower oxygen levels and air pressure at these elevations make it difficult for the bloodstream to absorb an adequate supply of oxygen. Listlessness, weakness, drowsiness and nausea are common symptoms of this affliction. When a victim shows these signs, he should stop and rest, breathe deeply for a few minutes, eat or drink some high energy food, and then travel to a lower elevation.

Hyperventilation is another reaction to high altitudes. This is caused by too rapid breathing which diminishes the carbon dioxide level of the blood. The victim will usually show signs of apprehension and excitedness accompanied with light headedness. It is important that the victim is helped to relax and breathe into a bag, glove or hat until normal breathing is restored.

Good physical condition will diminish the likelihood of altitude sickness occurring. Avoid beginning any sort of vigorous exercise without allowing time for your body to acclimate to elevations that are higher than those at which you normally reside.

Dehydration: Dehydration is the result of your body not having ample water. Strenuous activity uses up to four quarts of water daily. There is a 25% reduction in stamina if the body loses 1 1/2 quarts of water. To avoid dehydration always have plenty of fluids on hand and drink frequently, especially after active exertion. Avoid eating snow, as explained earlier, but travel equipped to melt and treat snow for drinking.

Lost or Injured: If you are lost, injured or your equipment has failed, the first rule of the wilderness is to remain calm. Review your situation and develop a plan. If you have a compass or map, pinpoint your location. Back-track if possible. If not, remain in place and build a fire and shelter to stay warm. Stay together with your group if possible, but if not, send at least two people for help. Mark your base camp so that it is visible from the air using the distress signals discribed below.

DISTRESS SIGNALS

1. Crossed skis placed upright in the snow.

2. Three blasts of a whistle, three shouts, three puffs of smoke or flashes of light

3. Ground to Air Signals can be stamped in the snow or formed with evergreen bows in large open areas. The most common Ground to Air signals are as follows:

SOS	**I**	**F**
Help	Require Doctor Serious Injury	Require Food and Water
Y	**N**	**LL**
Yes	No	All is Well
II	**↑**	**X**
Require Medical Supplies	Proceeding in this Direction	Unable to Proceed

Skier's Responsibility Code
(Officially endorsed by National Ski Areas Assn., Ski Industries of America)

There are elements of risk in skiing that common sense and personal awareness can help reduce.

1. Ski under control and in such a manner that you can stop or avoid other skiers or objects.
2. When skiing downhill or overtaking another skier, you must avoid the skier below you.
3. Do not stop where you obstruct a trail or are not visible to other skiers.
4. When entering a trail or starting downhill, yield to other skiers.
5. Wear retention straps or other devices to help prevent runaway skis.
6. Keep off closed trails and posted areas, and obey all posted signs.
7. Do not ski while "under the influence" of drugs or alcohol.
8. If you are involved in a collision, or are a witness, do not leave the scene until the ski patrol has talked to you.

This is only a partial list. Be safety concious !!!

TRAIL ETHICS

The aesthetics of the winter environment are basic to nordic skiing. There are thousands of acres of wilderness open to ski touring and ski mountaineering. A great many cross-country skiers prefer the ease and structure of the groomed and tracked trails. All nordic skiers enjoy the beauty and adventure of this ever growing sport, but in order to preserve this tranquility, there are some basic rules to follow:

1. Obey all trail signs and warnings.

2. Step out of the trail for skiers coming downhill.

3. Step out of the way for a faster skier. If someone yells "Track", step to the right and let the person pass.

4. Step off the trail when pausing for a break.

5. Look up and note what's ahead of you on the trail.

6. Ski safely, with control.

8. Pick up litter. Carry out what you carry in.

9. Do not leave human waste in concentrated areas or near any water sources, trail or camp.

10. Avoid ski tracks if you are hiking or skiing with a dog.

Dogs, hikers, and snowmobilers are generally prohibited from using cross-country trails. Dogs tend to leave their marks on cross-country trails. Their pawprints begin the process of erosion and eventually create hazardous holes in the trail. Their other reminders, "brown Kleister", are not pleasant to ski through. Also, many serious accidents have be a result of a fast moving skier colliding with an unresponsive dog.

Hikers should also avoid groomed cross-country trails. A hiker's footprint is often large enough to catch a ski tip. This frequently results in the skier taking a painful fall.

Snowmobilers can present an even more serious hazard for skiers. Their noise level and high speed prevent the driver from noticing skiers until they are too close for a proper reaction. Snowmobilers should remain in areas designated for their use.

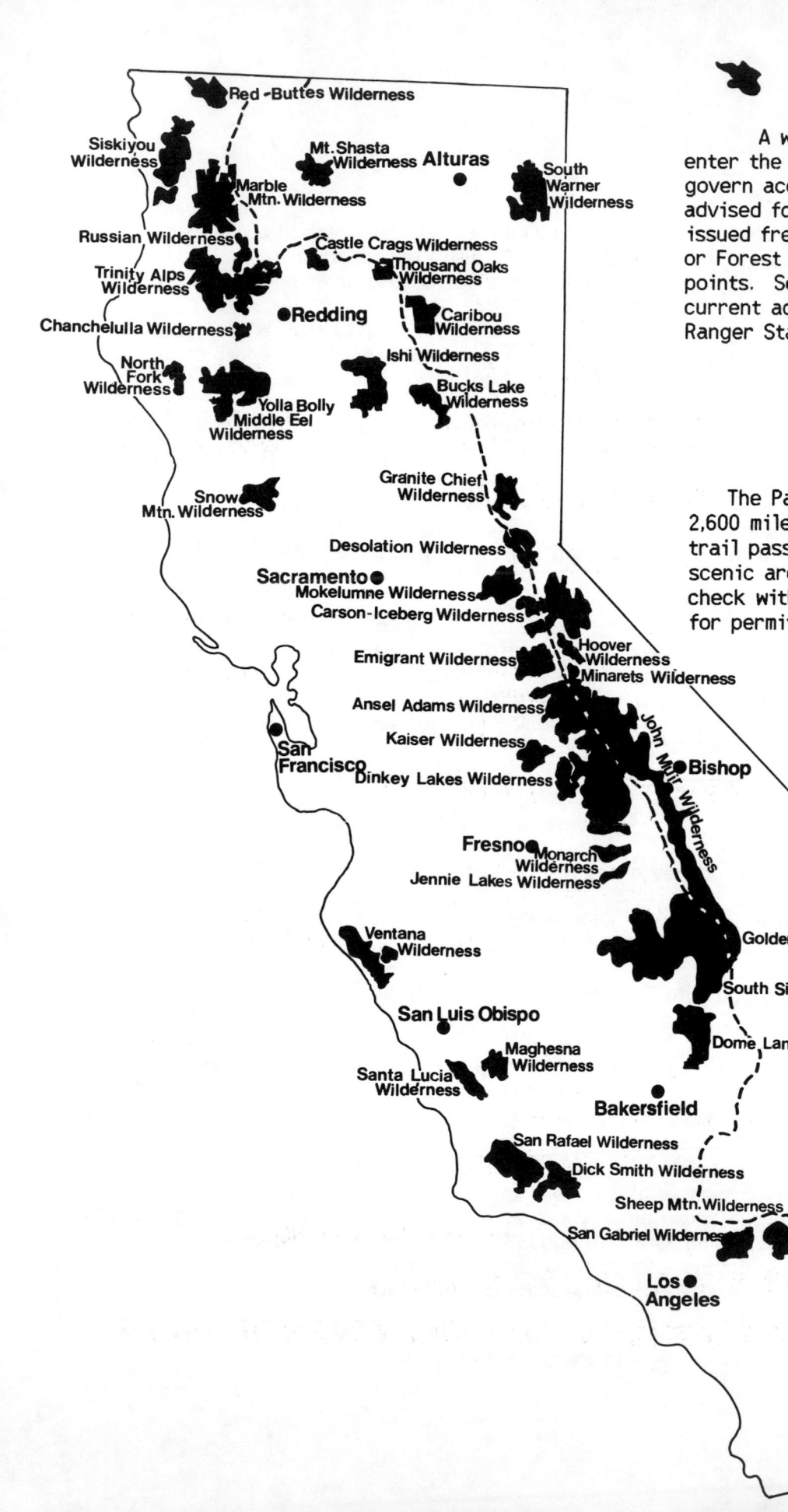

WILDERNESS AREAS

A wilderness permit is required to enter the Wilderness Areas. Regulations govern access. Advance reservations are advised for some areas. Permits are issued free of charge at Ranger Stations or Forest Service Offices near entry points. See following section for current addresses and phone numbers of Ranger Stations.

PACIFIC CREST TRAIL

The Pacific Crest Trail extends 2,600 miles from Canada to Mexico. The trail passes through some of the most scenic areas of California. Be sure to check with the nearest Ranger Stations for permits and information.

Red-Buttes Wilderness

Siskiyou Wilderness

Mt. Shasta Wilderness   Alturas

South Warner Wilderness

Marble Mtn. Wilderness

Russian Wilderness   Castle Crags Wilderness

Trinity Alps Wilderness   Thousand Oaks Wilderness

Chanchelulla Wilderness   ●Redding   Caribou Wilderness

North Fork Wilderness   Ishi Wilderness

Yolla Bolly Middle Eel Wilderness   Bucks Lake Wilderness

Snow Mtn. Wilderness   Granite Chief Wilderness

Desolation Wilderness

Sacramento●   Mokelumne Wilderness

Carson-Iceberg Wilderness

Emigrant Wilderness   Hoover Wilderness
Minarets Wilderness

Ansel Adams Wilderness

San Francisco   Kaiser Wilderness

Dinkey Lakes Wilderness   Bishop●

John Muir Wilderness

Fresno●   Monarch Wilderness

Jennie Lakes Wilderness

Ventana Wilderness   Golden Trout Wilderness

South Sierra Wilderness

San Luis Obispo   Dome Land Wilderness

Maghesna Wilderness

Santa Lucia Wilderness   Bakersfield

San Rafael Wilderness

Dick Smith Wilderness

Sheep Mtn. Wilderness   San Bernardino

San Gabriel Wilderness   Cucamonga Wilderness

San Gorgonio Wilderness

Los Angeles●   San Jacinto Wilderness

Santa Rosa Wilderness

Agua Tibia Wilderness

Pine Creek Wilderness

Hauser Wilderness

RANGER STATIONS AND FOREST SERVICE OFFICES

CALIFORNIA REGION OF THE U.S. FOREST SERVICE

GENERAL INFORMATION, MAPS AND WILDERNESS PERMITS MAY BE OBTAINED AT THE FOLLOWING LOCATIONS:

ANGELES NATIONAL FOREST

Head Office
701 N. Santa Anita Ave.
Arcadia 91006
Ph: 818-574-5270
818-574-1613

Arroyo-Seco Ranger District
Oak Grove Park
Flintridge 91011
Ph: 818-790-1151

Mt. Baldy Ranger District
110 N. Wabash Ave.
Glendora 91740
Ph: 818-335-1251

Saugus Ranger District
27757 Bouquet Canyon Rd.
Saugus 91350
Ph: 805-252-9710

Tujunga Ranger District
12371 N. Little Tujunga Cny.
San Fernando 91342
Ph: 818-899-1900/(1447)

Valyermo Ranger District
34146 Longview Rd.
Pearblossom 93553
Ph: 805:944-2187

CLEVELAND NATIONAL FOREST

Head Office
880 Front St., Rm.
San Diego 92188
Ph: 619-293-5050

Descanso Ranger District
3348 Alpine Blvd.
Alpine 92001
Ph: 619-445-6235

Palomar Ranger District
332 S. Juniper
Escondido 92025
Ph: 619-745-2421 or
619-566-0130

Trabuco Ranger District
1147 E. Sixth Street
Corona 91720
Ph: 714-736-1811

EL DORADO NATIONAL FOREST

Information Center
3070 Camino Heights
Camino 95709
Ph: 916-644-6048

Amador Ranger District
26820 Silver Dr. & Hwy. 88
Star Route 3
Pioneer 95666
Ph: 209-295-4251

Pacific Ranger District
Pollock Pines 95726
Ph: 916-644-2348

Georgetown Ranger District
Georgetown 95634
Ph: 916-333-4313

. . . Continued. . .

. . . Continued. . .

INYO NATIONAL FOREST

Head Office
873 No. Main St.
Bishop 93514
Ph: 619-873-5841

Mt. Whitney Ranger District
P.O. Box 8
Lone Pine 93545
Ph: 619-876-5542

Mammoth Ranger District
P.O. Box 148
Mammoth Lakes 93546
Ph: 619-934-2505

White Mountain Ranger District
798 NO. Main Street
Bishop
Ph: 619-873-4207

Mono Lake Ranger District
P.O. Box 10
Lee Vining 93541
Ph: 619-647-6525

KLAMATH NATIONAL FOREST

Head Office
1312 Fairlane Road
Yreka 96097
Ph: 916-842-6131

Oak Knoll Ranger District
2254 Hwy. 96
Klamath River 96050
Ph: 916-465-2241

Ukonom Ranger District
P.O. Box 410
Orleans 95556
Ph: 916-627-3291

Goosenest Ranter District
37805 Hwy. 97
Macdoel 96058
Ph: 916-398-4391

Salmon River Ranger District
Sawyers Bar 96027
Ph: Ft. Jones Operator and
ask for Sawyers Bar 4600 or
P.O. Box 280
Etna 96027
Ph: 916-467-5757

Happy Camp Ranger District
P.O. Box 377
Happy Camp 96039
Ph: 916-493-2243

Scott River Ranger District
11263 S. Hwy. 3
Fort Jones 96032
Ph: 916-468-5351

LAKE TAHOE BASIN MANAGEMENT UNIT

THIS UNIT COVERS PARTS OF EL DORADO, TAHOE AND TOIYABE NATIONAL FORESTS.

Head Office
P.O. Box 8465
870 Emerald Bay Rd.
South Lake Tahoe 95731
Ph: 916-544-6420

Tahoe Visitor Center
1/2 Mi. from Camp Richardson
Ph: 916-541-0209
Open Summers Only

William Kent Info. Station
William Kent Campground
West Shore
Ph: 916-583-3642
Open Summers Only

LASSEN NATIONAL FOREST

Head Office
55 South Sacramento St.
Susanville 96130
Ph: 916-257-2151

Hat Creek Ranger District
P.O. Box 220
Fall River Mills 96028
Ph: 916-336-5521

Almanor Ranger District
P.O. Box 767
Chester 96020
Ph: 916-258-2141

Engineering Department
1800 Main St.
Susanville 96130
Ph: 916-257-5507

Eagle Lake Ranger District
472-013 Johnstonville Rd.
Susanville 96130
Ph: 916-257-2595 or 2161

. . . Continued . . .

. . . Continued . . .

LOS PADRES NATIONAL FOREST

Head Office
6144 Calle Real
Goleta 93117
Ph: 805-683-6711

Monterey Ranger District
406 S. Mildred
King City 93930
Ph: 408-385-5434

Mt. Pinos Ranger District
Star Route, Box 400
Frazier Park 93225
Ph: 805-245-3731 or 3462

Ojai Ranger District
1190 E. Ojai Ave.
Ojai 93023
Ph: 805-646-4348

Santa Lucia Ranger District
1616 N. Carlotti Dr.
Santa Maria 93454
Ph: 805-925-9538 or 39

Santa Barbara Ranger Dist.
Star Route, Los Prietos
Santa Barbara 93105
Ph: 805-967-3481 or 82

MENDOCINO NATIONAL FOREST

Head Office
420 E. Laurel St.
Willows 95988
PH: 916-934-3316

Corning Ranger District
22000 Corning Rd.
Corning 96021
Ph: 916-824-5196

Covelo Ranger District
Route 1, Box 62-C
Covelo 95428
Ph: 707-983-6118

Stonyford Ranger District
Stites Ladoga Road
Stonyford 95979
Ph: 916-963-3128

Upper Lake Ranger District
Middlecreek Rd.
P.O. Box 96
Upper Lake 95485
Ph: 707-275--2361

Chico Tree Improvement
Center
2741 Cramer Lane
Chico 95926
Ph: 916-895-1176 or 77

MODOC NATIONAL FOREST

Head Office
441 N. Main St.
Alturas 96101
Ph: 916-233-5811

Big Valley Ranger District
P.O. Box 885
Adin 96006
Ph: 916-299-3215, 16, 17

Devil's Garden Ranger Dist.
P.O. Box 5
Canby 96015
Ph: 916-233-4611, 12, 13, 14

Doublehead Ranger District
P.O. Box 818
Tulelake 96134

Warner Mountain Ranger District
P.O. Box 220
Cedarville 96104

PLUMAS NATIONAL FOREST

Head Office
P.O. Box 1500, 159 Lawrence
Quincy 95971
Ph: 916-283-2050

Beckwourth Ranger District
Mohawk Ranger Station
P.O. Box 7
Blairsden 96013
Ph: 916-836-2575

Greenville Ranger District
P.O. Box 329
Greenville 95947
Ph: 916-284-7126

La Porte Ranger District
Challenge Ranger Station
P.O. Drawer F
Challenge 95925
Ph: 916-675-2462

Milford Ranger District
Laufman Ranger Station
Milford 96121
Ph: 916-253-2223

Oroville Ranger District
875 Mitchell Ave.
Oroville 95965
Ph: 916-534-6500

Quincy Ranger District
1400 E. Main, Box 69
Quincy 95971
Ph: 916-283-0555

. . . Continued . . .

SAN BERNARDINO NATIONAL FOREST ... Continued ...

Head Office
144 N. Mt. View Ave.
San Bernardino 92408
Ph: 714-383-5588

Arrowhead Ranger District
Rimforest 92378
Ph: 714-337-2444

Big Bear Ranger District
P.O. Box 290
Fawnskin 92333
Ph: 714-866-3437

Cajon Ranger District
Lytle Creek Ranger Station
Star Route
Fontana 92335
Ph: 714-887-2576

San Gorgonio Ranger District
Mill Creek Station
Route 1, P.O. Box 264
Mentone 92359
Ph: 714-794-1123

San Jacinto Ranger District
Idyllwild Ranger Station
P.O. Box 518
Idyllwild 92349
Ph: 714-659-2117

SEQUOIA NATIONAL FOREST

Head Office
900 W. Grand Ave.
Porterville 93257
Ph: 209-784-1500

Cannell Meadow Ranger District
P.O. Box 6
Kernville 93238
Ph: 619-376-3781

Greenhorn Ranger District
Federal Bldg., Rm. 322
800 Truxtun Ave.
Bakersfield 93301
Ph: 805-861-4212

Hot Springs Ranger District
Route 4, Box 548
Ca. Hot Springs 93207
Ph: 805-548-6503

Hume Lake Ranger District
36273 E. Kings Canyon Rd.
Dunlap 93621
Ph: 209-338-2251

Tule Ranger District
32588 Highway 190
Porterville 93257
PH: 209-539-2607

SHASTA-TRINITY NATIONAL FOREST

Head Office
2400 Washington Ave.
Redding 96001
Ph: 916-246-5222

Big Bar Ranger District
Star Route 1, Box 10
Big Bar 96010
Ph: 916-623-6106

Hayfork Ranger District
P.O. Box 159
Hayfork 96041
Ph: 916-628-5227

McCloud Ranger District
District
Drawer 1
McCloud 96057
Ph: 916-964-2184, 85

Mt. Shasta Ranger District

204 West Alma
Mt. Shasta 96067
Ph: 916-926-4511

Shasta Lake Ranger

6543 Holiday Drive
Redding 96003
Ph: 916-275-1587

Weaverville Ranger District
P.O. Box T
Weaverville 96093
Ph: 916-623-2131 or 21

Yolla Bolla Ranger District
Platina 96076
Ph: 916-352-4211

NCSC
6106 Airport Road
Redding 96002
Ph: 916-246-5285

SIERRA NATIONAL FOREST

Head Office
Federal Building
1130 "O" St.
Fresno 93721
Ph: 209-487-5155

Bass Lake Ranger District
41969 Highway 41
Oakhurst 93644
Ph: 209-683-4665

Kings River Ranger District
Trimmer Route
Sanger 93657
Ph: 209-855-8321 or 22

Mariposa Ranger District
P.O. Box 747
Mariposa 95338
Ph: 209-966-3638

Minarets Ranger District
North Fork 93643
Ph: 209-877-2218 or 19

Pineridge Ranger District
P.O. Box 300
Shaver Lake 93664
Ph: 209-841-3311

Kings River Ranger District
Dinkey Ranger Station, Dinkey Route
Shaver Lake 93664
PH: 209-841-3404 (Summer Only)

... Continued ...

SIX RIVERS NATIONAL FOREST

Head Office
507 "F" Street
Eureka 95501
Ph: 707-442-1721

Mad River Ranger District
Star Route, Box 300
Bridgeville 95526
Ph: 707-574-6233

Zenia Fire Station
General Delivery
Zenia 95495
Ph: Zenia Toll Station
#6069 – through Operator

Gasquet Ranger District
P.O. Box 228
Gasquet 95543
Ph: 707-457-3131

Orleans Ranger District
Drawer B
Orleans 95556
Ph: 916-627-3291

Big Flat Station on:
Gasquet Ranger District
(Summer Station Only)
No Phone or Mail Service

Lower Trinity Ranger Dist.
P.O. Box 668
Willow Creek 95573
Ph: 916-629-2118

Salyer Fire Station
(No Mail Service)
Lower Tr. Rd.
Salyer 95563
Ph: 916-629-2114

Humboldt Nursery
4886 Cottage Grove
McKinleyville 95521
Ph: 707-839-3256

STANISLAUS NATIONAL FOREST

Head Office
19777 Greenley Rd.
Sonora 95370
Ph: 209-532-3671

Mi-Wuk Ranger District
Highway 108 E
P.O. Box 100
Mi-Wuk Village 95346
Ph: 109-586-3234

Calaveras Ranger District
Highway 4
P.O. Box 500
Hathaway Pines 95233
Ph: 209-795-1381

Summit Ranger District
Highway 108 E at Pinecrest
Star Route, Box 1295
Sonora 95370
Ph: 209-965-3434

Groveland Ranger District
Highway 120
P.O. Box 709
Groveland 95321
Ph: 209-962-7825

TAHOE NATIONAL FOREST

Head Office
Highway 49 & Coyote St.
Nevada City 95959
Ph: 916-265-4531

Nevada City Ranger District
12012 Sutton Way
Grass Valley 95945
Ph: 916-273-1371

Downieville Ranger District
N. Yuba Ranger Station
Star Route, Box 1
Camptonville 95922
Ph: 916-288-3231

Sierraville Ranger District
P.O. Box 95, Hwy. 89
Sierraville 96126
Ph: 916-994-3401

Foresthill Ranger District
22830 Auburn-Foresthill Rd.
Foresthill 95631
Ph: 916-367-2224

Truckee Ranger District
P.O. Box 399
Truckee 95734
Ph: 916-587-3558

NATIONAL PARKS

Lassen Volcanic National
Park
Mineral 96063
Ph: 916-595-4444

Sequoia-Kings Canyon
National Park
Three Rivers 93271
Ph: 209-565-3341

Yosemite National Park
P.O. Box 577
Yosemite National Park
95389
Ph: 209-372-4461

OVERALL INDEX

ORDER FORM

SEND TO: SAIL SALES PUBLISHING
P.O. Box 1028
Aptos, CA 95001

☐ **"Winter Recreation in California" – First Edition**

$10.95 Book
.71 Tax
1.84 Postage & Handling
$13.50 CHECK ENCLOSED

☐ **"Recreation Lakes of California" – Seventh Edition**

$10.95 Book
.71 Tax
1.84 Postage & Handling
$13.50 CHECK ENCLOSED

☐ **"Recreation on the Colorado River" – First Edition**

$9.95 Book
.65 Tax
1.25 Postage & Handling
$11.85 CHECK ENCLOSED

☐ **All Publications (Free Postage & Handling)**

$31.85 Books
2.07 Tax
$33.92 CHECK ENCLOSED

NAME: _____

ADDRESS: _____

_____